Public Relations and the Public Interest

T0330893

This book has the potential to open up debate on the positioning of public relations in society—one that has been simmering under the surface for a considerable time. It calls the 'profession' to account—to justify its claims to be working in the public interest. And it adds to the growing scholarly critiques of the discipline, which in turn, contribute to PR's growth as a field of academic research and as an ethical practice.
—*Leanne Glenny, University of South Australia, Australia*

This important work puts the 'public' where it belongs in public relations, providing perspectives that cross paradigms, cultures and disciplines to provide a compelling vision for public interest public relations.
—*Kenn Gaither, Elon University, U.S.A.*

Critical scholarship in public relations demands new thinking, urging exploration into alternative theories and paradigms. In such an environment, this book examines the ubiquitous and complex nature of 'the public interest,' a concept that is as old as Aristotle but as new as today's practice. Johnston examines the much contested yet widely used concept of the public interest, arguing that it deserves greater attention within the discipline of public relations, just as it has received in the law, media, anthropology, planning and public policy. The book draws on the work of leading theorists including Dewey, Habermas, Flathman, Foucault, Freire, Bourdieu and Dutta, as well as the origins of the public interest and interest-based theories, to examine the public interest's intersections with communication, culture, social capital, ethics and law. It examines how interests are negotiated and managed, the role of pluralism and discourse, and how context and time-dependency can provide the foundation for applying theory to practice. Rich in illustrations and dedicated 'snapshots,' it includes international examples and contexts—from cultural activism to government-community partnerships; from *pro bono publico* to global corporate expansion—focusing particularly on the role of social change and participation in the public interest and featuring an international study of the public interest in public relations industry codes.

Jane Johnston is Associate Professor, Public Relations and Communication at the University of Queensland, Australia. She has written and (co)edited several key texts including *Public Relations: Theory and Practice* and *Media Relations: Issues and Strategies,* both in several editions. Her diverse research interests include the intersection of justice, media and communication.

Routledge Research in Public Relations

Public Relations and the Public Interest

Jane Johnston

Routledge
Taylor & Francis Group

NEW YORK AND LONDON

First published 2016
by Routledge
711 Third Avenue, New York, NY 10017

and by Routledge
2 Park Square, Milton Park, Abingdon, Oxon OX14 4RN

First issued in paperback 2017

Routledge is an imprint of the Taylor & Francis Group, an informa business

Library of Congress Cataloging-in-Publication Data

Names: Johnston, Jane, 1961–
Title: Public relations and the public interest / by Jane Johnston.
Description: New York: Routledge, 2016. | Series: Routledge research in
public relations; 7 | Includes bibliographical references and index.
Identifiers: LCCN 2015040932
Subjects: LCSH: Public relations.
Classification: LCC HD59 .J64 2016 | DDC 659.2—dc23
LC record available at http://lccn.loc.gov/2015040932

ISBN 13: 978-0-8153-8657-5 (pbk)
ISBN 13: 978-1-138-83084-4 (hbk)

Typeset in Sabon
by codeMantra

Contents

List of Box, Figures and Tables

Acknowledgments

This book took me on a journey into one of the most ubiquitous concepts in modern (and not so modern) life—the public interest. My exceptional journey was with scholars, philosophers and even a few practitioners, who have exulted and praised, critiqued and questioned the public interest; among them are Jeremy Bentham, Jürgen Habermas, John Dewey, Aristotle, Robert Coleman, JAW Gunn, Pierre Bourdieu and Robert Flathman. For a subject that is so vaguely defined and often contested, the public interest continues to excite and engage those who have a passion for examining people, society and politics. For me, it has begun an exciting, if challenging, ongoing journey of research and investigation.

This book is intended to be positioned within the growing and flourishing literature of critical public relations which, since the 1990s, has demanded public relations 'go beyond' and question the status quo, examining business, politics, government, civil society and activism with reflexivity and a broad mind. At a discipline level, I thank the critical public relations trailblazers who have carved out a literature that continues to develop and thrive, allowing 'new' concepts and theories, such as the public interest, to germinate within it.

I thank Routledge's anonymous readers who saw the potential for the book and gave it an enthusiastic green light several years ago, and to the public relations scholars who encouraged and challenged the topic when it was first aired at international conferences in 2015. Throughout the process, I have enjoyed wonderful support from colleagues and friends who have brought their critical eyes, research assistance, editing skills and advice to the project—Nigel Krauth, Caroline Grahame, Michele Clark, Karen Irwin—and those who have contributed to the snapshots, tables and photographs from many corners of the world. My sincere thanks to Routledge, and my editors and support staff, for their commitment to the book, and to Bond University and the University of Queensland for supporting it and seeing its potential at various stages of production.

I dedicate the hard work and intellectual growth brought throughout the writing of this book to my loved ones—past and present—my dear parents, Stan and Karen Roots; my soul-mate and partner, Nigel Krauth; and my exceptional children Matthew, Sean and Tess.

'We must learn to live with, even welcome, a concept that remains continually in contest' (Mansbridge 1998).

1   The Public Interest, Public Relations and Society

The public interest: 'the X factor'.
(Sorauf 1957, p. 617)

Introduction

The public interest is a complex concept. During the mid-1900s, amid serious interrogation by political scholars, Sorauf argued that 'a concept as nebulous as the public interest invites not definition but absorption' (1957, p. 618). Decades later, this book invites the same; a journey into and around the public interest that is infused with possibilities, theories, illustrations and examples—and one that provides a revised perspective for thinking about public relations. The public interest is generally understood via criteria, values and contexts rather than definitions, located in historic and contemporary practice, and examined through a range of theoretical frameworks, ultimately providing a new lens through which to locate and analyze the role of public relations in society. The book does not naïvely propose that, in trying to locate the public interest, consensus will always be achieved or, indeed, sought. Instead, it demonstrates that the public interest can be vexed and complex, often caught up in competing interests that are not easily reconciled. As Dewey wrote eloquently in 1935 (cited in Bozeman 2007, p. 105), 'Of course there are conflicting interests: otherwise there would be no social problems.'

Theories and paradigms of the public interest have emerged from political, philosophical, legal, media and anthropological discourses. Its intersections with democracy, public policy, public administration, legislation and free speech have seen it closely examined from various directions, in many contexts, and over many time periods (Dewey 1927; Lippmann 1955; Sorauf 1957; Cassinelli 1958; Flathman 1966; Benditt 1973; Cochran 1974; Meyerson 2007; Moravcsik & Sangiovanni 2003; Wheeler 2006; Bozeman 2007; Leveson 2012; Ho 2011, 2013) all of which will come under some attention in this book. It has been teased out and analyzed over and over again, often with the same conclusion: that it defies a single definition and is best considered within specific social, legal, cultural and time contexts.

Analysis of the public interest has fallen largely at the margins of public relations research and discourse, with relatively few scholars considering it in depth or calling for greater inclusion within the field (Hill 1958; Heath 1992; Bivins 1993; Seib & Fitzpatrick 1995; L Grunig 1992; J Grunig 2001; L'Etang 2004; Weaver, Motion & Roper 2006; Messina 2007; Edwards 2011; Pendleton 2013; Preston 2013). Others have cited the public interest in passing, within broader contexts (Ehling 1992; Cutlip 1995; Theaker & Yaxley 2013), but fallen short of analysis. Still others have used the public interest in definitions or codes of ethics/practice/conduct (see definitions following and codes of ethics in chapter 8) without any real examination of what it actually means for the industry or society. There is surely a certain irony that 'the public interest' and 'public relations' have escaped any concerted and sustained examination *together* given the existence of 'the public' or 'publics' in both. Meanwhile, many other fields that intersect with public relations, such as public policy, politics and media, have for decades engaged with the public interest. Thus the public interest is like the elephant-in-the-room for public relations. It is axiomatic, a logical fit, for public relations scholars and practitioners to investigate and engage with the concept of the public interest from critical, theoretical and functional perspectives. The public interest and public relations share another commonality: they are both poorly understood and have public image problems, making them a challenging combination but one which, this book suggests, can provide a fruitful union.

In recent years public relations (PR), as a discipline, has experienced an uprising from within as it has moved into a period of self-reflection and critique. The international surge of critical analysis of public relations through the 1990s and expanding in the 2000s has brought issues of power, hegemony, truth, transparency, spin, propaganda and advocacy into a vibrant and expanded discourse. One of the key messages from this wave of critical thinking is that public relations needs to be open to new ideas, approaches and theories and become more reflexive in examining itself. This book provides a logical vehicle through which to continue the examination of a multi-paradigmatic discipline and further extend the critical debate. A central proposition of the book is that public relations, in its roles within policy development, communication, and in contributing to governance practices, can engage with the public interest in a focused and productive way. It is premised on a broad understanding of what public relations is, because not only is the industry varied—comprised of advisory roles and knowledge management, in developing discourses and producing communication materials and policy advice—but it is also part of civil society, involved in organized activism (Holtzhauzen 2012; Demetrious 2013) and is more dependent on function and skill than titled PR operators (Moloney 2000; Opdycke Lamme & Miller Russell 2010). In short, public relations is understood in both its formal, institutional function (e.g. in paid corporate and government positions), and equally in its informal, non-institutional function (e.g. in non-paid advocacy and activist positions which may not carry a PR 'title') and also, occasionally, driven by other fields which seek stronger relations with the public.

While the term 'public interest public relations' was historically used to describe the work of public interest groups (Pires 1983) or aligned with the public sector (L'Etang 2004) this book incorporates these, and then expands our understanding to incorporate the public interest more broadly. It suggests that in much the same way as the media, the legal system, government administrators and other fields use the public interest to navigate and articulate industry activity and standards, public relations can use the concept as a reflexive tool and to better understand itself and its place in society. This initial chapter will briefly examine the public interest from a range of perspectives and in a range of contexts, first providing an overview of the public interest, followed by its role in the better known fields of law and media, a summary of the public relations literature and, finally, an outline of the chapters of the book.

Understanding the Public Interest

In order to fully investigate the role of the public interest in public relations, it is useful to more fully understand what is meant by the mutable, ambiguous concept of 'the public interest.' Although the expression is widely used, it is poorly understood and rarely defined. Bozeman (2007, p. 84) refers to it as a conundrum: 'nearly everyone is convinced that the public interest is vital in public policy and governance, but there is little agreement as to exactly what it is.' While legal case law, legislation, public policies, scholarly literature and historical documents are littered with the expression 'the public interest,' this simplest of phrases is rarely explained. As one government ombudsman surmised in his attempt to explain it:

> Firstly, while it is one of the most used terms in the lexicon of public administration, it is arguably the least defined and least understood ... secondly, identifying or determining the appropriate public interest in any particular case is often no easy task.
>
> (Wheeler 2006, p. 12)

Indeed, the public interest is a somewhat mercurial concept, an expression that takes its shape from the context in which it is used. Frank Sorauf called it 'the X factor, the imponderable and unknown, in the political equation' (1957, p. 617). That Wheeler and Sorauf, some 50 years apart, are both drawn from public administration and politics is no surprise. They represent a large body of scholars and public administrators who have sought to unravel the concept of the public interest, based on its application by governments. As Sorauf explained, 'it has come to signify that public policy alternative that most deserves enactment' (1957, p. 616). As such, it is a central concept within democratic systems of government. Decades of examination have positioned it within democratic frameworks and, for this reason, this book is primarily focused within this political space. Most attempts to describe the public interest use words like community, common good, general welfare, and public values (Locke 1767; Wheeler 2006; Bozeman 2007). Where definitions or descriptions of the public interest are advanced, even within one country, they illustrate how varied its meaning can be. In Australia, for example, it has been described as:

> ... a convenient and useful concept for aggregating any number of interests that may bear upon a disputed question that is of general—as opposed to merely private—concern (Australian Senate Committee on Constitutional and Legal Affairs in Wheeler 2006, p. 14).

And also,

> The expression 'in the public interest' directs attention to that conclusion or determination which best serves the advancement of the interest or welfare of the public, society or the nation and its content will depend on each particular circumstance ... (Federal Court of Australia in Wheeler, p. 14).

In order to advance our understanding of not only the public interest, but also public interest theory, we can look to four categories of public interest proposed by Cochran (1974) and Mitnick (1980) and examined more recently by Bozeman (2007). These provide a foundation for understanding the key areas in which the public interest is understood by scholars, which will be reviewed in more detail in chapter 2. They are the following:

- Normative theories of public interest based on understandings of the general good of society. This approach tends toward an idealistic understanding of the 'whole community';
- Abolitionist theories which deny the public interest as an 'idea ghost' because they are not empirically measurable and are not achievable anyway because there can be no single public interest;
- Process theories which can take several forms but the most instructive is the procedural approach, which sees the public interest as a process of compromise and accommodation, based on multiple or pluralist publics;
- Consensualist theories which incorporate a communitarian approach, accepting basic rules of political conduct and principles of democratic society, such as political deliberation and public discourse.

If abolitionist theories are rejected, by effectively rejecting themselves, then there are three to consider. Those professing the process approach find many publics, rather than a single public, and many interests, rather than one held by the whole (Cochran 1974, p. 339). As such, they find consistency with the understanding of pluralist publics and public segmentation in public relations. As we will see in the next chapter, a combination of process and consensual approaches often provides the most workable, practical outcomes. Normative theories apply more to the ideal, and while theorists argue that 'balancing' of interests can defy logic because the public interest is in the interest of all citizens (Bozeman 2007, p. 91), the normative can also combine elements of process, plurality and consensuality, depending on time and context.

The public interest, as we will see throughout this book, is often about balance and counterbalance: in legal contexts, balancing public interest and the rights of the majority with individual rights; in economic terms, balancing the public interest with economic individualism; in philosophical and critical analysis, balancing the minority and weaker against the stronger, more powerful. Within national borders and internationally, the public interest is often balanced against rights of the individual and sovereignty. The Human Rights Act 1998 (UK), the European Convention for the Protection of Human Rights and Fundamental Freedoms (1953) and the Canadian Charter of Rights and Freedoms (1982), for example, aim to strike this balance (Meyerson 2007). In public interest terms, these laws effectively consider whether 'interference with one of the qualified rights must be necessary in a democratic society' (Meyerson 2007, p. 877). At their core are questions of proportionality, that is: 'do the gains to the public justify the interference with the right?' (Meyerson 2007, p. 878). The European Court of Human Rights, for instance, asks 'whether the measure is likely to be effective in achieving the government's purpose, whether there are less restrictive ways of achieving the purpose, and whether the cost to the right is justified by the public interest or public benefit' (Meyerson 2007, p. 877). A sliding scale of this balance of individual rights and public interest has been called the 'law of balancing' (Alexy 2002 in Meyerson 2007, p. 879).

However, the public interest is not simply pitted against human or other group rights. Wheeler suggests viewing 'the public,' in the context of 'the public interest,' may be any of the following:

- members of the community as a whole or a large part of it (such as a nation);
- groups or sub-classes (such as migrants);
- private rights of individuals which are seen as so fundamental that they in turn represent a public interest (such as education) (Wheeler 2006, p. 16, my examples).

In other words, the public interest should not necessarily be considered as the interests of the wider community, or indeed always in competition with each other, but may also be about values that are accepted by the wider community but affect only a few. The concept of balance and counterbalance provides a sort of equilibrium; however, in the weighing of competing interests, a judgment of one interest over another does not necessarily discount either, as the Australian High Court defined:

> The interest of a section of the public is a public interest but the smallness of the section may affect the quantity or weight of the public interest so that it is outweighed by [another public interest]. It does not, however, affect the quality of that interest (Australian High Court in Wheeler 2006, p. 17).

These words are echoed by Lord Justice Leveson, who delivered the report into *The Culture, Practices and Ethics of the National Press* in Britain in 2012 (discussed later in this chapter). In considering competing public interests, Justice Leveson argued: 'It will often be a matter of balancing a number of outcomes which would be for the common good, but which cannot all be achieved simultaneously' (2012, p. 69).

Obviously then courts and others in policy decision-making roles need to strike a balance. Where consensus cannot be found, the most compelling public interest argument may be adopted. However, there can also be consensus. In such cases the public interest may be 'best conceived as the preservation and improvement of the community itself' (Cochran 1974, p. 355). The public interest may therefore be achieved via various pathways, for example, in the following approaches which seek a public interest outcome.

- *Competing public interests which, after open, transparent and fair debate, find one interest prioritized for the benefit of a community;*
  For example: the self-determination of same-sex marriage in Ireland, resulting from a Constitutional Convention and referendum.
- *The public interest achieved where a societal or community need is advanced where there is no (significant) conflict or opposition;*
  For example: public education relating to adult literacy programs in Aotearoa New Zealand.
- *Multiple public interests being achieved, that is, two or more public interest imperatives may be achieved contemporaneously.*
  For example: the preservation or reintroduction of traditional or indigenous languages, concurrent with modern languages.

These pathways, together with previous comments by the likes of Justice Leveson and the Australian High Court, provide contexts for understanding the public interest. However, lack of specificity and apparent pliability and subjectivity have nevertheless seen major criticisms railed against the public interest. Such criticisms rest largely with the lack of empirical or quantitative evidence that can be provided by or about the public interest. Bozeman argues this is caused by a 'taproot problem': the public interest's ambiguity (Bozeman 2007, p. 84), which has been central to it falling out of favor with empirically focused, quantitative social scientists. Despite this, its importance in public policy, governance and law continues to command its place at the table by many scholars from many disciplines. As one of the foremost researchers of the public interest, political scientist Richard Flathman argued more than 60 years ago: 'The problems associated with the "public interest" are among the crucial problems of politics ... we are free to abandon the *concept*, but if we do so we will simply have to wrestle with the *problems* under some other heading' (1966, p. 13, his italics).

If we follow the approach of Flathman, and many others, we will see that the public interest, like the public sphere, can advance our qualitative understandings of public relations, beyond that which is empirically measurable or positivist in approach. Such approaches are not new to critical public relations scholarship, which increasingly favors an interface with social justice and social change (see, for example, Curtin & Gaither 2012, p. 301) and works beyond the functionalist approach to advance the field.

The Public Interest and Society

It has been argued that public relations and the public interest cannot be reconciled (Messina 2007); that defining the public interest, its subjectivity, questionable validity, potential for conflict and the intractable problem of letting public relations practitioners decide what is in the public interest make it too difficult a concept to pin down, let alone be managed by public relations practitioners. Messina dismisses it as 'unachievable and must be abandoned' (Messina 2007, p. 38). How then, do other professions and sectors of society manage to grapple with the complexities of the public interest? As complex and nebulous as it may be, the public interest is incorporated into the frameworks and discourse of politics, media, public policy, law, anthropology, planning and accounting—so why not public relations?

We will tackle the initial question first, and the second question will be considered later in the chapter. So, *how* and *where* does the public interest 'fit' into society and, specifically, into other professions? Lawyers, politicians, public officials, journalists and scholars around the world use the expression liberally within hundreds of thousands of court cases, pieces of legislation, government documents, policies and guidelines. In one Australian state alone (New South Wales) the public interest is included in almost 200 Legislative Acts (Wheeler 2006, p. 22). At the same time, anthropologists have developed a stream of dedicated 'public interest anthropology' which examines the public interest role in culture and society, while accountants have turned to the public interest as a business model. Each of these fields will come under focus in the book, collectively illustrating the ubiquitous and widely connected nature of the public interest across society.

Arguably the two fields best known for their association with the public interest are the media and the law. These provide some general training grounds for understanding the public interest which can be extrapolated to more general implications for other sectors of society. An analysis of these two areas will therefore be particularly useful as we gather a firmer grasp of the public interest within contemporary society and other fields of practice and scholarship such as public relations.

Media

The public interest was thrust into the international spotlight earlier this decade following the *News of the World* scandal in the United Kingdom. What began as the closure of the 168–year-old *News International* newspaper on 7 July 2011 for hacking the phone of a murdered schoolgirl spiralled into a national inquiry and Lord Justice Leveson's report *The Culture, Practices and Ethics of the Press* (Leveson 2012). The scandal had a ripple effect on media all over the world, focusing on ethical and legal media culture and practice, with particular implications for the balance of free speech and individual rights. At the center of investigations, court proceedings, media analysis and subsequent public documents was the question of whether the public interest justified the media's behavior. When court proceedings occurred, the British Crown Prosecution Service (CPS) handed down a guidance document to assist understanding of the public interest: *Interim Guidelines for prosecutors for assessing the public interest in cases affecting the media*. This document, and the broader issues surrounding it, highlighted the slippery nature of the public interest. While there was no shortage of reference to the public interest within this document, unlike the traditional approach to legal or government documents which define the terms of reference, there was no definition of the public interest. Indeed, the CPS notes: 'The public interest served by freedom of expression and the right to receive and impart information has never been defined in law' (Crown Prosecution Service 2012, p. 8). It uses instead examples of conduct that may serve the public interest, such as: 'Conduct which is capable of raising or contributing to an important matter of public debate' (2012, p. 9).

The vexed issue of defining the public interest was not lost on *The Observer*'s Peter Preston who lampooned the lack of definition:

> … this interest is damnably difficult to define. If it serves 'public debate' then it may be OK, whatever rules or precedents say. Remember that the bulk of journalism itself is in the public interest. Proceed cautiously case by case—and suck a long thumb. Engage prosecutorial brain, exalt common sense, and don't look for rigid lines in a flexible world.
> (Preston 2012, n.p.)

General analysis at the time suggested the public interest could, for all intents and purposes, be whatever anyone wanted it to be. One commentator noted: 'The meaning has rather lost shape in that it has become a get-out-of-jail-free card in whichever direction it is facing' (ONO 2012, n.p.). The entire shambolic episode provided, for our purposes, the greatest review of the public interest in recent British history, with implications for global media, but also for a broader, more general sense of what the public interest means. That there is no universal understanding of the concept of the public interest was illustrated when *The Guardian* made a call for a definition from members of the public, finding no real common ground from 150 responses (ONO 2012).

Of the existing guidelines and policies, the BBC's is among the most comprehensive and widely cited. Its policy on the public interest, which falls under its Privacy Guidelines, reads:

> Private behaviour, information, correspondence and conversation should not be brought into the public domain unless there is a public interest that outweighs the expectation of privacy. There is no single definition of public interest. It includes but is not confined to:

- exposing or detecting crime
- exposing significantly anti-social behaviour
- exposing corruption or injustice
- disclosing significant incompetence or negligence
- protecting people's health and safety
- preventing people from being misled by some statement or action of an individual or organisation
- disclosing information that assists people to better comprehend or make decisions on matters of public importance.

> There is also a public interest in freedom of expression itself. When considering what is in the public interest we also need to take account of information already in the public domain or about to become available to the public. When using the public interest to justify an intrusion, consideration should be given to proportionality; the greater the intrusion, the greater the public interest required to justify it (BBC 2013).

Moreover, the call for definitions suggested one further clause be added: '... disclosing information that assists people to better comprehend or make decisions on matters of public importance' (ONO 2012, n.p.).

The British Press Complaints Commission (PCC) includes selected points in common with the BBC, focusing on three key areas. It reads:

> The public interest includes, but is not confined to:
>   i Detecting or exposing crime or serious impropriety.
>   ii Protecting public health and safety.
>   iii Preventing the public from being misled by an action or statement of an individual or organisation (PCC 2012).

It is interesting that the PCC also notes that where the media invoke the public interest as a defense they should be able to argue how, and with whom, the public interest was established *at the time,* effectively that it should have been a motivating factor *prior to* any action rather than an afterthought (PCC 2012). This suggests the need for an *ex ante* (before) approach coupled with an *ex post* (after) examination, within specific time constraints and contexts. Additionally, there is the expectation that the public interest must be dealt with on a case-by-case basis, that it must also be time-specific, and reflect the social mores of the time. *The Guardian's* award-winning blogger Andrew Sparrow summed it up:

> I'm wary about attempts to define it or to pin it down, partly because I think this could end up being restrictive, but mainly because our view of what the public interest entails changes quite dramatically over time and I think, as journalists, we should be willing to fight the public-interest battle on a case-by-case basis. For example, 50 years ago it was assumed that there was a public interest in knowing that an MP was gay, but little or no public interest in whether he drove home drunk, hit his wife or furnished his house using wood from non-sustainable sources. Now, obviously, it's the other way round. Society does—and should—constantly redefine what the public interest entails and journalism should be part of that (ONO 2012).

As we will see in the next chapter, this 'public-interest-as-changeable' approach is also at the center of a theoretical and critical understanding of the concept (Bozeman 2007, p. 13). But though it may need to be viewed as changeable and dynamic, by necessity the public interest does need to be addressed at certain times to ascertain its parameters. The massive four-volume Leveson Report found the lack of attention to the public interest in contemporary society and media practice had fallen below acceptable standards, suggesting that it needed to be both defined in law and reflect the views of the British public. Within the report, a number of experts suggested that more thought needed to be given to the meaning of 'public interest' in the context of a new Media Standards Authority code.

> ... there needs to be a wider debate on the definition of the public interest, in particular if it is to gain enhanced status as a defence in the courts. The Carnegie Trust agrees that understanding the public interest in the context of the code requires more thought and recommends ongoing research to understand citizens' views on the matter. Lord Soley also raises issues of concern around both the definition of the public interest in the code and its application.
>
> (Leveson 2012, p. 1684)

This attention to the definition is echoed by media scholars, particularly in examining government policy over diversity. At a time of extreme concentration of media ownership, public interest tests are applied to determine diversity of news and plurality of voices in media organizations all over the world. British media professor Steve Barnett has argued for 'a more wide-ranging and properly implemented interpretation of the public interest, related specifically to diversity of output' (Barnett 2009, p. 13). This, he argued, would enhance civic and local journalism. Barnett was responding to the Ofcom report *Digital Britain: Final Report* (2009), which totals 245 pages and mentions the public interest only seven times, at no point defining it.

Barnett, Leveson and others have therefore called for a greater focus and closer analysis of the public interest concept, which is intractably tied to responsible media and the balancing of rights, embedded within the political economy. Their concerns are instructive in a number of ways: first, they illustrate the importance of greater understanding of the concept of the public interest; second, they argue the importance of re-evaluating and updating the public interest to reflect social expectations and mores; third, they provide theoretical and practical assistance in determining how the public interest can be used as a framework for balancing competing interests in communication practice. That it is defined in places such as the BBC and the Press Complaints Commission also provides some assistance in establishing industry-relevant criteria.

Law

The next field of practice that regularly intersects with the public interest is the law. The use of the public interest as a media defense within the law is already illustrated in the previous section. More broadly, the complexity and the intrigue it holds within legal and jurisprudential scholarship are highlighted in a publicly funded project in the United Kingdom intended to consolidate its meaning and enhance its understanding. The project—Public Interest in UK Courts—holds the core objectives of developing a taxonomy of its uses as well as a more concrete understanding of the concept (Public Interest in UK Courts 2011, n.p.).

However, while the public interest is used within the law as a defense, it is also used by the legal profession to define the sub-practice of what has become known as 'public interest law' and it is this second interface on which we will now focus. The use of the term 'public interest lawyers' was popularly coined in 1970 in a *Yale Law Journal* article called 'The new public interest lawyers.' Separate from lawyers who had hitherto worked in a public interest capacity for the government, these were a new type of social-justice driven lawyers. They were involved in three different pursuits:

- aiding the poor;
- representing political and cultural dissidents and new radical movements; and,
- furthering substantive but neglected interests such as environmental quality and consumer protection ('The new public interest lawyers' 1970, p. 1072).

Descriptions of this new breed of lawyers mirror those of activists more generally in responding to environmental and social issues of the time. This rise in activism with its emergence across public relations' ambit is examined by Demetrious (2013) who noted a merging with mainstream government bodies and policy makers as well as the rise of non-governmental organizations (NGOs) during this period. The public interest lawyer, meantime, was seen to attack problems and pursue long-term goals, engaging in a wide range of strategies and activities including:

> Counselling, lobbying, research and investigation, use of propaganda and the press, mobilizing community demonstrations, and organizing citizens' lobbies and community groups ('The new public interest lawyers' 1970, pp. 1146–47).

This job description might well have depicted a form of public interest/public relations; such was the role of the public interest lawyers. They were 'committed ultimately to causes, not clients … but also arbiters of social priorities' (1970, p. 1146).

Nowadays, public interest law has become synonymous with *pro bono*, human rights, community and minority law. It has become embedded as a speciality within university education (see, for example, the top 11 public interest law schools in the United States in Weyenberg 2009); it is a sub-set of mainstream law and can be accredited with national or international bodies. In Australia, for instance, the Queensland Public Interest Law Clearing House (QPILCH) is accredited with the National Association of Community Legal Centres (NACLC), which lists the State's Chief Justice as its patron. QPILCH works as a referral service for the homeless, refugees, not for profit groups, people with mental health issues and others, providing information and services across a wide range of legal fields from Strategic Lawsuits against Public Participation (SLAPPs) to anti-discrimination (QPILCH 2012). It also advocates for professional alliances, calling on volunteers *outside* the legal profession, noting: 'Sometimes … our clients … also require help from psychiatrists, psychologists, town planners, medical experts and others to help resolve their case' (QPILCH 2012). Logical 'others' in these contexts would include media advocates, communication specialists or those with public relations skills.

These developments in public interest law raise compelling possibilities for non-legal professionals, including public relations: first, we note that the public interest is now a specialized field of university study, illustrating how it has gained traction as a specialization in the legal profession; second, accreditation and association with national or international industry bodies can provide both legitimacy and networking benefits and possibilities for public relations; third, cross-disciplinary alliances provide opportunities for public relations, communication and policy-oriented professionals to work with legal and other specialists to assist in public interest work.

The Public Interest and Public Relations

To return to our second, earlier question: What then of the public interest's role in public relations? Though it has achieved relatively little attention in public relations literature, the public interest's application to public relations has nevertheless drawn mixed responses from scholars within the discipline. Among the most cited is Thomas Bivins's article *Public Relations, Professionalism and the Public Interest* (1993) in which he proposes four potential public interest paradigms:

- Paradigm I: If every individual practicing public relations acts in the best interest of his or her client, then the public interest will be served.
- Paradigm II: If, in addition to serving individual interests, an individual practicing public relations serves public interest causes, the public interest will be served.
- Paradigm III: If a profession or professionals assure that every individual in need or desiring its/their services receives its/their services, then the public interest will be served.
- Paradigm IV: If public relations as a profession improves the quality of debate over issues important to the public, then the public interest will be served (Bivins 1993, pp. 120–24).

Not surprisingly perhaps, Bivins suggests that the last of these paradigms is the most workable, arguing that ultimately: 'Public relations will have no choice but to define the public interest in a way that society will accept' (1993, p. 126). In criticizing the industry as a whole for failing to formalize its own doctrine of public service, he also suggests this role would alternately fall to the individual practitioner. Following Bivins, Seib and Fitzpatrick (1995) also advance the idea of public relations as a service profession.

Critiques of the public interest and public relations emerged over many decades from both the United Kingdom and the United States. In the United States, John W. Hill (1958, 1963) foreshadowed the foundation of Bivins's fourth paradigm, noting: 'the better informed the people are, the more capable they are of judging where the public interest lies' (1963, p. 256). Hill's work centered very closely on the public interest, suggesting it is one of the three requirements for essential public relations. Collectively, he suggested these are (1) truth and integrity; (2) soundness of policies, decisions, and acts which are in the 'general' public interest, and (3) the use of honest facts that are understandable, believable and imaginative (1958, pp. 6–7). Hill's corporate-centered approach, reflected in the book's title *Corporate Public Relations,* situated in part within a post–New Deal context in the United States, sits in contrast to those in Britain who locate the public interest in the public sector rather than the corporate sector (L'Etang 2004; Theaker & Yaxley 2013).

Jacquie L'Etang's (2004) critique of the public interest in her *History of Public Relations in Britain* notes an early reference to the public interest in the British Institute of Public Relations (IPR) Code of Professional Conduct in 1966. Three issues raised in a 1972 article in the journal *Public Relations* resonate strongly with contemporary thinking: the public interest must reflect contemporary community values; it must be guided by the law of the day; and the public interest is not easy to define (L'Etang 2004, p. 171). Significantly, L'Etang notes that the public interest as part of the code of ethics at the time was to separate two conceptual models of public relations which emerged:

> one of public relations as advocacy on behalf of clients and employers, the other of public relations as public information and social responsibility acting in the public interest. The implicit tensions between these two positions has not received the attention it deserves given its wider political implications ... Acting in the public interest was a crucial justification for the existence of public relations and an implicit (and sometimes explicit) way for practitioners to distinguish their occupation from propaganda (2004, p. 170).

L'Etang thus saw the corporate or 'client-consultant' path as the one most closely associated with propaganda and others, following, were to focus on the sector or type of public relations as impacting on its public interest capacity. Weaver, Motion and Roper (2006) focused their attention on how corporations construct the public interest as intrinsically connected to corporate interests; however, they concluded that public relations had the potential to challenge dominant perceptions and hegemonic power and thus work for the public interest (Weaver, Motion & Roper 2006, p. 20). And Moloney (2006, p. 14), meanwhile, was to caution that non-capitalist, non-big-business PR—notably activist and advocacy PR—also effectively uses propaganda and advances self-interest so there can be no absolute distinction.

Robert Heath's (1992, p. 318) early work on the public interest suggested that interests compete against each other, outlining what he called a 'negotiated self-interest model' of public relations. He premised this on systems being self-regulated and self-correcting in keeping with the theory of political economist Adam Smith and his 'natural harmony of individual wills' or 'invisible hand' laissez-fair approach (Smith 1976, p. 31). In essence, Heath argued that free enterprise and public policy will balance out 'to the extent that each assertion of self-interest produces various counter assertions' (1992, p. 318). The result, he said, is that the self-interest paradigm is not antithetic to the symmetry paradigm.

The duality of serving both the organization and its publics' interests is central to early iterations of Excellence Theory whereby 'public relations should be practiced to serve the public interest, to develop mutual understanding between organizations and their publics, and to contribute to informed debate about issues in society' (L Grunig 1992, p. 9). However, the body of critical public relations analysis which emerged following this position (see, for example, L'Etang & Pieczka 1996, 2006; Pieczka 2006; Moloney 2006; Weaver, Motion & Roper 2006) saw an adjustment to the proposed harmony and mutuality. As such, arguments of equally serving 'everyone' were refined, and *balanced interests* were subsequently advocated: 'Symmetry means that communicators keep their eyes on a broader professional perspective of balancing private and public interests ... they must consistently remind themselves and management that they might not be right and, indeed, that their organizations might be better off if they listen to others' (J Grunig 2001, p. 28).

While Heath (1992) proposed a political economy approach to reconciling the public interest with public relations, others, over the decades (Hill 1958; Bivins 1992; Seib & Fitzpatrick 1995; Messina 2007; Grunig 2001; Pendleton 2013; Preston 2005, 2013) were more focused on the ethics of the public interest and public relations. Preston's 2005 and 2013 entries on the public interest in Heath's *Encyclopedia of Public Relations* provide a short review of the US literature since Hill's early analysis (1958). She cites Scott Cutlip, Allen Center and Glen Broom's (1985, p. 482) text, which calls on the industry to serve 'the larger good over short-term private interests.' Ten years later, in his US history of public relations, Cutlip was to lament the lack of public interest in both public relations and journalism—the final paragraph of his history noting 'it is time for the journalist and practitioner to take stock of their work and to determine if what they are doing is truly in the public interest as both journalists and practitioners profess to serve' (1995, p. 284). Preston also lists the deep concerns raised by leading US practitioner Harold Burson over the relative rejection of the public interest by public relations scholars, a commentary that is examined in more detail below.

While the majority of the relatively scant literature is either optimistic of a public interest presence in public relations or concerned for its limited application, Alex Messina (2007) emphatically rejects the capacity of public relations to effectively engage with it. Drawing heavily on Flathman's (1966) work on the public interest, Messina determined that public relations could *not* work in the public interest in part because 'no public relations practitioner could preemptively decipher the public interest' and that the ethics of the public interest could only be determined 'later by the political process' (2007, p. 38). He argued that the public interest could only be determined *ex post* (after), rather than *ex ante* (before), an action is carried out (Messina 2007, p. 38) and further saw public relations occurring *outside* the political process. This book, meanwhile, takes a different view: first, in situating public relations as *part of* the political process; second, in arguing that public relations practitioners are capable of navigating the public interest, just as lawyers, journalists, policy makers and anthropologists can; and, finally, in arguing that an *ex ante* approach may be consistent with the planning process of public relations activity and should therefore not be excluded as a possibility. Others, notably economist Lok Sang Ho (2011, 2013), have proposed the public interest *should* be pursued *ex ante*.

What's in a Name: PR Definitions and the Public Interest

The public interest has come under attention in recent years for both its inclusion and exclusion from official definitions of public relations. When a group of Canadian public relations fellows were quoted on a blog in 2012—'Can public relations be in the public interest?' (Begin 2012, n.p.)—they were referring to an overwhelming lack of attention to the public interest within international public relations. Among their concerns was the omission of the term 'public interest' from most definitions of public relations (Begin 2012). In response to the criticism of 'no public interest' the Canadian Public Relations Society (CPRS) embraced the term in a revised definition, which reads:

> Public relations is the strategic management of relationships between an organization and its diverse publics, through the use of communication, to achieve mutual understanding, realize organizational goals, and serve the public interest.
>
> (Gregory & Valin in CPRS 2013)

At around the same time, the Public Relations Society of America (PRSA 2011, 2012) used a crowdsourcing approach to redefine public relations, resulting in the following definition:

> Public relations is a strategic communication process that builds mutually beneficial relationships between organizations and their publics.

Notably, there is no reference to the public interest. The PRSA (2012) reported that of the 900 definitions submitted in the redefining process, the term the 'public interest' did not rate a mention. The most popular words included the following: organization (388 submissions), public (373), communication (280), relationship/s (260), stakeholders (172), create (170), mutual (158), understand (153), build (152), audiences (147), inform (144) and management (124) (PRSA 2012). The new definition drew criticism from leading practitioner Harold Burson, who saw it as inadequate. Responding to the new definition, Burson (2012, n.p.) argued that 'we who choose careers in public relations also have an implied obligation to what we call the public interest' and that it is incumbent on the role of public relations to reconcile employer goals with the public interest. For Burson, public relations must *begin* with the public interest. 'Yes, communications and establishing relationships are part of the mix, but the process must start with appropriate behaviour that serves the public interest,' he said (Burson 2012, n.p.).

The redefining of public relations in Canada and the United States put the public interest firmly onto the contemporary international public relations agenda. Though definitions are inherently restrictive, they can and do provide both a launch-pad for further discussion, and send a message. And while it has been argued that 'experienced people ignore conversations about definitions' (Moloney 2006, p. 178), these shorthand scripts do nevertheless assist with understanding how the industry both views itself and is viewed externally. At the very least, locating the public interest in definitions provides a litmus test of how scholars and industry view its relevance. Several are included in Box 1.1, following.

Box 1.1 – Five Definitions of Public Relations that include the Public Interest

Public Relations – Public Interest Definitions

'*Experts in the field almost uniformly agree that public relations is concerned with building goodwill or with establishing a policy of good deeds in the public interest by means of the media or communication*' (Nayyar 2010, p. 18).

'*Good corporate public relations depends first, upon sound policies truly in the public interest and second, upon clear and effective communication, explanation, and interpretation of policies and facts to the public*' (Hill 1958, p. 163).

'*Public relations is a distinctive management function which helps establish and maintain mutual lines of communication, understanding, acceptance and co-operation between an organization and its publics; involves the management of problems or issues; helps management to keep informed on the response to public opinion; defines and emphasises the responsibility of management to serve the public interest; helps management keep abreast of and efficient utilise change, serving as an early warning system to help anticipate trends: and uses research and ethical communication techniques as its principal tools*' (Harlow 1976 in Cain 2009, p. ix).

'*Public relations practice is the art and social science of analysing trends, predicting their consequences, counselling organization leaders, and implementing planned programs of action which serve both the organization's and the public's interest*' (World Assembly of Public Relations' Mexican Statement 1978 in Cain 2009, p. 136).

Conclusion and Navigating This Book

We have seen in this chapter calls for greater attention to the public interest. These calls may be strongest from other disciplines but have nevertheless registered since the 1950s within the field of public relations. To paraphrase Andrew Sparrow: society does—and should—constantly redefine what the public interest entails; public relations should be part of that process. Likewise, scholars and practitioners might take advice from Justice Leveson who has argued for a review of the public interest in light of recent media activity in Britain. As communicators, and those who contribute to public policy and debate, it would be prudent for public relations to embrace his advice, accepting 'there needs to be a wider debate on the definition of the public interest' (Leveson 2012, p. 1684).

As a practice and function that has an arsenal of tools available to it, in formal and informal positions—as consultant, in-house practitioner, activist or volunteer—the power public relations holds is wide-ranging and the benefits it provides can be substantial, but these should be tempered with reality checks of public values, benefits and interests. A deeper understanding and consideration of the public interest can provide an avenue for reflexivity, just as it does for other industries and sectors of society. Burson's powerful voice, those from the CPRS, and a handful of public relations scholars over the decades have placed the concept onto the contemporary public relations agenda and engaged with its potential or argued for its inclusion. Accordingly, there is clearly a case for more fully and critically examining the public interest within the context of contemporary public relations critique and practice. This book now moves on to consider the public interest through a range of different prisms which intersect with public relations. Each chapter includes examples and 'snapshots' to illustrate and amplify chapter themes, and though each chapter may stand alone, common themes of the book become apparent.

Chapter 2 examines the origins and dedicated theories of the public interest, including an overview of the public interest literature and an analysis of its role within the political economy. It incorporates normative and critical perspectives, drawing from Habermas, Dewey and others, and introduces regulatory concepts of capture and slack, as well as reviewing the established and well-known theories of ideal speech and communicative and strategic action, as each applies to the public interest. It raises important issues and themes, such as timing, context, participation and plurality, which resonate throughout the book. Chapter 3 examines key intersections between the public interest and the field of public relations which have emerged from within the existing communication and public relations literature: the first is the role of the public information officer (PIO) as distinct from the public relations practitioner (RPR); the second is the development of public interest groups as they emerged in response to social challenges; the third is the part played in developing partnerships and alliances to advance public interests; and the fourth, is the concept of *pro bono publico,* which translated means 'for the public good.' It considers the role of agency and how this applies to public relations and the public interest, using examples from the third sector and government agencies as snapshots.

Chapter 4 uses political economy and critical theory lenses to view how communication and media work both within and against the public interest. In examining the production, distribution and the ideological dimensions of media and communication, it provides critical and functional perspectives of speech acts, discourse, source-media relationships, social media and online knowledge with illustrations and snapshots including the production of media guides and public relations' interface with Wikipedia. The chapter draws on a broad base of theory, including the work of Habermas, Picard and Fuchs.

Chapter 5 examines the public interest's intersections with culture and public relations. It draws on existing public relations and communication scholarship about culture, subalternity and postcoloniality and examines new points of entry for the public interest including the work of Paulo Freire and public interest anthropology. Themes that emerge in this chapter which resonate throughout the book are the role of praxis in facilitating change, links between culture, communication and power, the importance of bottom-up participation in cultural understanding and the role of pedagogy in moving toward participatory models of transformational culture.

Chapter 6 uses the field of social capital, as situated within all capitals—industrial, financial, intellectual, human, social and natural—to examine the role of the public interest within public relations, particularly as it relates to communities. In particular it draws on the work of Putnam, Coleman and Bourdieu to examine social capital as it applies to individuals and communities, finding synonymies with public relations, and locating the public interest within this analysis. The chapter explores the inter-relatedness of all capitals, including the accounting paradigm of 'cognitive capitalism' and the importance of capacity building. It also expands on earlier themes of community participation and the role of governments in the process, using 'snapshots' of mental health lobbying and rural renewal.

Chapter 7 examines the intersections of the public interest with the law, picking up on earlier themes of social change, and introducing social order and how these intersect with public relations. It considers how the public interest can be a 'shape-shifter,' how it evolves and adapts to the social values of time and context, and how freedom of information laws can provide a touch-point for better understanding the theory in practice. It incorporates normative and critical theories from Habermas, Luhmann, Rawls and Foucault in drawing together concepts of social justice, social change and order, power and communication, illustrated with examples and snapshots of the Irish referendum on same-sex marriage, 'on country' justice for Indigenous claims to native title, and the role played by public relations in communicating the role of the courts.

Chapter 8 takes the public interest journey into the field of values, ethics and moral philosophy, examining the fields of utilitarianism, deontology, virtue ethics and codes of practice. Included are works and critiques of Aristotle, Bentham, Kant and others—philosophers and scholars who have sought to explicate interest theory from a variety of positions including a defense of Bentham's approach to interests, and views of public relations scholars on the application of Aristotle's virtue ethics to the industry. It proposes the idea of an 'outsider' or 'third party' to judge the veracity of interest claims and reinforce accountability and openness to scrutiny. Finally, the chapter presents an original analysis of 84 global codes of public relations ethics and practice, finding 34 codes that use the expression 'the public interest,' presenting a table of how the term 'the public interest' is used and concluding with a brief discussion of ethical codes more generally.

Finally, chapter 9 draws together the themes and issues raised throughout the book, providing a reflexive response and modeling of ideas for moving forward. In examining the public interest from normative, critical and functional perspectives, it synthesizes the issues and arguments raised throughout elsewhere, proposing how public relations, as both an institutionalized industry and as a function that exists outside formal environments, might engage less tentatively with the concept of the public interest just as other disciplines have done. It suggests the public interest not only can provide balance in discourse and decision making but also can raise levels of public understanding, knowledge and participation, thus providing an important concept for conducting public relations activity and critiquing the complex field of public relations within contemporary scholarship.

References

Barnett, S 2009, *Journalism, democracy and the public interest: Rethinking media pluralism for the digital age*, Reuters Institute for the Study of Journalism working paper, Ofcom, viewed 15 December 2013, https://reutersinstitute.politics. ox.ac.uk/fileadmin/documents/Publications/Journalism_Democracy_Public_ Interest_for_website.pdf.

BBC 2013, *Editorial Guidelines Section 7: Privacy*, viewed 15 December 2013, http://www.bbc.co.uk/editorialguidelines/page/guidelines-privacy-introduction/# the-public-interest.

Begin, D 2012, 'Can public relations be in the public interest?' *Where to begin: life as my muse* [weblog], viewed 20 November 2013, http://www.wheretobegin.ca/ can-public-relations-be-in-the-public-interest/.

Benditt, TM 1973, 'The public interest', *Philosophy and Public Affairs*, vol. 2, no. 3, pp. 291–311.

Bivins, TH 1993, 'Public relations, professionalism, and the public interest', *Journal of Business Ethics*, February, vol. 12, no. 2, pp. 117–26.

Bozeman, B 2007, *Public values and public interest: counterbalancing economic individualism*, Georgetown University Press, Washington, DC.

British Crown Prosecution Service 2012, *Interim guidelines for prosecutors for assessing the public interest in cases affecting the media*, Crown Prosecution Service, London, viewed 14 June 2014, http://www.cps.gov.uk/consultations/ mg_consultation.pdf.

Burson, H 2012. 'A "modern" definition of public relations? Why?' 5 March 2012. Harold Burson [weblog], viewed 10 June 2014, http://www.burson-marsteller. com/harold-blog/a-modern-definition-of-public-relations-why/.

Cain, S 2009, *Key concepts in public relations*, Palgrave Macmillan, London.

Canada Public Relations Society (CPRS) 2013, *Mission, definition and values*, viewed 15 December 2013, http://www.cprs.ca/aboutus/mission.aspx.

Cassinelli, CW 1958, 'Some reflections of the concept of the public interest', *Ethics*, vol. 69, no. 1, pp. 48–61.

Cochran, CE 1974, 'Political science and the public interest', *The Journal of Politics*, vol. 36, no. 2, pp. 327–55.

Crown Prosecution Services, 2012, *Interim guidelines for prosecutors for assessing the public interest in cases affecting the media*, April, viewed 5 June 2015, http://www.cps.gov.uk/consultations/mg_consultation.pdf.

Curtin, PA & Gaither, TK 2007, *International public relations: Negotiating culture, identity and power*, Sage, Thousand Oaks, CA.

Cutlip, SM 1995, *Public relations history: from the 17th to the 20th century*, Routledge, New York.

Cutlip, SM, Center, AH & Broom, GM 1985, *Effective public relations*, Prentice Hall, Englewood Cliffs, NJ.

Demetrious, K 2013, *Public relations, activism and social change: speaking up*, Routledge, London.

Department of Business, Innovation and Skills 2009, *Digital Britain: Final Report*, British Government, viewed 20 December 2013, https://www.gov.uk/government/uploads/system/uploads/attachment_data/file/228844/7650.pdf.

Dewey, J 1927, *The public and its problems*, Holt, New York.

Edwards, L 2011, 'Questions of self-interest, agency and the rhetor', *Management Communication Quarterly*, vol. 25, no. 3, pp. 531–40.

Ehling, WP 1992, 'Estimating the value of public relations and communication to an organization', in J Grunig (ed.), *Excellence in public relations and communication management*, Lawrence Erlbaum, Mahwah, NJ, pp. 617–38.

Flathman, R 1966, *The public interest*, John Wiley & Sons, New York.

Grunig, LA 1992, 'How public relations/communication departments should adapt to the structure and environment of an organization … and what they actually do', in JE Grunig (ed.), *Excellence in public relations and communication management*, Lawrence Erlbaum Associates, Mahwah, NJ.

Grunig, JE 2001, 'Two-way symmetrical public relations: past, present, and future', in RL Heath & G Vasquez (eds.), *Handbook of public relations*, Sage, Thousand Oaks, CA.

Heath, RL 1992, 'Visions of critical studies in public relations', in EL Toth & RL Heath (eds.), *Rhetorical and critical approaches to public relations*, Lawrence Erlbaum Associates, Mahwah, NJ.

Heath, RL 2009, 'The rhetorical tradition', in RL Heath, EL Toth & D Waymer (eds.), *Rhetorical and critical approaches to public relations II*, Routledge, New York, pp. 17–47.

Hill, JW 1958, *Corporate public relations: arm of modern management*, Harper & Bros, New York.

Hill, JW 1963, *The making of a public relations man*, David McKay, New York.

Ho, LS 2011, *Public policy and the public interest*, Routledge, London.

Ho, LS 2013, *Health policy and the public interest*, Routledge, London.

Holtzhausen, D 2012, *Public relations as activism: postmodern approaches to theory and practice*, Routledge, New York.

L'Etang, J 2004, *Public relations in Britain*, Lawrence Erlbaum, Mahwah, NJ.

L'Etang, J & Pieczka, M 1996, *Critical perspectives in public relations*, International Thomson Business Press, London.

L'Etang, J & Pieczka, M 2006, 'Introduction', in J L'Etang & M Pieczka (eds.), *Public relations: critical debates and contemporary practice*, Lawrence Erlbaum, Mahwah, NJ, pp. 1–3.

L'Etang, J & Pieczka, M (eds.) 2006, *Public relations: critical debates and contemporary practice,* Lawrence Erlbaum, Mahwah, NJ.

Leveson, Lord Justice 2012, *An inquiry into the culture, practice and ethics of the press,* 29 November, viewed 29 May 2013, http://www.levesoninquiry.org.uk.

Lippmann, W 1955, *Essays in the public philosophy,* Little Brown, Boston.

Locke, J 1767, *The second treatise of civil government,* 6th edn, viewed 15 June 2015, https://ebooks.adelaide.edu.au/l/locke/john/l81s/index.html.

Messina, A 2007, 'Public relations, the public interest and persuasion: an ethical approach,' *Journal of Communication Management,* vol. 11, no. 1, pp. 29–52.

Meyerson, D 2007 'Why courts should not balance rights against the public interest', *Melbourne University Law Review,* 31 (3), pp. 873–903.

Mitnick, B 1980, *The political economy of regulation,* Columbia University Press, New York.

Moloney, K 2000, *Rethinking public relations: the spin and the substance,* Routledge, London.

Moloney, K 2006, *Rethinking public relations,* Routledge, London.

Moravcsik, A & Sangiovanni, A 2003, 'On democracy and the "public interest" in the European Union,' *Working Paper No. 93,* Center for European Studies, viewed 20 October 2013, http://aei.pitt.edu/9135.

Nayyar, D 2010, *Public relations and communication,* Global Media, Jaipur.

Opdycke Lamme, M & Miller Russell, K 2010, 'Removing the spin: toward a new theory of public relations history', *Journalism Communication Monographs, Association for Education in Journalism and Mass Communication,* vol. 11, no. 4.

Organization of News Ombudsmen (ONO) 11 June 2012, *How do we define the public interest,* viewed 5 November 2013, http://newsombudsmen.org/columns/how-should-we-define-in-the-public-interest.

Pendleton, J 2013, *Public relations, discourse practice and the public interest: analysis of a health communication campaign,* PhD thesis, RMIT University.

Pieczka, M 2006, 'Paradigms, systems theory, and public relations', in J L'Etang & M Pieczka (eds.), *Public relations: critical debates and contemporary practice,* Lawrence Erlbaum, Mahwah, NJ, pp. 331–59.

Pires, MA 1983, Texaco: Public interest groups, *Public Relations Journal,* April, pp. 16–19.

Press Complaints Commission (PCC) 2012, *Editors' code of practice,* viewed 10 November 2013, http://www.pcc.org.uk/cop/practice.html.

Preston, A 2005, 'Public interest', in R Heath (ed.), *Encyclopedia of public relations,* Sage, Thousand Oaks, CA, pp. 673–75.

Preston, A 2013, 'Public interest', in R Heath (ed.), *Encyclopedia of public relations,* 2nd edn, Sage, Thousand Oaks, CA, pp. 717–19. doi.org/10.4135/9781452276263.n392.

Preston, P 2012, 'Public interest defined: er, it's hard to pin down. Use your common sense' *The Guardian/The Observer* 22 April, viewed 20 December 2013, http://www.theguardian.com/media/2012/apr/22/public-interest-defined-hard-to-pin-down.

PRSA 2 December 2011, *Snapshot#PR defined word cloud,* viewed 18 December 2013, http://prdefinition.prsa.org/index.php/2011/12/02/snapshot-of-the-public-relations-defined-initaitve-submission-day12.

PRSA 11 April 2012, *Public relations defined: a modern definition for a new era of public relations,* viewed 18 December 2013, http://prdefinition.prsa.org.

Public Interest in UK Courts 2011, Economic and Social Research Council, viewed 7 June 2015, http://publicinterest.info.

Queensland Public Interest Law Clearinghouse 2012, *Other volunteers,* viewed 19 December 2013, http://www.qpilch.org.au/cms/details.asp?ID=633.

Seib, P & Fitzpatrick, K 1995, *Public relations ethics,* Harcourt Brace, Orlando, FL.

Sorauf, FJ 1957, 'The public interest reconsidered', *The Journal of Politics,* vol. 19, no. 4, pp. 616–39.

Smith, A 1976, *The theory of moral sentiments,* Liberty Classics, Indianapolis.

'The new public interest lawyers 1970', *The Yale Law Journal,* vol. 79, no. 6, pp. 1069–1152.

Theaker, A & Yaxley, H 2013, *The public relations strategic toolkit,* Routledge, London.

Weaver, CK, Motion, J & Roper, J 2006. 'From propaganda to discourse (and back again): truth, power, the public interest, and public relations', in J L'Etang, & M Pieczka (eds.), *Public relations: critical debates and contemporary practice,* Lawrence Erlbaum, Mahwah NJ, pp. 7–23.

Weyenberg, M 2009, 'Best public interest law schools', *The National Jurist,* viewed 1 June 2014, http://www.nationaljurist.com/content/best-public-interest-law-schools.

Wheeler, C 2006, 'The public interest: we know it's important, but do we know what it means', R Creyke & A Mantel (eds.), Australian Institute of Administrative Law *AIAL Forum no. 48,* viewed 1 September 2013, http://www.aial.org.au/Publications/webdocuments/Forums/Forum48.pdf.

2 Theoretical Scaffolding and Critical Perspectives

An appeal to the public interest settles nothing as such, but its invocation helps to distinguish matters ... from purely sectional, individual or idiosyncratic points of view.
(McQuail 1992, p. 29)

Introduction

This chapter provides an opportunity to develop many of the theoretical currents that emerged in chapter 1. As noted, the popularity of the public interest as a political construct has ebbed and flowed over the decades, with scholars such as Hill (1958), Flathman (1966), Cochran (1974), Douglass (1980), Levine and Forrence (1990) and Bozeman (2007) arguing for its retention despite its underlying ambiguity and inherently subjective nature. As a fundamentally political, legal and economic theory, it has been adapted and adopted into public policy, media, sociology and anthropology and, to a lesser extent, public relations. For the media, the public interest has become its mantra, its virtual *raison d'etre* and locus of ethical activity—its legal and moral claim to a universal 'right-to-know.' Media scholar Denis McQuail argues that the reason he chose to re-examine what he calls 'the unresolved issue' of the public interest in his book *Media Performance: Mass Communication and the Public Interest* was to help in identifying 'specific manifestations of public benefit from communication that go *beyond* the immediate purposes of the media themselves, of their clients or of their audiences' (1992, p. 21, my italics). In effect, McQuail argues that the public interest is *bigger* than the media. Indeed, it is claimed by government, corporate and civil sectors, and because public relations has a presence across all these, as advocate, enabler, advisor and communicator, it behooves those who practice, study and critique public relations to understand it more deeply—not only as it applies to its own field but also, like the media, as part of political, economic and civil society.

The chapter serves two separate but interlocking purposes within the book: it acts as a stand-alone chapter in presenting an historical analysis of public interest while also introducing important theoretical positions and distilling key concepts. Some of the theories will be very familiar to public relations scholars, whereas others, drawn from the public interest literature, will be less so. Themes that emerge include, but are not limited to, the shifting landscape of public and private interests, pluralist approaches to publics, intersections between the public interest and the public sphere (or multiple public spheres) and the role of communication in connecting and finding congruence among these. That these are examined within the fields of political science, economics and regulatory structures collectively defines the public interest as being part of a political economy framework (Mitnick 1980; Moloney 2000) which importantly provides context both historically and contemporaneously. As such, the chapter spans centuries-old developments through to present challenges raised in changing information and communication technology (ICT) environments.

Two caveats are made prior to beginning this exploration of theory and the origins of the public interest. First, selecting from the vast public interest literature risks a translation that could be interpreted as reductionist; the most any analysis can do is distill dominant and important threads and approaches—in this case in order to provide a deeper understanding for public relations scholarship and practice. Second, a broad reading of the public interest literature assumes a synonymy between the public interest and democracy. The existing literature is dominated by Western thinking, premised on democratic ideologies; thus the public interest is presented broadly within democratic contexts, with occasional alternative historical, political and cultural examples and sources in this chapter and elsewhere.

Public Interest Origins

There is no definitive account, no precise time in history, when 'the public interest' universally emerged as a philosophical, political or economic concept. Through Roman and medieval times, the 'common good,' 'common interest,' 'public good' and 'public interest' emerged in varying iterations, some argue interchangeably, while others see the public interest emerge in response to the common good. For Aristotle (384–322 BCE), while matters of 'common interest' may have been sought by the king, the aristocracy or the people, only matters of 'common good' represented the 'right' action (Taylor 1995). Thomas Aquinas (1222–1274) saw the upholding of a 'common good' as falling to government and law as 'nothing less than the fulfilment of all human persons and communities' (Finnis 2011, para. 5.2.3). John Locke (1632–1704) saw 'public good' as the purpose of government in protecting the rights of people, with political power 'only for the public good' (Locke 1767, chapter 1, p. 1). Jean-Jacques Rousseau (1712–1778) identified the 'common good' as the responsibility of government, found in the social contract—'no citizen shall be rich enough to buy another, and none so poor as to sell himself' (Rousseau 1762, para. 73). Jeremy Bentham (1748–1832) adopted the term 'the public interest' as the standard for public policy, determining the standard to be the 'the sum of the interests of the ... members of who compose it' ([1780] 1906, p. 3 in Mansbridge 1998, p. 9).

Each brought his own idea of the common good, the public interest or public good to what was the just and right way for societies to behave and scholars have found the meaning to be malleable and time-specific. Douglass views the 'common good' as emerging from the Ancient Greeks. He notes (1980, p. 105):

> They were moral goods in the Aristotelian sense: They contributed to the development and perfection of distinctively human qualities. They enabled men to live well, to experience the fullness of human life, as opposed to merely existing.

In medieval times, the idea of the common good was to provide for its people but, with the breakdown of medieval feudalism, the common good became increasingly identified with the interests of the crown as national monarchies sought justifications for expansion and to 'fuel foreign adventures' (Douglass 1980, p. 106).

This resulted in negative connotations associated with governments imposing what was deemed to be in the common good. 'These people might have chosen to contest the royalist interpretation of the common good' (Douglass 1980, p. 106) and indeed they did, by voicing their own ideas of what they felt to be in their own interests.

> As is often the case in the interaction between political ideas and political events, the insurgents chose to create a new alternative. Thus emerged the concept of the public interest. Particularly in the turbulent history of mid-seventeenth century England this shift in language and concepts was apparent.
>
> (Douglass 1980, p. 105)

The result was what may have been conceived of as an aggregation of private interests, but also a way of articulating an individualist conception of the public good as one 'that could not be hidden in the cabinets of kings' (Gunn 1968, p. 551; Douglass 1980). Douglass draws on the philosophy of Thomas Hobbes in forming an argument for how the public interest thus gained credence over what was understood as the wider government or common interest. The Hobbesian view suggests that there was no alternative to self-interested behavior in distinguishing it from government; indeed 'the politics of interest was universal' (Douglass 1980, p. 107). Others suggest that Hobbes may have believed 'the problems that befall human beings ... result[ed] from their being *too little* concerned with self-interest' (Williams n.d., his italics).

Accordingly, the concept of interest became influential as part of a liberal, democratic revolt against royalist impositions and the prerogatives of the king, carrying 'possessive individualist connotations.'

The more emphasis was placed on property rights and private benefits and the more democratic ideas grew in popularity, the more natural it became to contend that the definition of well-being should be left as much as possible to the individual.

(Douglass 1980, p. 108)

In this era, the concept of 'interest' was well accepted and became widely used in France, Spain, Italy and England. Indeed Gunn notes that seventeenth-century English politics 'employed the word in a way for which there was no precedent' (1968, p. 551). He points out:

From a term that had usually entered public life within the context of legal matters and discussions of positive rights, interest came to refer to all designs and concerns, whether or not sanctioned by legal recognition; furthermore, it also began to be applied to those groups that shared certain concerns.

Gunn explains the move within civil society, noting that by the 1650s public interest groups in England used pamphlets as tools for social action: 'The age of interests, in the sense familiar to modern political science, had arrived' (Gunn 1968, p. 552).

An alternative entry point comes from Mitnick (1980) who sees the common good and the public interest as interchangeable, emerging within government regulation, locating it within the political economy of medieval times. He identifies four 'forerunners' to the public interest (Mitnick 1980, p. 243), each aligned with government regulation, which were aimed to ensure a degree of equity to all citizens. In effect, these were closely aligned with the common good, as governments looked to providing services to achieve social and political goals. The first lay in the development of the concept of the 'just price,' developed by the Church in opposition to the 'natural price' that Roman law prescribed. The just price recognized the implicit coercion in exchanges that arose under difficult circumstances, such as famine. The second was the development of the guild system in medieval towns whereby guilds were allowed a monopoly in exchange for servicing at a reasonable price. Guilds took the form of merchant or craft guilds and members were called *confraternities*—brothers helping one another (Mitnick 1980, p. 245). The third was found in the royal charters and franchises, which also allowed monopolies during the age of mercantilism, ensuring certain services were made available. Fourth and finally, the concept of 'common callings' was a strong precursor to the public interest because it was based on the need for necessary services and occupations being made available to society at reasonable price; important in these were public utilities and occupations including surgeons, smiths, bakers, tailors, millers, innkeepers, ferrymen, wharfingers and carriers (Phillips 1965 in Mitnick 1980, p. 245). These 'common callings' were intended to balance the idea of the 'uncontrolled market place' which was 'affected with a public interest' (Mitnick 1980, p. 246). As such, certain industries were recognized in law and custom as affected with a public interest, often connected with transport and other utilities, including communication services. In such circumstances, public regulation was applied to ensure equity and efficiency, that is, in the fair and adequate provision of goods and services at reasonable prices (Mitnick 1980; McQuail 1992).

In turn, the courts, through the common law, developed a series of rights and obligations that attached to these public service businesses. These were incorporated into law and regulation, thus providing the foundation for the modern understanding of 'the public interest' in law as we know it today (Mitnick 1980). In summary, the rights and obligations of 'common callings' included the following:

Obligations:
- to serve all who request service;
- to give safe and adequate service;
- to serve all on an equal basis; and
- to require only a 'just and reasonable' price.

Rights:
- the right of protection of private property;
- the right to receive a reasonable price;
- the right to offer services and to terminate services;
- the right of eminent domain (adapted from Mitnick 1990, p. 244).

Ultimately 'medieval regulation gave way in the eighteenth century to a renewed emphasis on the ... "natural laws" ... of the market place' and the laissez-faire notion of Adam Smith and his 'invisible hand' which brought together self and public interest (Mitnick 1980, p. 246). 'A concept of the public interest is not abandoned to the private interest but, rather, said to be realized as the resultant of private action' (Mitnick 1980, p. 247). However, abuses and poor performance of the competitive era were not able to be remedied by the limited regulatory controls which had been put in place; hence a revised approach of the public interest was to appear in a more 'sophisticated notion of the public utility concept, as well as a set of regulatory mechanisms' (Mitnick 1980, p. 247) which would compensate for the failures of the market.

The early to middle of the twentieth century saw the public interest develop via a series of theories within political and economic fields, with notable scholars John Dewey (1927) and later Richard Flathman (1966) among those articulating various theoretical directions and models for the public interest. Educationalist and social theorist John Dewey's work, *The Public and Its Problems* (1927), examined the pressing challenges of the age of industrial capitalism. Here Dewey demonstrated a strong normative notion of the public interest while also identifying where he believed government regulation could assist with the market failure of the US political economy (Bybee 1997; Bozeman 2007). Dewey subsequently eloquently wrote in *Liberalism and Social Action*: 'Of course there are conflicting interests: otherwise there would be no social problems' (1935 cited in Bozeman 2007, p. 105). Thus, those engaging in political discussion should be under no illusions as to the existence of interest-politics.

His philosophy brought a pragmatic understanding to the public interest, which would resonate through the later writing on the topic in the 1960s and 1970s—primarily related to notions of the public interest being context-driven participant-oriented, incorporating what Bozeman calls 'public interest in action' that drew together ideas of balancing community values with the contextual nature of the public interest within a given historical context (2007, p. 104). His early work was said to be in response to Walter Lippmann's *The Phantom Public* (1927) in which Lippmann expressed disillusionment with democratic politics, calling the public a 'mere phantom' (1927, p. 67) later arguing in his *Essays on Public Philosophy* (1955, p. 42): 'There is no point in toying with any notion of an imaginary plebiscite to discover the public interest.' Yet, perhaps ironically, Lippmann's definition of the public interest remains one of the best known, as 'what men would choose if they saw clearly, thought rationally, [and] acted disinterestedly and benevolently' (Lippmann 1955, p. 42). Alternately, Dewey, as a fierce proponent of democracy, believed the movement to democracy was 'built into the social character of existence' (Bybee 1997, n.p.). Thus, for him, answers lay in the need to find balance between the individual's needs and the interests and goods that are held in common (Bybee 1997). 'Dewey sees democracy as the embodiment of community itself; it is not an ideal towards which society is moving, but rather a tendency built into the very structure of social activity' (Bybee 1997, n.p.).

In *Public Values and Public Interest* (2007) Bozeman draws on the work of Dewey to develop what he calls a 'Pragmatic Public Interest Theory,' premised on two foundational elements:

- First, as a method of democratic social inquiry modeled on the workings of the scientific community; and
- Second, as a focus on the role of deliberation, social learning, and interest transformation during this process.

As such, he was not averse to scientific inquiry, however he saw the public interest as a responsive concept, suggesting an *ex post* approach to democratic deliberation, reacting to social inquiry, public discussion and debate. Though he was inspired by science, he felt it had 'forgotten its direct relationship with human experience and its role as servant to human interests' (Bybee 1997, n.p.). He believed that by holding narrow or special interests up to the scrutiny of the wider community, 'their merits could be assessed from the perspective of the emergent "more inclusive interests" of the public, identified through open discussion and free debate' (Dewey in Bozeman 2007, p. 105). In consequence, private interests masquerading as public ones would ultimately be exposed through 'the glare of publicity' and, in turn, the process of debate and deliberation would enable the community to test alternatives, ascertain social consequences and identify the most widely shared good for its citizens (Bozeman 2007, p. 105). Like Habermas, as we will see below, Dewey advocated cooperative undertakings 'in which both parties learn by giving the other a chance to express itself ' (Bozeman 2007, p. 107). He further considered that social and political knowledge was not innate but reliant on education, association and communication and this 'democratic social intelligence' would ultimately allow citizens to chart their own political course (Bozeman 2007, p. 111).

Not surprisingly, Dewey has been criticized for representing an idealized political environment, a point which he countered by arguing how the public interest is not an absolute or universal good. 'It is constructed in each policy and problem context' (in Bozeman 2007, p. 108). 'It follows then that there will be many publics just as there will be many public interests in various times and places' (Bozeman 2007, p. 108). However, while he acknowledged self-interest and competing interests, a further, logical criticism lies in the lack of attention given to power differentials among the publics in the deliberation process.

Dewey's approach was to foreshadow the criticism that was developing within the scientific community in rejecting the public interest. By the mid-1900s the concept of the public interest had met with considerable resistance in large part due to its lack of empirical clout. Scholars (see, for example, Sorauf 1957; Schubert 1961; Downs 1962) began arguing for its rejection because it was 'too vague, too value-laden, too utopian, and too inconsistent with the policies of group accommodation to be of much value' (Bozeman 1979, p. 72). This 'hasty retreat' is ascribed to the rise in quantitative and behavioral approaches of the time, the public interest being left in the wake, seen as unscientific and metaphysical.

In response, Richard Flathman (1966) and others (Cassinelli 1958; Benditt 1973; Cochran 1974) were critical of the scientific rejection. Flathman argued of false logics: 'It is my hope that use of materials for philosophy will not only be helpful in dealing with the substantive problems of public interest and value theory but will also aid in dispelling the view that Logical Positivism reigns supreme in philosophy' (Flathman 1966, pp. xi–xii). He acknowledged that the use of the public interest for propagandist purposes was 'as old as politics' citing propaganda used in the Peloponnesian War, accepting that its use will be subjective but, nevertheless, argued against banishing the term from analytic vocabularies. What gained traction, in its place, argues Bozeman, was economic individualism. While Bozeman is referring particularly to the United States, noting 'market values have been elevated to a normative level perhaps unsurpassed in U.S. history' (2007, p. 3), he also cites China, Russia and Western European nations as increasingly focused in this direction. Thus, regulatory systems again moved to a market-oriented approach, associated with the rise of the 'Regan Revolution and Thatcherism' of the 1980s (Bozeman 2007, p. 5). Within these political economies, individual interests and the public interest were thus in constant tension with each other, adapting and changing according to capacities and the rising expectations of citizens.

Regulation and Competing Interests

Levine and Forrence (1990) note that virtually all accounts of public interest regulation are premised on the exercise of collective power through government in order to cure market failures and protect society from monopolies and the abuse of private economic power or the effects of external forces. Early regulatory theory saw regulation as a 'public-interest-inspired attempt, supported by aggrieved groups, and perhaps ultimately of a balancing or compromise nature, to control "abuse" and thus solve "problems"' (Mitnick 1980, p. 102). Regulation grew in response to consumer demand and social change and was also developed as a safety net for ensuring services were made available that were not profitable but nevertheless in the public interest, such as airline services to regional localities and publicly funded broadcasting. As such, governments regulate the actions of business to balance competitive pursuit of advantage with public needs, which take the form of barriers which can be a factor in an industry's competitive structure. Young (2008) notes how in the United States, for example, more than 500 occupations require licensing. On the one hand, licensing can facilitate honest and fair exchange by monitoring and controlling quality and standards; however, it may also be a barrier that limits competition, economic opportunity and wealth creation (Young 2008).

Such a dialectic is epitomized in the rise of the 'sharing economy,' also called the 'peer-to-peer economy' and 'collaborative consumption,' illustrated in the non-regulated taxi alternative of Uber and the accommodation option Airbnb, which globally have presented mammoth regulatory and public interest challenges. The sharing economy has emerged as an economic-technological phenomenon, 'fuelled by developments in information and communications technology (ICT), growing consumer awareness, proliferation of collaborative web communities as well as social commerce/sharing' (Hamari, Sjöklint & Ukkonen 2015, p. 1). While opinion is divided over the benefits and drawbacks of at least some sectors of the sharing economy, much of the criticism rests with the lack of regulatory checks and balances in industries such as accommodation and transport. At the same time, it is argued that the focus on this new economy has facilitated a necessary global review of regulation. One leading scholar and economist argues that while 'many existing regulations should be changed, as they were originally designed to serve narrow interests and/or have outlived their usefulness ... it doesn't make sense to essentially exempt entire classes of business from safety regulations or taxes just because they provide their services over the internet' (Baker 2014, n.p.). And communication and media scholars draw our attention to risks associated with 'venerating the technology ... [noting] technology is anything but benign and equalizing' (Picard 2014, n.p.). We will return to the sharing economy in the context of the following analysis of regulation and the public interest.

Within regulatory frameworks, the concept of 'capture,' otherwise known as 'special interest theory,' is introduced by scholars as it relates to government regulation (Levine & Forrence 1990; Mitnick 1980; Mitnick & Getz 2008; Young 2008; Rubin 2012). 'The capture view holds that the regulatory mechanism is basically workable and desirable but is somehow "captured" by regulated parties so that it serves their interests rather than the public interest' (Mitnick 1980, p. 95). Capture can occur at several levels: venality, incompetence or in a basic form. At the extreme, capture as 'venality' exists when it is corrupted for self-interest (Mitnick 1980, p. 94) though it is noted that 'actors in the process are sometimes motivated by self-interest and sometimes by a concern for others' (Levine & Forrence 1990, p. 173). Venality can see regulators as corrupt, taking bribes or being involved in otherwise illegal activity. Under such systems, public values are challenged. Incompetence sees the quality of personnel within regulation as sub-standard for one reason or another, possibly due to inadequate training, mediocrity or simply not being up to the job (Mitnick 1980). Basic capture finds the regulatory system is workable but still failing because it is 'captured' by interests other than the public interest. This occurs in regulatory pathways through co-option, co-ordination, control and reward systems from external interests. As such, interest groups lobby, persuade and contribute to the political process, thus swaying the opinion of policy makers (Downs 1962; Mitnick 1980; Mitnick & Getz 2008).

Alternately, when regulatory systems work in the public interest, they efficiently and openly balance external interests—for example, systems which are put in place against fuel price fixing or media monopolies. Kalt and Zupan (1990) and Levine and Forrence (1990) introduce the additional concept of 'slack' that exists within regulatory systems, which enables regulators to act without being observed by the polity, effectively enabling 'discretion which can be used to favour special-interest groups' (Levine & Forrence 1990, p. 177). With slack, scrutiny can be poor and, in part, due to gaps in information or communication, slack becomes inevitable (Levine & Forrence 1990).

To this point, the focus has been on how the regulatory system can work to negotiate public and special interests, all of which can have implications, either directly or indirectly, for public relations. The following analysis, however, places public relations activity squarely in the middle of the public interest capture-slack model. Levine and Forrence (1990) argue that, within this environment, ideological language and public interest rhetoric serve to assure those within the polity that complicated regulatory acts, which in the absence of slack would otherwise need to be ratified, are in the general or public interest. As a result, the very reasons that regulators use public interest rhetoric to secure public support can make it *unclear* whether:

- The acts and politics of the regulator are in the general interest;
- The regulator is acting in an other-regarding (selfless) manner and believes the acts and policies are publicly desirable;
- The regulator is acting in a self-regarding manner on behalf of self-regarding special interests, but wishes to reduce the likelihood of detection (Levine & Forrence 1990, p. 181).

Therefore, distinguishing between the public interest and capture can be dependent on public interest language or institutional discourse. In critical theory terms, as discussed below, this has congruency with strategic communication and it is not difficult to imagine discourses spiralling into obfuscation, spin and cover-ups. Levine and Forrence (1990) point out how key institutional features can reduce slack. These include self-publicity, political competition, organizations and institutions that function protectively and proactively, critical scholarship and public policy intelligentsia and the news media. The supply of information represents a 'public good' in managing slack and capture because it places issues on the public record and opens them up to scrutiny. Those issues placed on the public agenda are more likely to have a public interest outcome, while those not on the public agenda are more likely to be corrupted by capture.

What then of the sharing economy which, on the face of it, presents a utilitarian benefit at odds with that of organized labor and capital-intensive business? Here, twentieth-century regulatory theory meets a twenty-first-century issue which has governments around the world grappling to locate the public interest as, among other factors, the unregulated markets represent huge financial tax losses. Arguably, the public interest is already a winner as the sharing economy has irrevocably forced regulators and legislators to review, redefine and update policy and regulatory models for the modern era. This may result in what Mitnick and Getz (2008, p. 1794) call implementing a 'precautionary principle,' thus placing the burden of proof of safety on those introducing a new service. Hayes argues, 'In time, regulation will catch up with the innovative use of technology as it is being put to use ... and while there will still be some losers, the great majority of society will be better off' (2014, n.p.). Meantime, the online peer-reviewing system of the sharing economy—particularly those which bring associated fees and costs—has located similarities with any other business. As one blogger notes (Hacker news, n.p.):

> The term 'sharing economy' was coined just for the marketing aspect, to make it sound like something nice, to have the connotation of 'sharing meals with a friend'. It's not. It's a cold-hearted business

transaction—there's nothing wrong with business transactions, but please if it's business, just don't try to get emotional on me.

Online critiques such as these are reflective of the issues raised in chapter 4 (see, for example, Picard 2014), which call into question the true public interest of models spawned out of the internet and social media. Irrespective, the 'sharing economy,' facilitated by ICTs, has become a new public sphere, based on shifts in consumption patterns and 'a yearning for social embeddedness' (Hamari et al. 2015, p. 1).

The Public Sphere

Like the public interest, the public sphere has been identified as both complex and difficult to delineate (Craig 2004, p. 53); like the public interest, the public sphere is societally driven and in a state of ongoing fluctuation (Polan 1993); and, like the public interest, the public sphere is identified around multiple publics, presenting a plurality of organized interests within society (Fraser 1993). Several points of intersection have already been identified in the previous discussion, including the role played by deliberation, open dialogue and civil society. In seeking to further advance our understanding of the public interest and interest theory, we now turn to a broader analysis of this field of theory.

The public sphere is a particularly useful theory to consider in examining the public interest, because the public sphere is, at its core, about bringing together competing ideas to form public opinion within publicly accessed spaces. Within this space, and in its purest form, there is an expectation of a common good coming from deliberation within the public sphere and the ruling out of private interests (Fraser 1993). Traditionally, the public sphere provided a forum for the mediation between the authority of the state and civil society, but the strict separation between the two began to decline during the 1800s because of the intervention of the state into private affairs and the penetration of civil society into the state, thus upsetting the clear distinction (Holub 1991). Habermas (1974, p. 55) suggests reasons for this transformation and how these tied into special interests:

> At one time the process of making proceedings public was intended to subject persons or affairs to public reason, and to make political decisions subject to appeal before a court of public opinion ... but often enough the process of making public serves the arcane policies of special interests.

Over time, scholars such as Nancy Fraser (1993) argued against the concept of a single public sphere. Fraser argued that 'any conception of the public sphere that requires a sharp separation between (associational) civil society and state will be unable to imagine the forms of self-management, inter-public coordination, and political accountability that are essential to a democratic society' (1993, p. 26). Fraser questioned the ideal nature of what the public sphere might have been and repositioned, instead, a series of public spheres as more realistic. In her view there could be no one, single public sphere in any egalitarian, multicultural society: 'That would be tantamount to filtering diverse rhetorical and stylistic norms through an overarching lens' (Fraser 1993, p. 17). Her criticism and others (Fraser 1993; Outhwaite 1994) was that a single public sphere was exclusionary, with people restricted from the public sphere based on sex, status and race. Fraser argued that the force of public opinion was strengthened when a body representing it was empowered to translate opinion into authoritative decisions, highlighting how some dominant publics had access to this process and other weak or subaltern publics did not.

Habermas's revised approach to multiple public spheres in his later work *Between Facts and Norms* therefore presented a theory of pluralism and a civil society made up of non-governmental and non-economic interest groups. He argued, 'Civil society is composed of those more or less spontaneously emergent associations, organizations, and movements that, attuned to how social problems resonate in the private life spheres, distil and transmit such reactions in amplified form in the public sphere' (1996, p. 367). While he argued that civil society is not the largest and most conspicuous part of the public sphere, he notes that it forms the organizational substratum of the general public of citizens. This substratum is crucial to pluralist democracies which project 'the social balance of power onto the distribution of political power in such a way that politics remains sensitive to a broad spectrum of values and interests' (1996, pp. 331–32). This is epitomized in the way educational scholars Kemmis and McTaggart have developed a modern take on pluralist public spheres in which participants 'aim to change the climate of debate, the ways in which things are thought about and how situations are understood' (2005, p. 590). Their ten-point summary provides a clear way of seeing how interests may be managed within social structures (Kemmis & McTaggart 2005, their italics):

- Public spheres are *constituted as actual networks of communication among actual participants;*
- Public spheres are *self-constituted.* They are formed by people who get together *voluntarily;*
- Public spheres frequently come into existence in response to *legitimation deficits* (i.e. because potential participants do not feel that existing laws, policies, practices, or situations are legitimate);
- Public spheres are constituted for *communicative action* and for *public discourse;*
- Public spheres aim to be *inclusive;*
- As part of their inclusive character, public spheres tend to involve communication in *ordinary language;*

- Public spheres presuppose *communicative freedom;*
- The communicative networks of public spheres generate *communicative power* (i.e. mutual understanding and consensus);
- Public spheres do not directly affect social systems (e.g. government, administration) (i.e. their impact on systems is *indirect);*
- Public spheres frequently arise in practice through, or in relation to, the communication networks associated with *social movements* (Kemmis & McTaggart 2005, ch. 8, adapted from Habermas 1996).

And, if we return to the sharing economy as a new public sphere, while open to 'capture' through, for example, co-option by big business or changed business models, the sharing economy provides social and economic alternatives, provided the discursive environment is driven by publicness and self-regulation, responsive to 'how other people reflect' within the review process (Hamari et al. 2015, p. 9). As such, it is easily identifiable through most, if not all, elements of Kemmis and McTaggart's pluralist public sphere outline.

Ideal Speech, Language and Discourse

Habermas sees the concept of ideal speech as a logical extension of the public sphere, defined as '[r]ational discourse that is free from both domination and linguistic pathology, and oriented towards intersubjective understanding and consensus [which] is precisely the type of activity appropriate to the public sphere' (Holub 1991, p. 8). In the *Pragmatics of Communication* (1998), Habermas links the concepts of ideal speech, discourse and truth, providing a basis for understanding ideal speech in a broader context. He notes that it is characterized by:

> Openness to the public, inclusiveness, equal rights to participation, immunization against external or inherent compulsion, as well as the participant's orientation toward reaching understanding ... a proposition is true if it withstands all attempts to refute it under the demanding conditions of rational discourse.
>
> (Habermas 1998, p. 364)

For Habermas, philosopher and linguist, discourse is that 'peculiarly unreal' form of communication in which the participants subject themselves to the 'unforced force of the better argument' (Habermas in McCarthy 1981, p. 2020). Supporters of the ideal speech theory suggest that it can make sense of argumentation (McCarthy 1981) and that it was never intended as a 'concrete utopia' (Outhwaite 1994, p. 45). Rather, it 'can serve as a guide for the institutionalisation of discourse and as a critical standard against which every actually achieved consensus is measured' (McCarthy 1981, p. 308). Kemmis and McTaggart (2008) argue that what is projected is not an ideal against which actual communications and utterances are to be judged; instead, it can be taken for granted unless speech is '*deliberately* distorted or challenged' (Kemmis & McTaggart 2008, p. 294, my italics). Likewise, Cook (in Habermas 1998, p. 14) defends its normative value, providing a logical synergy with public interest process theory outlined below:

> Habermas ... now focuses on the idealizing suppositions guiding the *process* of rational argumentation rather than on the idealizing suppositions marking its *outcome*. The former idealizations pertain to the conduct of discourse rather than to the agreement to which participants in discourse aspire.

Habermas argues that through discourse public relations' representation of private interests challenge the authority of the state while, at the same time, the state and public authority have to compete with private interests for space within the public sphere:

> ... the kind of integration of mass entertainment with advertising, which in the form of public relations already assumes a 'political' character, subjects even the state itself to its code. Because private enterprises evoke in their customers the idea that in their consumption decisions they act in their capacity as citizens, the state has to address its citizens like consumers. As a result, public authority too competes for publicity (1989, p. 195).

In one of the few critiques that brings together the public interest, the public sphere and public relations, Weaver, Motion and Roper (2006) consider how corporations construct the public interest as intrinsically connected to narrow corporate interests. They question the potential for achieving the public interest as it applies to powerful hegemonies, while noting, as Habermas does, the potential for public relations to also challenge dominant perceptions and thus work in the public interest through representation within a pluralist system.

Communicative and Strategic Actions

Central to Habermas's theory of achieving ideal speech is the notion that discourse must be 'properly' motivated: it can only be reached through *communicative action* rather than *strategic action*. A distinction between strategic and communicative actions locates strategic actions as distorted or manipulated while actions aimed at reaching an understanding are communicative. One of the central elements of Habermas's *Theory of Communicative Action* (1998) is the distinction between the genuinely communicative use of language to attain common goals and the strategic use of language that will not achieve this. Communicative action can only be legitimately achieved when people are free to choose:

- What is comprehensible to *them* (whether in fact they understand what others are saying);
- What is true in the light of *their own* knowledge (both their individual knowledge and the shared knowledge represented in the discourse used by members);
- What participants *themselves* regard as sincerely and truthfully stated (individually and in terms of their joint commitment to understanding);
- What participants *themselves* regard as morally right and appropriate in terms of their individual and mutual judgment about what it is right, proper, and prudent to do under the circumstances in which they find themselves (Kemmis & McTaggart 2008, p. 294).

To achieve communicative action, discourse must exclude structural constraints on argumentative reasoning, both internally and externally, and there must be equal chances for dialogue. If these conditions are not met, then the discourse is open to the charge of being less than rational, or being the result not of the force of the better argument but of domination by strategic motivations (McCarthy 1981). Using this distinction, extreme strategic forms of communication such as lying and misleading result in 'pseudo-communication' (Kunneman in Outhwaite 1994, p. 119). In such a discursive environment, public relations may be escalated to manage problems or issues through speech patterns which construct reality for special interests, incorporating 'capture' or 'slack,' thereby antithetical to the public interest.

Alternatively, Kemmis and McTaggart (2005) provide a pathway to the public interest through communicative action by expanding the participatory role within civil society. In adopting a critical participatory approach, which calls on many actors to enable successful communicative action outcomes, they argue that public interest outcomes can be best achieved, providing the following public interest success stories:

> Rebuilding education in South Africa, in literacy campaigns in Nicaragua, in developments in nursing practice in Australia, in improving classroom teaching in the United Kingdom, in community development in the Philippines, in farms in Sri Lanka, in community governance in India, in improving water supplies in Bangladesh (2005, p. 599).

'These people might not have changed the world, but they have changed their world. Is that not the same thing?' (Kemmis & McTaggart, 2005, p. 600). The participatory approach, using communicative and strategic action, and ideal speech, within pluralistic public spheres and discursive environments, are further examined throughout the various snapshots in this book.

Public Interest Theories

The final section of the chapter examines the dedicated public interest theories. These share one fundamental element: they emerge out of political systems. Explaining this, Held argues that 'meaningful use of the term public interest presupposes the existence of a political system, however primitive or complex' (1970, p. 164). Accordingly, claims-to-interest are fundamentally based on sets of principles and norms within political systems with an understanding that the claim has wider merit than satisfying individual wants (Held 1970; McQuail 1992).

Typologies

As noted in chapter 1, there are many ways of organizing how the public interest can be categorized and conceptualized. Although various typologies have been suggested (Downs 1962; Held 1970; Cochran 1974; Mitnick 1980; Bozeman 2007), this book follows those outlined by Cochran (1974) and developed by Bozeman (2007). Whichever way these are categorized, we should keep in mind that each has many strands and the categories can be quite porous, but they can be broadly described as:

- Abolitionist;
- Normative;
- Consensualist or communitarian;
- Process.

Abolitionist

As noted earlier, many critics have argued for the abandonment of the concept of the public interest; indeed there have been calls for researchers to 'banish the concept from their analytic vocabularies' (Flathman 1966, p. 9). The harshest critics are concerned that the public interest is too ambiguous, unrealistic, imprecise and anachronistic due, in large part, to its lack of empiricism (see, for example, examinations by Sorauf 1957; Douglass 1980; Goodin 1996; Bozeman 2007). Because the public interest is principally understood as a political science theory, this lack of empirical and positivist potential is undeniably the locus of its problem, based on '… the belief that scientific understanding is the only appropriate path to true knowledge and that "facts" and "values" are separate kinds of reality' (Cochran 1974, p. 352). Public interest scholar Clarke E. Cochran notes how criticisms of non-scientific inquiry can be traced to the beginning of the twentieth century when 'idea ghosts' were rejected in favor of facts. Thus, for some at least, the public interest was cast as such an 'idea ghost.'

Cochran suggests that the abolitionists also reject the public interest because groups compete solely to advance their own interests, invoking the public interest merely as a strategy. Essentially, the abolitionists argue that there can be no public interest because no community or public has any *single* interest and that interests are conceived analogous to wants or desires with no distinction between selfish or altruistic interests (Cochran 1974). While proponents of the public interest accept these criticisms, they do not see it as a reason for abandoning the concept; instead, alternative theories are offered.

Normative

In contrast to the abolitionists, the normative approach focuses on a 'common good'—a term which is often used interchangeably with the public interest, as outlined above. This approach sees people as social beings who form associations in order to gain a better (common) life, not based on personal gain or benefit (Cochran 1974). Bozeman (2007, p. 89) explains further:

> A normative concept of the public interest assumes that there is a common good that is different than the aggregate of private benefit and, as usually expressed, that common good is something that is in the interest of the community as a whole.

Cochran (1974) and Bozeman (2007) suggest this field of theory as advancing 'the public interest as an ethical standard for evaluating public policies as a goal public officials should pursue' (Bozeman 2007, p. 89). Likewise, economics scholars Levine and Forrence (1990, p. 168) argue that public interest theory is both a positive theory about what motivates policy makers but also a normative theory about what *should* motivate policy makers. Bozeman (2007) argues it is useful to maintain the ideal concept of the public interest because it provides a benchmark—one approached but almost never attained. He compares this approach of the public interest to that of a perfectly competitive market. 'Having the target in mind keeps one on course, even if it is not possible precisely to hit the target' (Bozeman 2007, p. 90). Likewise, Cassinelli is cast as a normative scholar, based on his 1958 polemic which brings a critical approach to the ideal. He sees the public interest as the counterpoint to private or self-interests, with each being mutually exclusive (1958, p. 55).

Essentially, this approach does not allow private interests to be in the public interest *per se,* nor does the public interest recognize the role played by 'competing interests.' Accordingly, the public interest is ultimately seen as unattainable as outlined by Cochran, who views it synonymously with the common good.

> In short, a sound theory of the common good must consider it to be an end or a goal which is normatively defined and, hence, not perfectly attainable; for no society, subject to pride, self-interest, and worldly contingencies, can ever actualize fully its moral and social potential.
> (Cochran 1974, p. 355)

In response, other approaches 'shift the focus away from identification of a substantive "good" to identification of institutions and procedures that can help formulate an acceptable idea of "good"' (Bozeman 2007, p. 99). As such, this is more responsive to a case-by-case basis which can provide a more workable understanding of the public interest. In moving beyond the normative, we see the development of the consensualist and communitarian approach.

Consensualist-Communitarian

This typology focuses on the majority interest and that which reaches consensus. Two elements that set it apart from the normative is that the consensualist approach is 'neither invariant nor self-evident' (Bozeman 2007, p. 91). What this means is that contexts, and varying criteria, can define what is deemed good or beneficial at a given time. While moral philosophers such as Plato, for example, emphasized the limited role of context in determining what is 'good,' a consensual approach accepts that public interest criteria will change over time and place (Bozeman 2007). As such, it is not only time-specific but also culturally sensitive and aware. Downs (1962), for example, suggests the idea of 'minimal consensus' as necessary for the operations of a democratic society. This approach further suggests 'anything that is in the long term detrimental to the majority of citizens cannot be in the public interest, unless it is essential to the protection of those individual rights included in the minimal consensus' (Downs 1962, p. 9). He lists essential protections as 'basic rules' and 'fundamental social policies' that a government seeks to carry out and which a citizenry must follow (Downs 1962, p. 5). By its nature, the consensualist-communitarian approach calls for a focus on the majority while, at least, being aware of minorities. Within this category, Sorauf describes the public interest as having a 'hair shirt' function (1957, p. 639), which reminds those in decision-making positions that they must recognize and consult interests of the 'unorganized, unrepresented or underrepresented.' As such:

> ... the public interest may represent the interests of freedom, equality, and opportunity—the widely-held and unorganized interests. The public interest then becomes a symbol for the attempt to recognize and consult interests that might be forgotten or overlooked in the pressure of political combat.
>
> (Sorauf 1957, p. 639)

Communitarianism has much in common with consensualism, described by Habermas as 'a shared consciousness that arises from the identification with the ... traditions of one's own political and cultural community' (Habermas 1996, p. 499). Communitarianism is premised on a shared moral culture and an expectation of positive rights which are available to everyone; rights such as education, health care and environmental security which we might align with overriding public interests. Support for this approach comes from philosopher John Rawls who argues that a society should 'be non-aggressive towards other communities, and internally it must have a 'common good' conception of justice,' a 'reasonable consultation hierarchy,' and it must secure basic human rights' (Rawls in Bell 2012, n.p.). Rawls's idea of an 'overlapping consensus' would see agreement over basic human rights across all societies.

Communitarianism is often associated with traditional social and political structures and values, which provide alternatives to neoliberal thinking. For example, Bell (2012) argues the concept of 'Asian values,' as espoused in the 1990s, saw emphasis upon family, social harmony and community values, eschewing the individualism of Western liberal societies. According to the communitarian-consensualist view, pluralism, as we will see in the next category, undermines the single most important value in society—the sense of being part of a whole and, through self-determination, providing the individual's rightful place in the political culture (Bozeman 2007, p. 93).

Process Theories

These theories consider how the public interest is served during *the process* of compromise or accommodation (Cochran 1974, p. 342). Those supporting this typology also find many publics, rather than a single public, and many interests, rather than a single interest, as held by the whole (Cochran 1974, p. 339). Under this approach, there can and will be 'conflicts of interest' because of the nature of individuation. It also sees the need to provide practical and logical *reasons* for decision making beyond moral principles (Cochran 1974, p. 350; Flathman 1966).

Process theories are divided into three overlapping sub-categories:

- Aggregative—the public interest as the sum of individual interests
- Pluralist—the public interest made up of competing perspectives
- Procedural—the public interest as related to 'method or function' (Cochran 1974; Bozeman 2007)

However, there is a significant porosity across these as pluralism, by its nature, demands a process to evaluate the public interest across multiple interests.

The aggregative approach is the most compatible with the idea of economic individualism, explained by Bozeman as seeing the human or individual as paramount over the collective. It presumes that the best society prioritizes individual choice as 'governments that govern least govern best' (Bozeman 2007, p. 4). As such, the aggregative model sees the public interest equating with an alternative to government interests. Its limitations lie in the inability to provide a valid aggregation of *equal* interests, due to power imbalances, plus in the subjective meaning of what is 'good' and what therefore takes primacy within the process of aggregation.

Following Smith (1960), the pluralist approach is said to sit in contrast with normative theory because it rests on the idea of multiple publics rather than an idealized single public. Smith suggests that the public interest is compatible with the idea of the need to balance interests and is also consistent with democratic notions of interest-conflict, providing the process is responsive to community consensus (Cochran 1974). The risk with this category is that all public policy can therefore be seen as *ipso facto* in the public interest because it is *perceived* as representing all publics in one way or another (Sorauf 1957).

The final category—the procedural—sees the public interest as *part of a process* rather than as a substantive outcome. Moreover, it also might be considered a method rather than a theory. Proponents argue that it is central to the democratic process; Herring explains: 'the concept is to the bureaucracy what the "due process" clause is to the judiciary' (1968, p. 23). Part of the procedural approach is the development of a standard for balancing interests (Herring 1968; Wheeler 2006); however, it might also be said that interest-conflict is no more or less an issue for this typology than any other. Nevertheless, Cochran (1974, p. 345) argues that any process that guarantees access should also guarantee that the values and interests of the community as well as those of interest groups are considered. Critics of this approach argue that the public interest is, by its nature, deficient because, unlike the other theories, it has no specific moral content. Cochran (1974) raises the conundrum that if the procedure already has a result in mind, then the envisaged result should not be defined in terms of the process. Conversely, if there is no substantive result in sight, then it is aiming at nothing and cannot justify the term of public interest. Lowi simply calls process theories 'vulgarised versions of the pluralist model' (1969, p. 12). His comment reminds us that there is overlap and porosity across categories. Indeed, in *The Political Economy of Regulation* Mitnick (1980) discusses the body of theory that links process to competing interests. Because group activity is interpreted in relation to other groups, and in tension with other groups, these other groups must be considered in the process; ergo we return to the pluralist approach.

Conclusion

The chapter provides an examination of public interest theories and considers some historical connections to medieval times, including Hobbesian theory and theories of regulation. In examining some of the earlier political and economic theories of the public interest, it suggests the public interest emerged in history out of an aggregation of individual interests in response to royalist interpretations of the common good and the rise of social action. An alternate view sees it linked to the public services and utilities that were founded on certain rights and duties within society. Such common callings—from medicine to postal services—were ultimately incorporated into law and regulation, forming the underpinnings of 'the public interest.' Here we have drawn on Mitnick and others who locate balance and the public interest in modern neoliberal societies, latterly challenged by altered social norms and technology, illustrated within the contemporary public sphere of the sharing economy.

The chapter outlines public interest typologies: the abolitionist, the normative, the consensualist or communitarian and process theories, each providing different, though sometimes overlapping, ways of understanding the public interest, linking these to strands of critical social theory. Drawing on Dewey, Bozeman calls for a 'pragmatic idealism,' which he describes as 'keeping in mind an ideal of the public interest, but without specific content, and then moving toward that ideal, making the ideal more concrete as one moves toward it' (2007, p. 13). There is clearly overlap between this approach, process theories and Habermas's ideal speech, noted earlier by Cook (cited in Habermas 1998) as 'guiding the *process* of rational argumentation rather than on the idealizing suppositions marking its *outcome.*' In such an *ex ante* approach, there is a strong case for considering the potential for the public interest *before* taking action or making an interest claim; however, this should not preclude the efficacy that can be brought through *ex post* approaches which incorporate reflexivity. Bozeman (2007, p. 13) neatly describes the public interest as 'an ideal that is given shape on a case-by-case basis.' This presents us with the crucial element of context for consideration. Because there can be no universal public interest for all places, at all times, for all people, in context we find social, cultural and political differences, located in specific time frames, which need to be considered for their part in determining public interest claims.

References

Baker, D 2014, 'Don't buy the "sharing economy" hype: Airbnb and Uber are facilitating rip-offs', *The Guardian,* 27 May, viewed 20 July 2015, http://www.theguardian.com/commentisfree/2014/may/27/airbnb-uber-taxes-regulation.

Bell, D 2012, 'Communitarianism', *Stanford encyclopaedia of philosophy,* viewed 21 May 2014, http://plato.stanford.edu/entries/communitarianism/.

Benditt, TM 1973, 'The public interest', *Philosophy and Public Affairs,* vol. 2, no. 3, pp. 291–311.

Bivins, TH 1993, 'Public relations, professionalism, and the public interest', *Journal of Business Ethics,* February, vol. 12, no. 2, pp. 117–26.

Bozeman, B 1979, *Public management and policy analysis,* St. Martin's Press, New York.

Bozeman, B 2007, *Public values and public interest: counterbalancing economic individualism,* Georgetown University Press, Washington, DC.

Bybee, CR 1997, 'Media, public opinion and governance: burning down the barn to roast the pig', University of Leicester, [weblog] viewed 10 July 2015, http://www.infoamerica.org/teoria_articulos/lippmann_dewey.htm.

Cassinelli, CW 1958, 'Some reflections on the concept of the public interest', *Ethics,* October, vol. 69, no. 1, pp. 48–61.

Cochran, CE 1974, 'Political science and the public interest', *The Journal of Politics,* vol. 36, no. 2, pp. 327–55.

Craig, G 2004, *The media, politics and public life,* Allen & Unwin, Sydney.

Dewey, J 1927, *The public and its problems,* H. Holt & Co., New York.

Douglass, B 1980, 'The common good and the public interest', *Political Theory,* February, vol. 8, no. 1, pp. 103–17.

Downs, A 1962, 'The public interest: its meaning in a democracy', *Social Research,* Spring, vol. 29, no. 1, pp. 1–36.

Finnis, J 2011, 'Aquinas' moral, political and legal philosophy,' *Stanford encyclopedia of philosophy,* viewed 6 June 2015, http://plato.stanford.edu/entries/aquinas-moral-political/.

Flathman, RE 1966, *The public interest: an essay concerning the normative discourse of politics,* John Wiley & Son, New York.

Fraser, N 1993, 'Rethinking the public sphere: a contribution to the critique of actually existing democracy', in B Robbins (ed.), *The phantom public sphere,* University of Minnesota Press, Minneapolis, pp. 1–33.

Goodin, RE 1996, 'Institutionalizing the public interest: the defense of deadlock and beyond', *The American Political Science Review,* June, vol. 90, no. 2, pp. 313–43.

Gunn, JAW, 1968, 'Interests will not lie: a seventeenth century political maxim', *Journal of the History of Ideas,* vol. 29, no. 4, pp. 551–64.

Habermas, J 1974, 'The public sphere: an encyclopedia article (1964)', *New German Critique,* vol. 1, no. 3, pp. 49–55.

Habermas, J 1989, *The structural transformation of the public sphere: an inquiry into a category of bourgeois society,* MIT Press, Cambridge, MA.

Habermas, J 1996, *Between facts and norms: Contributions to a discourse theory of law and democracy,* MIT Press, Cambridge, MA.

Habermas, J 1998, *On the pragmatics of communication,* MIT Press, Cambridge, MA.

Hacker news, n.d., https://news.ycombinator.com/item?id=8008716.

Hamari, J, Sjöklint M & Ukkonen A 2015, 'The sharing economy: why people participate in collaborative consumption', *Journal of the Association for Information Science and Technology,* published online, viewed 4 September 2015, http://www.researchgate.net/publication/255698095_The_Sharing_Economy_Why_People_Participate_in_Collaborative_Consumption.

Hayes, A 2014, 'Winners and losers in the sharing economy', *Investopedia,* viewed 20 July 2014, http://www.investopedia.com/articles/investing/120214/winners-and-losers-sharing-economy.asp.

Held, V 1970, *The public interest and individual interests,* Basic Books, New York.

Herring, P 1968, 'Public interest', *International Encyclopedia of the Social Sciences,* vol. 13, pp. 170–75.

Hill, JW 1958, *Corporate public relations: arm of modern management,* Harper & Bros., New York.

Holub, R 1991, *Jurgen Habermas: critic in the public sphere,* Routledge, London.

Kalt, J & Zupan, M 1990, 'The apparent ideological behaviour of legislators: testing for principal-agent slack in political institutions', *Journal of Law and Economics,* vol. 94, pp. 103–31.

Kemmis, S & McTaggart, R 2005, 'Participatory action research: communicative action and the public sphere', in NK Denzin & YS Lincoln (eds.), *The Sage handbook of qualitative research,* 3rd edn, Sage, Thousand Oaks, CA, pp. 559–603.

Kemmis, S & McTaggart, R 2008, 'Participatory action research: communicative action and the public sphere, in NK Denzin & YS Lincoln (eds.), *Strategies of qualitative inquiry,* 3rd edn, Sage, Thousand Oaks, CA, pp. 271–330.

Levine, ME & Forrence, JL 1990, 'Regulatory capture, public interest, and the public agenda: toward a synthesis', *Journal of Law, Economics & Organization,* vol. 6, Special Issue [Papers from the Organization of Political Institutions conference, April 1990], pp. 167–98.

Lippmann, W 1927, *The phantom public,* Harcourt, Brace and Co, New York.

Lippmann, W 1955, *Essays in the public philosophy,* Little Brown, Boston.

Locke, J 1767, *The second treatise of civil government,* 6th edn, accessed 14 January 2015, https://ebooks.adelaide.edu.au/locke/john/181s/index.html.

Lowi, T 1969, *The end of liberalism,* WW Norton, New York.

Mansbridge, J 1998, 'On the contested nature of the public good', in WW Powell & ES Clemens (eds.), *Private action and the public good,* Yale University Press, New Haven, pp. 3–19.

McCarthy, T 1981, *The critical theory of Jurgen Habermas,* MIT Press, Cambridge, MA.

McQuail, D 1992, *Media performance: mass communication and the public interest,* Sage, London.

Mitnick, B 1980, *The political economy of regulation,* Columbia University Press, New York.

Mitnick, B & Getz, KA 2008, 'Regulation and regulatory practices', in RW Kolb (ed.), *Encyclopedia of business ethics and society, vol. 5,* Sage, Thousand Oaks, CA, pp. 1787–1802.

Moloney, K 2000, *Rethinking public relations: the spin and the substance,* Routledge, London.

Outhwaite, W 1994, *Habermas: a critical introduction,* Polity Press, Cambridge.

Picard, RG 2014, 'The humanisation of media? Social media and the reformation of communication', Keynote speech at the *Australia & New Zealand Communication Association 2014 Conference,* Melbourne, 9 July.

Polan, D 1993, 'The public's fear: or, media as monster in Habermas, Negt and Kluge', in B Robbins (ed.), *The phantom public sphere,* University of Minnesota Press, Minneapolis.

Rousseau, JJ 1762, *The social contract: book 2,* Rousseau archive, viewed 4 September 2015, https://www.marxists.org/reference/subject/economics/rousseau/social-contract/ch02.htm#16.

Rubin, P 2012, 'Regulation of information and advertising', in R van den Bergh & AE Pacces (eds.), *Regulation and economics,* Edward Elgar Publishing, Northampton, MA, pp. 138–63.

Schubert, G 1961, *The public interest,* Free Press, Glencoe, IL.

Smith, M G 1960, Social and cultural pluralism, *Annals of the New York Academy of Science,* vol 83, no. 4, pp. 763–79.

Sorauf, FJ 1957, 'The public interest reconsidered', *The Journal of Politics,* vol. 19, no. 4, pp. 616–39.

Weaver, CK, Motion, J & Roper, J 2006, 'From propaganda to discourse (and back again): truth, power, the public interest, and public relations', in J L'Etang & M Pieczka (eds.), *Public relations: critical debates and contemporary practice,* Lawrence Erlbaum, Mahwah, NJ, pp. 7–23.

Wheeler, C 2006, 'The public interest: we know it's important, but do we know what it means', in Australian Institute of Administrative Law *AIAL Forum no. 48*, pp. 12–26, R Creyke & A Mantel (eds.), viewed 1 September 2013, http://150.203.86.5/aial/Publications/webdocuments/Forums/forum48.pdf.

Williams, G n.d., 'Thomas Hobbes: moral and political philosophy', *Internet encyclopedia of philosophy*, Lancaster University, UK.

Young, G 2008, 'Competition', in RW Kolb (ed.), *Encyclopedia of business ethics and society*, vol. 5, Sage, Thousand Oaks, CA, pp. 385–89.

3 Locating the Public Interest in Public Relations

Agency, Alliances and *pro bono publico*

... the public interest, myth or not, serves a 'hair shirt' function.
(Sorauf 1957, p. 639)

Introduction

Public relations scholarship has moved into a phase of strong self-critique in recent years with many critical studies incorporating polemical and alternative approaches to its construction and functions, including public relations as propaganda (Moloney 2006; Weaver, Motion & Roper 2006; L'Etang 2006) or viewed through socio-political or socio-cultural lenses (Mickey 2003; Bardham & Weaver 2011; Curtin & Gaither 2007, 2012; Holtzhausen 2012; Demetrious 2013). The field has thus been rethought, reconceptualized and reconfigured over time which has, in turn, moved our understanding and the discussion forward. As a result, public relations now draws from a wide range of theories including critical theory, postcolonialism, modernism and postmodernism, structuralism and poststructuralism, informed by many and diverse fields such as anthropology, media, law and moral philosophy. Many of these intersections are explored and developed in this book which, germanely, proposes the public interest can add theoretical and paradigmatic concepts and dimensions to public relations thinking.

Johnston and Zawawi (2000) point out that communication in public relations is the tip of the iceberg, that public relations is far more multi-faceted than this. Moloney, meanwhile, aptly describes it as both a portable set of attitudes and techniques and a structured industry (2000) and Opdycke Lamme and Miller Russell (2010) note that, more important than the title of PR for individuals who perform public relations functions, is the capacity for consistent and critical skills and knowledge. While Demetrious notes (2013, p. 8) that it is the unity of public relations that 'struggles to convince society it has intrinsic worth,' it may be the very lack of unity, as both industry and practice that exist within political economies around the world, that provides the entry points for examining the public relations-public interest nexus.

This chapter identifies several key intersections for examining this nexus, each having emerged within the existing communication and public relations literature (though it does not propose this is representative of the discipline as a whole). The first is the role of the public information officer (PIO)—as distinct from the public relations practitioner (RPR)—and considers its place in public interest engagement. It then examines the development and contemporary role played by public interest groups as they emerge in response to social challenges and in seeking social change. It also analyses how *pro bono publico*, which translated means 'for the public good', plus the role of partnerships, can provide neat interfaces between public interest and public relations. In the previous chapter, Mitnick (1980) suggested agents can provide a mechanism to make the public interest workable: to advocate, defend and manage issues of public interest. He argued: 'As long as agents exist to believe in and act for the public interest, construction of public interest theories should be feasible' (1980, p. 91). Building on this idea, the chapter also examines the concept of agency, and how it applies to both public relations and to interest theory.

The Role of Agency

In the *Encyclopedia of Business Ethics and Society*'s dozens of entries, there are precisely 779 mentions of the word 'agency,' indicating its omnipresence within the literature. Agency is one of the oldest and most commonly codified relationships in social interaction (Ross 1973), with early iterations found in classic sociology writing by Weber (see Kiser 1999; Shapiro 2005) and the modern body of work originating in economic theory, based on principal-agent asymmetries, incentives and exchanges within institutional or organizational contexts (Hill & Jones 1992; Shapiro 2005; Mitnick 2008). Though Shapiro notes (2005, p. 263) the economic paradigm of agency theory continues to cast 'a very long shadow over the social sciences,' agency theory has nevertheless rhyzomed and developed, incorporating normative, institutional, cognitive, social and systemic factors within business, political science, law and sociology literature (Shapiro 2005; Mitnick 2008). Shapiro (2005) identifies how Mitnick, whose work we drew on in the previous chapter, has championed the development of agency theory within political science and sociology to move it from the economic assumptions of being acontextual, ahistorical and static. In turn, this expanded approach sees agency relationships as complex, dynamic, enacted within broad social, heterogeneous contexts, buffeted by outside forces such as competitors, interest groups, regulators, technology and the law (Shapiro 2005). Often under allied names—bureaucracy, organizations, professions, roles, markets, labor, government, family, trust, social exchange—agency relationships are called on for various reasons: because of the need to divide labor; to acquire specialized skill or knowledge; to bridge physical, social and temporal distances; to provide coordinated approaches or economies of scale; for protection from risk; or, (more cynically) as a symbolic show to defuse criticism (Shapiro 2005; Mitnick 2008). Most commonly, however, it is simply understood as the idea of 'acting for' (Jones 1995 in Mitnick 2008, p. 46).

In public relations and communication, agency appears to have been used more as an embedded concept than examined as a full-fledged theory (see, for example, Dutta 2011; Edwards 2011; Dutta, Ban & Pal 2012; Demetrious 2013) explained as 'the capacity of human beings to engage with structures that encompass their lives, to make meanings through this engagement, and at the same time, creating discursive openings to transform these structures' (Dutta, Ban & Pal 2012, p. 7). For Dutta (2011) agency is situated at the interaction between culture and structure, while Demetrious (2013) locates it at the point of social change, often driven by the individual's moral motivation and civic duty. Edwards (2011, p. 536) positions agency within an interest context, describing it as the ability to encourage organizational 'goodness' and, therefore, equally as serving organizational 'self-interest at others' expense.' Some have suggested combining stewardship with agency theory (Van Puyvelde, Caers, Bois & Jegers 2012) to better reflect common understandings of how agency is understood, especially in the non-profit sector. However, Mitnick (2008) maintains that since agency has two sides—control and service—it already includes stewardship through the service component and this can be elevated to the primary component if deemed appropriate. Either way, both perspectives provide logical paradigmatic axes for better understanding and critiquing the role of agency in public relations, whether from a critical, normative or functional point of view.

What goes along with this, in addition to the service role noted above, is the fiduciary duty that comes with a contract, usually in employment, in which agents must 'act diligently, with appropriate skills and with appropriate levels of effort … [whereby] No other interests must be permitted to interfere with that action' (Mitnick 2008, pp. 46–47). Problematic here, of course, is how conflicts of interest or unexamined self-interests may misalign with appropriate social behavior; what happens if an agent sees the need to act as a whistle-blower about illegal activity, or chooses *not* to act as a whistle-blower about illegal activity? Governance failings are clear indicators of where internal self-interests, recorded in spikes in some corporate and government activity in the 1980s and 2000s, have seen agents take the latter path. However, this is not a dilemma peculiar to public relations—or any one particular industry—indeed, in the medical context, for instance, 'Fiduciaries can produce not only the caring behaviors of health professionals but also the efficient implementation of the Holocaust's "final solution"' (Mitnick 2008, p. 47). In all industries and interest groups, it is therefore necessary to develop and study the normative structure of relationships which must work out the nature, forms and management of contracts or prescriptions to ensure that agents are not only efficient but also serve socially acceptable ends (Mitnick 2008). Mitnick explains this option in his earlier work when he positions agency within public interest theory. He argues how agents—for example, politicians and public interest groups—may satisfy their self-interest instrumentally 'but the theory requires that at least some preferences for the public interest be genuine and terminal' (1980, p. 91). There are, of course, choices for the agent, between those who 'adopt the skeptical, even paranoid, assumptions of agency theory and the costly control mechanisms it propounds and those who have a more hopeful view of human capacities for other-regarding behavior' inclusive of reciprocity, cooperation, embeddedness and trust (Shapiro 2005, p. 270). While rarely are choices so clear or easy, this dichotomy provides a foundation for theorizing how public relations agents, either institutionally or non-institutionally, may be considered by others or consider their own positions—of self-interest, within conflicts of interest, claiming a public interest, or as disinterested parties. The distinctions are relevant as we now continue examining the intersection of the public interest with public relations.

PIO versus PRP

Public relations as agency comes under many and varied titles. Negative and pejorative associations, particularly with its institutional presence, are well documented and widely discussed within critical literature (for example, see Moloney 2006; McKie & Munshi 2007; L'Etang 2004; Pieczka 2006; L'Etang & Pieczka 2006; Weaver, Motion & Roper, 2006; Lee 2000; Demetrious 2013). Undoubtedly partly due to this, some fields of practice have been carefully distanced from the title of 'public relations,' with the titles public information officer/manager (PIO), government information officer/manager (GIO, as it applies) or public affairs officer/manager, among those used in preference. In particular, an historic significance exists for the use of the titles PIO or GIO across some sectors. L'Etang points to early distinctions between PIO and public relations practitioner (PRP) models, as seen in the developing public relations codes of practice by the Institute of Public Relations (IPR) in Britain during the 1960s. She discusses two conceptual models of public relations:

> One as public relations as advocacy on behalf of clients and employers, the other of public relations as public information and social responsibility acting in the public interest.
>
> (L'Etang 2004, p. 170)

She further notes: 'Acting in the public interest was a crucial justification for the existence of public relations and an implicit (and sometimes explicit) way for practitioners to distinguish their occupation from propaganda' (2004, pp. 170–71). As such the role of the PIO became most commonly positioned within certain sectors of the public sphere, including its close association with government, public administration and courts (Lee 1998; Moravcsik & Sangiovanni 2003; Johnston 2005; Lee 2000; White 2012; Theaker & Yaxley 2013). In White's (2012) analysis and comparison of the

PIO and PRP she, like L'Etang, separates the two by public interest practice. For her, the PIO is firmly associated with science, describing the role as 'communication professionals within government agencies and educational research institutions who disseminate information about health/science issues, enabling better decision-making within the public sphere' (2012, p. 564). In her view, the PIO has a role of 'knowledge transfer between scientists and the public,' while the PRP is driven by 'inequality' and privileging the client (2012, p. 546) and she is supported in her argument that health and science communication functions at a public interest level (see, for example, Ankney & Curtin 2002; Mickey 2003; Guttman & Thompson 2011; Pendleton 2013).

On the face of it, there is a clear case to be made that much science/health communication and information *is* in the public interest because it literally relates 'to life and death' (Guttman & Thompson 2011, p. 252). Take, for example, public health campaigns, including the following:

- The Grim Reaper (AIDS/Australia 1987)
- World No Tobacco Day (WHO/International created 1987)
- Let's Move (USA 2010)
- It's About Time (Organ Donation/Wales 2014)
- Anti-Malaria Campaign (Sri Lanka 2012)
- Life Be in It (Australia 1975)
- 'Drop the Case' (*Medicine San Frontiers v Novartis* 2006/7)

However, claims that one sector or field should have a greater moral or ethical claim to the public interest have, rightly, also brought criticism. Accordingly, two issues need to be addressed in this distinction: the first rests with the claim to moral superiority of certain sectors, namely health in this instance; the second is whether the title PIO or GIO provides any significant difference to that of PRP simply because of its use in certain sectors or within government departments.

The issue is brought into focus through recent critiques of the public health marketing literature which emerged in the 1970s. Scholars have challenged assumptions and argued of an insufficient interrogation of the ethics and rightness of this field of inquiry noting that 'goals of public health are too often assumed or simply asserted, rather than cogently explained or justified' (Gostin, Boufford & Martinez 2007, p. 57; see also Hope 2001; Holden & Cox 2013). Holden and Cox (2013, p. 20) describe this as displaying 'moral myopia and muteness' through a lack of deep analysis and uninterrogated truths. Importantly, informing the distinction between the PIO/GIO and PRP, and associated government versus corporate differences, they question why the corporate model should be seen to be inferior simply because it makes a profit. They note how public health marketing also has to meet targets and budgets, that those involved focus on preserving their own employment, and, like a commercial marketer, serve multiple stakeholders and reflect multiple interests, while competing for government, philanthropic and public support. Their arguments raise the issue of competing interests and how these can be debated and potentially reconciled, confirming the idea that the public interest is context and culturally dependent. Take, for example, the issue of childhood immunizations, a 'hotly contested' topic around the world, which effectively pits public interests against each other or against individual rights. In many Western countries there is a tendency to favor the many, via immunization programs, over the few conscientious objectors who choose not to immunize. However, the interest conflict can be culturally or nationally complicated: Japan, for instance, bans the use of the measles, mumps, rubella (MMR) vaccine (Holden & Cox 2013; Hope 2001) while other countries, for example, Australia, place disincentives on those who do not vaccinate. Rothschild argues that 'because all societies attempt to manage the behaviour of their citizens at some level, the question is not whether to manage public health and social issue behaviour but rather how to do so appropriately' (1999 in Holden & Cox, p. 36). As such, Holden and Cox's call for a greater willingness to engage in philosophical and ethical dialogue, and to challenge claims of absoluteness within the field of public health marketing, move the issue of the public interest in the direction of this book, that is, toward more intense scrutiny, deeper debate and informed choices, rather than aligning the public interest or public benefit with any single claim to rightness, or indeed any one sector of the political economy.

Public Interest Groups

The second field of practice that has historically connected public relations to the public interest is 'the public interest group.' The contemporary idea of public interest groups is commonly associated with the social movements and 'general social upheavals' (Walker 1983, p. 403) of the 1930s and 1960s (see Schuck 1977; McCarthy & Zald 1977; Berry 1977; Walker 1983; Demetrious 2013; Schuck 2014). As noted in chapter 2, interest groups are part of pluralist civil societies, as presenting alternate public spheres, and as a departure from the broader understanding of the 'common good.' For many scholars their purpose has become synonymous with the roles of lobbying, advocacy, grassroots activism, civil society organizations or stakeholder groups. While contemporary literature has moved toward the latter titles, 'public interest groups' or 'interest groups' still has currency and holds historical significance. Notably, in determining the nomenclature for developments in the European Union, Obradovic and Viscano (2007, p. 13) defined 'collectively organised non-state actors' as 'civil society organisations' which, they argued, were also understood synonymously with 'interest groups.'

Like the public interest itself, these vehicles for action and reform hold various meanings, with the term widely 'used, abused, exploited and derided' (Schuck 1977, p. 133). Early descriptions of public interest groups saw them as separate from professional, occupational or party-political groups, relating to consumers, taxpayers, citizens or 'members of the biosphere,' defined as 'an organizational entity that purports to represent very broad, diffuse, non-commercial interests which traditionally have received little explicit or direct representation in the processes by which agencies, courts, and the legislatures make public policy' (Schuck 1977, p. 133). Nevertheless, they were not without power. Schuck explains the rise in these groups in the United States as moving beyond mere community groups to politically savvy groups which behave in a conventional political mode. 'They identify issues, mobilize political support, form alliances, bargain and accommodate, accumulate and expend political favors, and nurture their organizational base' (Schuck 1977, p. 134). Because their role was (and remains) to fill a void within the traditional pluralistic bargaining process, political systems are thus seen as their *raison d'etre* (Schuck 1977).

Despite deficiencies which come from limited budgets, lack of internal expertise and access restrictions—which might arguably be seen as strengths if they assure political and corporate independence—public interest groups provide a critical, informal safeguard within the political structure, achieved through three measures:

- First, by systematically monitoring a government agency, there is persistent potential for embarrassing its officials and policies. Moreover, the public interest group is a natural repository for whistle-blowers from within the system;
- Second, through their access to the media (*and, by extension, their audiences*);
- Third, the mere existence of these groups can affect the behavior of government policy makers in much the same way as industry regulators can, as a check and balance system (Schuck 1977, p. 138, my italics).

As Schuck's analysis was written well before social media, we might add a fourth measure: the widespread use of social media and the capacity to bypass the traditional media to reach targeted audiences. Some suggest public interest groups can bring a process of 'incremental erosion' in effecting change in corporate or government sectors. In their examination of the anti-smoking lobby, Condit and Condit (1992, p. 242) examined the battle between the public interest group 'Coalition on Smoking or Health' (ConSORH—made up of the American Heart Association, the American Lung Association and the American Cancer Society) and the corporate tobacco industry. This David and Goliath battle is now well documented within the public relations literature (see, for example, Pratt 2001). The coalition's strategy of 'incremental erosion' in dealing with the bigger, better-funded, self-interested organizations of Big Tobacco used 'rhetorical exigencies' to place demands on the opposition and 'rhetorical constraints' to impose legal or financial limits where possible (1992, p. 42). Condit and Condit argued that because of their 'altruistic nature,' public interest groups carry more credibility within the public than do self-interested industries (1992, p. 255). Thus, public interest groups can, and do, provide the 'hair shirt' function that Sorauf (1957) suggests is a requisite function of the public interest. Or, as Dutta (2011) points out, they represent the inevitable resistance that seeks to transform structures of injustice and inequality. Yet their limited resourcing, when compared to more powerful organizations or governments, and their potential for cooptation, represent serious limitations, as we will discuss later in the chapter.

Public interest alliances have become increasingly important as interest groups develop creative ways of capacity building, sharing costs, locating synergies, accomplishing goals and achieving individual missions (Yankey & Willen 2005). For example, the Refugee Council of Australia is a national center for refugees and the groups and individuals who support them, made up of more than 200 organizational and more than 900 individual members. The following snapshot outlines their response to the Australian government's asylum seeker policies, illustrating the collective resistance that is being brought to bear in support of this largely 'voiceless' population.

Snapshot

Giving Voice to the Voiceless: Refugees and Asylum Seekers

Background

According to the figures of the United Nations High Commissioner for Refugees, 2013 saw the largest number of asylum seekers worldwide of this century (UNHCR 2015). As the issue continued to escalate in the years that followed, these figures increased dramatically worldwide. Asylum seeker and refugee policy remains a highly contentious issue all over the world—one which has been at the center of ongoing struggle and division across many countries. Australia is among the nations that have been widely criticized at international, national and local levels by the United Nations, Amnesty International, and Human Rights Watch plus hundreds of non-profit, interest and community groups (Johnston 2016). Many of these groups have 'banded together' to challenge government policies relating to the forced indefinite detention of people seeking asylum, particularly those housed offshore in the neighboring islands of Nauru and Papua New Guinea (PNG).

Children in Detention

In 2015, the Australian Human Rights Commission (AHRC) tabled a damning report into 'Children in Immigration Detention' that argued the 'indefinite mass detention of children is a national disgrace' (Triggs 2015), finding:

- A total of 1,068 children were detained in immigration detention centers on mainland Australia, Christmas Island and Nauru;
- These children came from over 20 different countries;

(Continued)

- The largest group of children were born in Iran;
- The second largest group are identified as 'stateless' and were predominantly of Rohingya ethnic origin; and
- Other major groups of children were from Sri Lanka, Vietnam, Iraq, Afghanistan and Somalia.

The role of the 'public interest' was explicitly stated in the relevant legislation, the Commonwealth Migration Act, noting that the minister can allow people to live in the community rather than detention centers in such cases as 'the Minister thinks that is in the public interest to do so' (Triggs 2015, p. 241). While the report noted that the current Australian government had in fact used this discretion to reduce the numbers of children in detention and increase those allowed into the community, the discretion had not been adequately applied. 'Only some asylum seekers are detained in locked detention facilities. And only the Minister for Immigration and Border Protection has the power to release children and their families into community arrangements' (Triggs 2015, p. 20). Implicit in this is the more acceptable public interest that would flow from *all* children being released into the community.

'Best Interests' Response

President of the AHRC, Professor Gillian Triggs, said the inquiry provided a 'process aimed at giving voice to the otherwise unheard—and now largely unseen—the asylum seekers detained in remote parts of Australia' (2015, p. 21). Moreover, it gave children in detention, and their families, the opportunity to speak out, telling their firsthand experience of life in immigration detention facilities. A total of 1129 interviews were conducted with children and their parents, revealing 233 cases of assault, 33 cases of sexual assault and 128 incidents of self-harm by children over a 15-month period.

The report caused a national outrage, with the Australian Refugee Council (ARC) delivering a joint statement on behalf of more than 200 Australian non-profit organizations to the Australian government demanding it change its policies on children in detention (ARC 2015). The alliance argued that children should be removed from detention and 'never again' returned (ARC 2015, p. 2). Members of the community, representing a vast range of interests, voiced their opinion loudly, supporting the rights of asylum seekers, in particular the rights of the children. For example, the Institute of the Sisters of Mercy of Australia and Papua New Guinea (ISMAPNG) declared:

> Our moral duty is clear: we welcome these children and end the practice of mandatory, arbitrary and indefinite detention once and for all. ISMAPNG has joined over 200 organisations calling for the immediate release of children from immigration detention (2015, n.p.).

Other public interest responses included the following:

- Supporters of Grandmothers Against Detention of Refugee Children (GADRC), who displayed 1,000 paper dolls at their first rally representing the 1,000+ children in detention, announced they would 'take their campaign into the community to friends, neighbours and every federal politician in Victoria' and would 'not rest until the children are freed' (GADRC 2014, n.p.).

- A theater group 'Apocalypse Theatre' called on writers to submit short plays about asylum seekers and chose 24 short works to run a series of plays called 'Asylum' in Sydney (Australian Broadcasting Corporation 2015).
- Fifty senior students at Bethlehem College in Sydney held protests in the school courtyard every day for a week, using tape to cover their mouths

Figure 3.1 The eight-meter-tall banner on St. Paul's Cathedral in the heart of Melbourne's central business district makes a strong public interest message.

Used with permission of the United Nations High Commission for Refugees (UNHCR).

(Continued)

and hanging images of refugees around their necks. The Catholic Archdiocese of Sydney condemned Australia's treatment of refugees and asylum seekers and encouraged students to speak up if uncomfortable with the government's policies (McNeilage 2014).

- Students at Saint Ignatius College, Sydney, where Australia's then Prime Minister Tony Abbott went to school, sent the prime minister a letter condemning the government's asylum seeker policies (McNeilage 2014).
- The display of an eight-meter-tall banner of a mother and child on St. Paul's Cathedral in Melbourne, Australia's second most populous city, calling on Australians to 'Let's fully welcome refugees.' The banner will remain in place until detention policies are changed (Johnston 2016).

The Mobilized Body

Johnston (2016) citing Dutta (2011) notes how 'silence' within subaltern sectors in neoliberal policy structures are deeply intertwined with marginalizing policies. But the 'silence' which surrounds asylum seekers, the policies of exclusion and detention, and the restricted discursive practices that accompany them have found a voice in the local, national and international resistance that has loudly and forcefully emerged. The groundswell of public opinion includes a mobilized force of large and small organizations, plus individuals, made up of media commentators and journalists, academics, authors, churches and community and activist groups, some using official public relations agents and others working through the process independently, loudly and openly expressing condemnation of policies and providing compelling alternative counterpoints through rallies, literature, public statements, music and even cut-out doll displays (Scott & Keneally 2013; Tsiolkas 2013; Australian Broadcasting Commission 2015; GADRC 2014). Such a response has been described as 'the informally mobilized body of non-government discursive opinion that can serve as a counterweight to the state' (Outhwaite 1994, p. 483). Ultimately, the formal and informal alliances that use their multiple means of communication and protest to declare consistent messages have woven human rights and the public interest so tightly together that they provide a compelling narrative of morality and justice.

Ultimately, says Schuck (1977, p. 139), public interest groups can represent major public policy benefits.

> Public policy emerges best from a process in which the generation of relevant data is maximized, basic assumptions are questioned, expert witnesses are cross-examined, and a broad spectrum of values are advanced. Public interest groups are a necessary, if not always sufficient, condition of this process.

In this role, the public interest group is thus tasked with forming a balance with state authorities and, when pitted against the corporate sector, alerting governments of improprieties. However, funding models and alliances to political ideologies or corporate power blocks can shift the balance. Access to funds and resources can undermine the normative public interest model of checks and balances and position it as a power broker which wields massive political influence. Indeed, Nownes and Ciglar (1995) argue that, for some public interest groups, their member base can wield so much power that they easily mobilize votes and sway public opinion, citing as an example the United States National Rifle Association. When civil becomes blurred with state or corporate, the public interest can thus give way to special interests. In particular, it is the lack of transparency and the co-opting by hegemonic power bases that can challenge the very core of the public interest group. Among the industries under the spotlight for their lobbying power in recent years has been the pharmaceutical industry, or 'Big Pharma' (Gosden & Beder 2001; Weissman 2008; Raven 2008; Brezis 2008). Critics argue that while the pharmaceutical industry overtly uses its political muscle within the political economy, it also uses far less transparent tactics to impact the international health agenda (Weissman 2008; Raven 2008). Weissman (2008) suggests that 'industry-funded or -connected organizations' that propagate 'Big Pharma's myths and deceptions can be far more effective in muddying policy debate' than the more predictable corporate spin of the industry (Weissman 2008, n.p.).

The issue of using 'front' groups has become increasingly problematic in recent years (Gosden & Beder 2001) and Brezis asks the question: 'How solvable is the conflict of interests between private enterprise and public health?' (2008, p. 83). He cites aggressive direct-to-consumer marketing, payments to celebrities for their stories, sophisticated targeting of consumer groups that will then effectively lobby insurers and regulators, plus 'disease mongering' which plays up symptoms to effectively 'create' a disease. Such tactics are by no means restricted to Big Pharma with chemical, tobacco and food industries using similar tactics such as 'buying researchers, infiltrating universities, boards, media and legislative agencies' (Brezis 2008, p. 83). These are among the most insidious examples of 'capture' as described elsewhere in the book, going beyond the co-opting of public interest groups to represent broader ethical and legal issues. As Brezis (2008, p. 87) further notes: 'Those most affected are the sick, the poor and the least educated, and, therefore, free market successes appear to pose unsolvable challenges to social justice in public health.' Though he advocates increased regulation, greater transparency, restrictions on direct 'education' and legitimate external pressure through *true advocacy groups*, he concedes that the situation represents 'unsolvable conflicts of interests' in the face of such co-option (Brezis 2008, p. 87).

Pro Bono Publico and Partnerships

The concept of *pro bono* work is most commonly associated with the legal profession and very much aligned with public interest law, as outlined in chapter 1. Latin for 'the public good,' *pro bono publico* (usually shortened to pro bono) is understood to be work by industry specialists or professionals, undertaken at no cost (or reduced cost), for worthy causes. The potential link to the public interest is therefore a logical one but, like the public interest, there has been scant attention paid to pro bono in the public relations literature. In Heath's (2013) *Encyclopedia of Public Relations*, 'pro bono' does not rate a listing, mentioned in passing under its public interest entry; in *Key Concepts of Public Relations* the heading for 'pro bono' immediately directs the reader to the entry on campaigns, which includes only passing reference to pro bono as a campaign option (Franklin, Hogan, Langley & Pill 2009). As such, the concept of pro bono, by its very omission from such encyclopedic listings, indicates a lack of priority in public relations scholarship, thus representing a field ripe for investigation.

Early research in the United States found most members of the Public Relations Society of America (PRSA) performed pro bono work on a regular basis. The study by Ferré examined attitudes toward pro bono work as well as pro bono practices of 271 members of the PRSA, noting practitioners 'honor more than half of the requests that they receive for reasons of conscience, contact and exposure, personal involvement, and pressure' (Ferré, 1993, p. 59). More recently, a localized study of pro bono work surveyed 1,100 non-profit organizations in Long Island, New York (Morosoff 2014). The research located a huge need within these organizations for PR support, noting 'nonprofits realize the value of good public relations, but few have the budgets for staff or tools to create and implement the public relations campaigns they would like with enough resources' (Morosoff 2014, p. 10) and that it was 'in the best interests of nonprofits to seek out corporate support by way of pro bono services' (2014, p. 11). Morosoff (2014, p. 11) called for a 'more serious commitment' to providing pro bono services to the non-profits and, though he noted anecdotal instances of pro bono listed by some public relations agencies, he confirmed a distinct lack of any systematic research into time spent by agencies on pro bono.

Despite limited attention in scholarly literature, there is strong anecdotal evidence of pro bono work among those employed in the field, especially within large public relations organizations and industry bodies, as reflected in individual campaigns, awards and staff acknowledgments. Additionally, dedicated departments and even separate offshoot organizations have been developed to conduct pro bono work, such as Porter Novelli's 'jack + bill' (Griffiths 2014), Capstrat's 'Boomerang Society' (Cripps 2011) and Weber Shandwick's 'Impact Project' (Weber Shandwick 2013). This is supported in a survey of 101 member organizations of the US-based trade organization PR Council, which reported more than 70 percent were currently serving pro bono accounts (2011).

Moreover, foundations such as Pro Bono Lab in France and the Taproot Foundation in the United States have been established to facilitate pro bono partnerships between causes and specialist areas such as strategic planning and marketing. Taproot notes how it is working with the Commit-tee Encouraging Corporate Philanthropy to create industry standards and benchmarking for pro bono service (2011). Such a study might assist in bet-ter understanding the way public relations (and other industries) interfaces with pro bono, answering the as yet unanswered questions of how much pro bono is undertaken, how pro bono hours compare with billable hours, how systematically public relations companies or practitioners undertake the role, who does the work, how it is handled internally and by managers, and so on. Meantime, Taproot Foundation found the field of highest demand is in the related field of marketing, with the following table indicating both supply and uptake of available resources and unmet demand or need for more resources (Table 3.1).

Table 3.1 Pro Bono need and demand

Field of work	Pro Bono Uptake	Un-met demand/need
Marketing	41%	52%
Human Resources	30%	35%
Financial and administrative support	27%	28%
Financial advisory/consulting	27%	43%
Information Technology	27%	37%
Organizational design/coaching	26%	45%
Board member or executive search	20%	46%

Adapted from FTI Consulting & Taproot Foundation Nonprofit survey: Leveraging Pro Bono Resources (2011)

In the absence of dedicated public relations research, the legal literature is instructive, providing both pro bono and public interest insights. Cummings and Rhode's extensive study (2010) of 200 large American law firms pro-vides empirical data about the institutionalized role of pro bono in law firms, thus outlining the first best-practice account of when and why pro bono services were used, their effectiveness and the issues raised. Important for this book is the legal synonymy between pro bono and the public interest (Cummings & Rhode 2010; Abel 2010). Specifically, pro bono departments are also referred to as 'public interest departments' and descriptions of public interest employ the term 'pro bono' virtually interchangeably. For example, Harvard Law says the pro bono model 'encompasses charities, education and public international organizations, private public interest law firms and private law firms performing pro bono work' (Harvard 2015; see also Cummings & Rhode 2010, p. 2371).

Cummings and Rhode found several key factors contributed to the devel-opment and maintenance of pro bono work: first was the relationship to prestige awarded through pro bono work via legal, corporate and other rankings and hierarchies which provides noneconomic benefits relating to professional standing; second was the role played by internal cultures within a legal organization which impacts on the uptake of pro bono work, including attachments to public interest organizations and the resulting propensity to favor some over others; and third was the role played by the individual in choosing to undertake pro bono work. This was seen to increase during certain periods such as the civil rights movement in the United States in the 1960s, death penalty appeals in some Commonwealth countries in the 1990s, and Guantanamo Bay detainees during the 2000s. Moreover, pro bono work expanded at the same time that 'women grew to constitute half of new associates' with women greatly overrepresented in public interest law (Abel 2010, p. 2447; Cummings & Rhode 2010).

The study found that due to the integration of pro bono into legal study, a grey area had emerged between pro bono and billable work, whereby training, recruitment and reputational functions were increasingly being integrated into the economic framework of large organizations. What this meant was that pro bono had become an important part of law firms' business models, despite there being no cost attached to it. At the same time, pro bono was set to achieve not only social justice (as per its original goal) but also pedagogical aims of young lawyers or law students in sharpening and strengthening skills and training. Emerging out of this was the idea that law firms follow an 'economy of scale' principle and work to their strengths, aiming to assist in pro bono areas where they already had expertise and partnerships with other disciplines and professions where there was mutual knowledge and frameworks. At the same time, Cummings and Rhode cautioned against the idea of using pro bono for rainmaking—that is, attracting other paid work—arguing of the potential to undermine the pro bono ethic. Of note, lawyers had a professional mandate to 'give back,' with pro bono work enhancing professionalism as 'an expression of professional responsibility' (Cummings & Rhode 2010, p. 2426), a point reflected in early research by Bivins (1993) into how the public interest can assist with the professionalization of public relations and also raised elsewhere (Harrison & Galloway 2005). Abel concluded, based on the work of Cummings and Rhode, that 'large-firm pro bono has played an essential role in realizing the promise of "Equal Justice under Law" and will continue to do so' (2010, p. 2449).

What does this mean for public relations? Two words come to mind: access and equality, which, for British public relations scholar Kevin Moloney (2006), simply represent a correction to current public relations practice. 'It is a correction to the historically observed PR condition of unequal distribution of communicative resources amongst interests in actual liberal democracy' (Moloney 2006, p. 170). Moloney's notion of 'equalizing' is not about finding absolute equality, 'but rather a distribution that meets a threshold level of capacity and which is proportionate to the organisation's or group's contribution to public interest discourse' (2006, p. 80). Indeed, Moloney suggests how the law and PR could work together, for example, in legal aid centers, by offering side-by-side specialized assistance and through providing guidance for citizens' advice bureaus, assisting in providing 'equal "voicing" among interests' (Moloney 2006, p. 87). These ideas are further developed by Fawkes and Moloney (2008) in proposing PR subsidy schemes or resource-transfer mechanisms which utilize the collective critical power of retired politicians and civil servants, think tanks, academics and practitioners, as well as using existing mechanisms such as *PRWatch* in the US and *SpinWatch* in the UK. Under such institutions or 'national propaganda detectors' (Fawkes and Moloney 2008, p. 211) (which are themselves run as pro bono), public relations agencies and organizations could provide pro bono services to those non-profits who otherwise have little or no voice to counter the powerful interests they stand against.

However, just as Cummings and Rhode flag the pitfalls for the law, Dutta cautions of the risk of pro bono work being undertaken for the benefit of the 'doing' organization (Dutta 2011). He suggests that both the selection and the philanthropy process can serve the interests of the organization that conducts the pro bono work, with potential for the 'co-optation' of the process (2011, p. 260). Although this can be (at least partially) alleviated through a participatory model in partnership arrangements, where participants are central to decision-making practices, maintain control of their own agendas and ensure their aims are met, it cannot always alleviate unequal power bases.

Despite the limitations, pro bono—and partnerships as discussed following—can undoubtedly contribute significantly to the public interest. Critiques from public relations, communication and law can be developed to provide a useful checklist for clarifying issues for public relations in pursuit of pro bono practice, including the following:

- the importance of not seeing pro bono as a 'lesser' field;
- internal recognition of pro bono, with senior staff as well as junior staff working on pro bono accounts;
- the need to fit the best people to the job, using strengths and passions to the benefit of the organization, staff and client;
- the importance of not seeing pro bono as strategic (or rainmaking) but rather as a truly civic investment;
- the potential for enhancing pro bono work through other associations and partnerships.

The potential for partnerships and alliances across the sectors delivers opportunities and challenges for public relations and public interest. Selsky and Parker (2005) point out how cross-sector social-oriented partnerships provide frameworks for organizations to jointly address issues such as economic development, education, health care, poverty alleviation, community capacity building and environmental sustainability. (Many partnerships are examined in detail as part of social capital in chapter 7). At the same time, following Dutta's warning above, Brinkerhoff cautions that partnerships are 'in danger of remaining a "feel good" panacea for governance without a pragmatic grasp of what it is and how it differs from business as usual' (2002, p. 20). Seitanidi and Ryan (2007) further address this issue, pointing to a change in language associated with corporate-nonprofit partnerships from 'social' to 'strategic' signalling 'the appropriation of the 'social partnership' in order to serve the purposes of business' (2007, p. 257). They note that while the use of the partnership language is increasing, the management of the relationship may still be viewed as companies maintaining 'the central power position' over the weaker non-profit. They further identify that non-profits in such partnerships are often in the weaker position and usually not in a position to act as 'equal' players, suggesting the following recommendations to enhance partnerships, based on understanding of the following basic conditions:

- Partnerships can contribute to the development of organisational and institutional trust if the partners articulate clearly their motivations and respect the limitations of both the social and business logic behind each form of corporate community involvement.
- Partnerships can realise their potential *only* when both partners recognise the power dynamics between the organisations and make a conscious effort to reclaim their responsibilities.
- Partnerships can be a sustainable form of corporate community involvement if a clear emphasis on *process* is placed along with acknowledging that differences are a source of benefits that can lead to organisational learning and change (Seitanidi & Ryan 2007, p. 262).

Accordingly, the importance of process, together with organizational learning and potential for change, provide synergy with public interest theory and is also consistent with theories and studies developed elsewhere in the book. An alternate view is offered by Brinkerhoff, who proposes that partnerships may be considered in terms of mutuality and organizational identity. 'Mutuality encompasses the spirit of partnership principles; and organization identity captures the rationale for selecting particular partners, and its maintenance is the basis of partnership's value-added' (Brinkerhoff 2002, p. 22). As such, she suggests partnerships will vary, with the most efficient and successful existing where mutuality is affirmed in the actors' acknowledged and shared objectives. These jointly negotiated partnerships assist both mutually dependent parties, for example, where a government agency provides the structures and systems and a non-profit provides access to the necessary stakeholders and cultural expertise. The concluding snapshot about Literacy Aotearoa provides an example of such a partnership. It illustrates the role of the public relations agent in utilizing a carefully selected mix of formal and informal communication methods in supporting and furthering the organization's public interest objectives.

Snapshot

Literacy Aotearoa: Combining Formal and Informal Public Relations Methods

Literacy Aotearoa, a national adult literacy organization in Aotearoa New Zealand,* engaged in formal and informal public relations in order to serve a diverse range of students and to demonstrate its credibility in an increasingly marketized and competitive public sphere. The organization utilized an innovative and challenging mix of public relations strategies, the success of which was generally as a result of the tenacity and dedication of its workers. At various times since its beginnings in the 1970s, Literacy Aotearoa (previously known as ARLA—Adult Reading and Learning Assistance) has contracted communication consultants and produced glossy posters, brochures and advertising. For the most part, these aided the organization in its appeals to state and corporate identities.

Much has been written about the increasing need for non-profit organizations to market themselves in a public sphere where it is difficult to communicate complex social needs. However, Literacy Aotearoa recognized the importance of using professional public relations to help secure relationships with government and corporate sponsors from its early days. As such, formal public relations helped the organization convince the government that adult literacy was a legitimate and credible social need.

At the same time, although formal publicity methods did help reach some learners, it was the organization's informal methods such as networking and relationship building in local areas that recruited most students. This work was performed by literacy workers throughout Aotearoa New Zealand in their local areas. This localized approach was also helpful in communicating the organization's 'multi-literacies' approach: the notion that literacy was much more than reading and writing. Literacy learning could include, for example, oral skills and critical thinking, a more complex literacy discourse that was difficult to communicate in formalized, 'glossy', marketed publicity. Literacy workers used their own networks and spent much time creating relationships both locally and nationally in order to reach as many students as possible. The organization's commitment to recognizing the special status of Māori, the indigenous peoples of Aotearoa, meant that their strategies also had to engage in meaningful relationship building with Māori. Similar to many other non-profit organizations, historically, this kind of informal, labor-intensive communication work has been significantly underfunded, putting pressure on an already stretched workforce.

At times, it was not easy to reconcile the organization's different audiences' needs. The commonsense understanding of literacy is generally reduced to the 3Rs and literacy students are generally seen as 'lacking' in some way. Literacy Aotearoa agreed with the importance of reading and writing but, using the multi-literacies approach, offered a service that responded to students' diverse needs and aimed to build on a learner's strengths. Being mostly government funded meant that the organization was often advocating for the state to use a

(Continued)

broader literacy definition, which presented difficulties in a marketized public sphere that depended on glossy publicity and straightforward solutions to complex social problems. The organization thus spent a generous amount of time engaging in state consultation about literacy services.

Literacy Aotearoa's public relations success in achieving state funding since the 1980s, engaging with corporate sponsors and, most importantly, reaching a diverse range of learners has been due to a broad range of formal and informal strategies used by external professional communication consultants, by Literacy Aotearoa National staff and, in large part, by local literacy workers across the country. Its commitment to serve its multiple audiences has come at considerable cost, as much of its informal work is underfunded and often not recognized as important communication work. Like other organizations advocating for the complex needs of the people it serves, Literacy Aotearoa faced challenges in operating in an environment where it had to compete for funding as well as provide quality services, facing these challenges with careful allocation of resources, building on workers' strengths in their own communities, and using an innovative mix of communication strategies. This meant that Literacy Aotearoa broadened its range of learners over the years, importantly engaging with more Māori, Pasifika and rural learners.

*Aotearoa is the indigenous name for New Zealand.

Snapshot by Fiona Shearer, Massey University, Aotearoa New Zealand, with grateful thanks to Literacy Aotearoa for its generous support of this research.

Conclusion

Ideas of the public interest are not new to public relations. The intersection between the two has been examined in public relations literature for more than 50 years. As a concept, the public interest is arguably as good a 'fit' with certain types of public relations as it is with certain types of law, notably public interest and pro bono law. This chapter has examined some key intersections with traditional and non-traditional public relations, considering their 'best fit' and also their 'misfit' within the context of the public interest. The very fact that public relations will provide agency for opposing interests—the green group and the oil company; the pro-life and pro-choice lobby, the left and right of politics—means that simple solutions, indeed identifying any clear public interest, will often be elusive and subjective. Indeed, there is no panacea, no easy fix for conflicts of interest or self-interest which excludes alternate voices; there will inevitably be jockeying for positions, power struggles and ethical dilemmas. As long as the public interest is seen as a holy grail that must be both defined and magically achieved, it will frustrate professions and individuals, as it has some of the scholars who have engaged with it. Alternately, if it is dismissed as too vague, speculative or unquantifiable, then its potential benefits, as a part of participation, process, consensus or struggle, may be overlooked.

Wheeler (2006) points out that while it is no simple task, for those determining the public interest, they must take into consideration the following questions:

- Who should be considered the relevant public?
- What are the relevant public interest issues?
- What relative weightings should be given to various identified public interests and how should conflicting or competing public interest be addressed?

Such questions will affect public relations practitioners, in formal or informal roles; they may be assessed by others or be the assessors—either way they will need to consider the objectives and outcomes that are being sought and the process involved in seeking the public interest.

References

Abel, R 2010, 'The paradoxes of pro bono', *Fordham Law Review*, vol. 78, no. 5, pp. 2443–50, viewed 30 January 2015, http://ir.lawnet.fordham.edu/flr/vol78/iss5/10.

Ankney, RN & Curtin, PA 2002, 'Delineating (and delimiting) the boundary spanning role of the medical public information officer', *Public Relations Review*, vol. 28, pp. 229–41.

Australian Broadcasting Corporation 2015, 'Asylum: a series of plays', *Books and Arts Daily* (radio broadcast), 2 February 2015, viewed 5 April 2015, http://www.abc.net.au/radionational/programs/booksandarts/asylum3a-a-new-play/6061468.

Australian Refugee Council (ARC) 2015, 'Refugees and asylum seekers', viewed 1 June 2015, http://www.refugeecouncil.org.au.

Bardham, N & Weaver, K (eds.) 2011, *Public relations in a global cultural context*, Routledge, New York.

Berry, JM 1977, *Lobbying for the people: the political behavior of public interest groups,* Princeton University Press, Princeton, NJ.

Bivins, TH 1993, 'Public relations, professionalism, and the public interest', *Journal of Business Ethics,* February, vol. 12, no. 2, pp. 117–26.

Brezis, M 2008, 'Big Pharma and health care: unsolvable conflict of interests between private enterprise and public health', *Israeli Journal of Psychiatry and Related Sciences*, vol. 4445, no. 2, pp. 83–94, viewed 30 January 2014, http://publichealth.doctorsonly.co.il/wp-content/uploads/2011/12/2008_2_3.pdf.

Brinkerhoff, JM 2002, 'Government–nonprofit partnership: a defining framework', *Public Administration and Development*, vol. 22, pp. 19–30. DOI: 10.1002/pad.203.

Condit, CM & Condit, DM 1992, 'Smoking or health: incremental erosion as a public interest group strategy', in *Rhetorical and critical approaches to public relations*, in EL Toth & RL Heath (eds.), Lawrence Erlbaum Associates, Mahwah, NJ.

Cripps, K 2011, 'The power of pro bono: why more firms are doing well and doing good,' PR Council [weblog], viewed 2 March 2014, http://prcouncil.net/voice/2011/the-power-of-pro-bono-why-more-firms-are-doing-well-and-doing-good.

Cummings, S & Rhode, D 2010, 'Managing pro bono: doing well by doing better', *UCLA School of Law*, viewed 30 March 2015, https://escholarship.org/uc/item/8c99w341#page-1.

Curtin, PA & Gaither, TK 2007, *International public relations: negotiating culture, identity and power*, Sage, Thousand Oaks, CA.

Curtin, PA & Gaither, TK 2012, *Globalization and public relations in postcolonial nations*, Cambria Press, Amherst, NY.

Demetrious, K 2013, *Public relations, activism and social change: speaking up*, Routledge, New York.

Dutta, M 2011, *Communicating social change*, Routledge, New York.

Dutta, M, Ban, Z & Pal, M 2012, 'Engaging worldviews, cultures, and structures through dialogue: the culture-centred approach to public relations', *Prism*, vol. 9, no. 2, pp. 1–10.

Edwards, L 2011, 'Questions of self-interest, agency and the rhetor,' *Management Communication Quarterly*, vol. 25, no. 3, pp. 531–40.

Fawkes, J & Moloney, K 2008, 'Does the European Union (EU) need a propaganda watchdog like the US Institute of Propaganda Analysis to strengthen its democratic civil society and free markets?', *Public Relations Review*, vol. 34, no. 3, pp. 207–14.

Ferré, JP 1993, 'Ethical public relations: pro bono work among PRSA members', *Public Relations Review*, vol. 19, no. 1, pp. 59–74.

Franklin, B, Hogan, M, Langley, Q, Mosdell, N & Pill, E 2009, *Key concepts in public relations*, Palgrave, London.

Gosden, R & Beder, S 2001, 'Pharmaceutical industry agenda setting in mental health policies', in *Ethical Human Sciences and Services*, vol. 3, no. 3, pp. 147–59.

Gostin, LO, Boufford, JL & Martinez, RM 2007, 'The future of the public's health', in R Bayer, LO Gostin, B Jennings & B Steinbock (eds.), *Public health ethics: theory policy and practice*, Oxford University Press, Oxford, pp. 57–69.

Grandmothers against the detention of refugee children (GADRC), 2014, viewed 29 March 2015, http://www.grandmothersadrc.org/home-1.

Griffiths, M 2014, 'jack + bill: pro bono PR's answer to a $55,000 crowdfunding question', *PRIA*, viewed 5 March 2015, http://www.pria.com.au/newsadvocacy/january-2015/jack-bill-pro-bono-prs-answer-to-a-55000-crowdfunding-question.

Guttman, N & Thompson, TL 2011, 'Ethics in health communication', in G Cheney, L May & D Munshi (eds.), *The handbook of communication ethics*, Taylor & Francis, New York, pp. 293–308.

Harrison, K & Galloway, C 2005, 'Public relations ethics: a simpler (but not simplistic) approach to the complexities', *Prism*, vol. 3, pp. 1–17, viewed 26 June 2015, http://www.prismjournal.org/fileadmin/Praxis/Files/Journal_Files/Issue3/Harrison_Galloway.pdf.

Harvard Law School 2015, *What is public interest law? Public service practice settings*, viewed 1 January 2015, http://www.law.harvard.edu/current/careers/opia/public-interest-law/practice-settings/index.html.

Heath, RL (ed.) 2013, *Encyclopedia of public relations*, 2nd edn, Sage, Los Angeles.

Hill, CWL & Jones, TM, 1992, 'Stakeholder-agency theory,' *Journal of Management Studies*, vol. 29, no. 2, pp. 131–54.

Holden, S & Cox, D 2013, 'Public health marketing—is it good and is it good for everyone?', *International Journal of Marketing*, vol. 52, pp. 17–26.

Holtzhausen, D 2012, *Public relations as activism: postmodern approaches to theory and practice*, Routledge, New York.

Hope, S 2001, 'Why Japan banned MMR vaccine', *Daily Mail* n.d., viewed 5 January 2015, http://www.dailymail.co.uk/health/article-17509/Why-Japan-banned-MMR-vaccine.html.

Institute of the Sisters of Mercy of Australia and Papua New Guinea (ISMAPNG) 2015, Children in detention, *Latest news*, viewed 5 March 2015, http://institute.mercy.org.au/newscentre/view_article.cfm?loadref=269&id=1540.

Johnston, J 2005, 'Communicating courts: A decade of practice in the third arm of government,' *Australian Journal of Communication*, vol. 32, no. 3, pp. 77–93.

Johnston, J 2016, 'Public relations, postcolonialism and the other', in J L'Etang, D McKie, N Snow, & J Xifra (eds.), *Critical perspectives of public relations, the Routledge handbook of critical public relations*, Routledge, London, pp. 130–42.

Johnston, J & Zawawi, C 2000, 'What is public relations?' in *Public relations: theory and practice*, J Johnston & C Zawawi (eds.), Allen & Unwin, Sydney, pp. 3–25.

Kiser, E 1999, 'Comparing varieties of agency theory in economics, political science, and sociology: an illustration from state policy implementation', *Sociological Theory*, vol. 17, pp. 146–70.

Lee, M 1998, 'Public relations *is* public administration', *The Public Manager*, vol. 27, Winter, pp. 49–52.

Lee, M 2000, 'Public information in government organisations: a review and curriculum outlines of external relations in public administration', *Public Administration and Management*, vol. 5, no. 4, pp. 214–46.

L'Etang, J 2004, *Public relations in Britain*, Lawrence Erlbaum, Mahwah, NJ.

L'Etang, J 2006, 'Public relations as propaganda' in J L'Etang & M Pieczka (eds.), *Public relations critical debates and contemporary practice*, Lawrence Erlbaum, Mahwah, NJ.

L'Etang, J & Pieczka, M (eds.) 2006, *Public relations: critical debates and contemporary practice*, Lawrence Erlbaum, Mahwah, NJ.

McCarthy, JD & Zald, MN 1977, 'Resource mobilization and social movements: a partial theory', *American Journal of Sociology*, vol. 82, no. 6, pp. 1212–41.

McKie, D & Munshi, D 2007, *Reconfiguring public relations: ecology, equity and enterprise*, Routledge, New York.

McNeilage, A 2014, 'Catholic school kids protest against asylum seeker policies', *Sydney Morning Herald* 15 August, viewed 15 March 2015, http://www.smh.com.au/national/education/catholic-school-kids-protest-against-asylum-seeker-policies-20140815-104iq1.html.

Mickey, RJ 2003, *Deconstructing public relations: public relations criticism*, Lawrence Erlbaum, Mahwah, NJ.

Mitnick, B 1980, *The political economy of regulation*, Columbia University Press, New York.

Mitnick, B 2008, 'Theory of agency', in RW Kolb (ed.), *Encyclopedia of business ethics and society, vol. 5*, Sage, Los Angeles, pp. 42–49.

Moloney, K 2000, *Rethinking public relations: the spin and the substance*, Routledge, London.

Moloney, K 2006, *Rethinking public relations*, Routledge, London.

Moravcsik, A & Sangiovanni, A 2003, 'On democracy and the "public interest" in the European Union,' *Center for European Studies*, Working Paper No. 93, 2014, viewed 6 January 2015, http://aei.pitt.edu/9135.

Morosoff, JS 2014, 'Making the case for pro-bono public relations services for non-profit organizations on Long Island, *Proceedings of the 71st New York State Communication Association*, vol. 2013, article 9.

Nownes, JN & Ciglar, AJ 1995, 'Public interest groups and the road to survival', *Polity*, vol. 27, no. 3, pp. 379–404.

Obradovic, D & Viscaino, JMA 2007, 'Good governance requirements concerning interest groups in EU consultations', in D Obradovic & H Pleines (eds.), *The capacity of Central and East European interest groups to participate in EU governance*, Ibidem Publishers, Stuttgart, chapter 4, viewed 2 February 2015, http://www.eu-newgov.org/database/DELIV/D24D08a_Book_Manuscript.pdf.

Opdycke Lamme, M & Miller Russell, K 2010, 'Removing the spin: toward a new theory of public relations history', *Journalism Communication Monographs, Association for Education in Journalism and Mass Communication*, vol. 11, no. 4.

Outhwaite, W 1994, *Habermas: a critical introduction*, Polity Press, Cambridge.

Pendleton, J 2013, *Public relations, discourse practice and the public interest: analysis of a health communication campaign*, PhD thesis, RMIT University.

Pieczka, M 2006, 'Paradigms, systems theory and public relations', in J L'Etang & M Pieczka (eds.), *Public relations critical debates and contemporary practice*, Lawrence Erlbaum, Mahwah, NJ, pp. 331–59.

Pratt, CB 2001, 'Issues management: the paradox of the forty-year US tobacco wars', in RD Heath (ed.), *Handbook of public relations*, Sage, Thousand Oaks, CA, pp. 335–47.

Raven, M 2008, 'Are drug companies hijacking consumer advocacy'? *Crikey.com* 20 November, viewed 3 February 2015, http://www.crikey.com.au/2008/11/20/are-drug-companies-hijacking-consumer-advocacy.

Ross, SA 1973, 'The economic theory of agency: the principal's problem', *American Economic Association*, vol. 63, no. 2, pp. 124–39.

Scott, R & Keneally, T 2013, *A country too far*, Penguin, Melbourne.

Schuck, P 1977, 'Public interest groups in the policy process', *Public Administration Review*, vol. 37, no. 2, pp. 132–40.

Schuck, P 2014, *Why government fails so often and how it can do better*, Princeton University Press, Princeton, NJ.

Selsky, J & Parker, B 2005, 'Cross-sector partnerships to address social issues: challenges to theory and practice,' *Journal of Management*, vol. 31, no. 6, pp. 849–73.

Seitanidi, MM & Ryan, A 2007, 'A critical review of forms of corporate community involvement: From philanthropy to partnerships', *International Journal of Nonprofit and Voluntary Sector Marketing*, vol. 12, pp. 247–66. DOI: 10.1002/nvsm.306.

Shapiro, SP 2005, 'Agency theory', *Annual Review of Sociology*, vol. 31, pp. 263–84. DOI: 10.1146/annurev.soc.31.041304.122159.

Shearer, F 2015, *Snapshot of 'Literacy Aotearoa'*, personal communication.

Sorauf, FJ 1957, 'The public interest reconsidered', *The Journal of Politics*, vol. 19, no. 4, pp. 616–39.

Taproot Foundation 2011, *Pro bono history*, viewed 30 January 2015, http://www.taprootfoundation.org/about-probono/pro-bono-history.

Theaker, A & Yaxley, H 2013, *The public relations strategic toolkit*, Routledge, London.

Triggs, G 2015, *The forgotten children: national inquiry into children in immigration detention 2014*, Australian Human Rights Commission, Sydney.

Tsiolkas, C 2013, 'Why Australia hates asylum seekers', *The Monthly*, viewed 15 December 2014, http://www.themonthly.com.au/issue/2013/september/1377957600/christos-tsiolkas/why-australia-hates-asylum-seekers.

United Nations High Commissioner for Refugees (2014) 2014 UNHCR regional operations profile—East Asia and the Pacific, viewed 15 December 2014, http://www.unhcr.org/cgi-bin/texis/vtx/page?page=49e487af6.

Van Puyvelde, S, Caers, R, Du Bois, C & Jegers, M 2012, 'The governance of non-profit organizations: integrating agency theory with stakeholder and stewardship theories', *Non Profit and Voluntary Sector Quarterly*, vol. 41, no. 3, pp. 431–54. DOI: 10.1177/0899764011409757.

Walker, JL 1983, 'The origins and maintenance of interest groups in America,' *The American Political Science Review*, vol. 77, no. 2, pp. 390–406.

Weaver, CK, Motion, J & Roper, J 2006, 'From propaganda to discourse (and back again): truth, power, the public interest, and public relations', in J L'Etang & M Pieczka (eds.), *Public relations: critical debates and contemporary practice*, Lawrence Erlbaum, Mahwah NJ, pp. 7–23.

Weber Shandwick 2013, *Corporate citizenship report*, viewed 6 January 2014, http://www.webershandwick.com/uploads/news/files/2013_CSR_Report.pdf.

Weissman, R 2008, 'Big Pharma digs in', *Huff Post Business,* 1 May, viewed 6 January 2015, http://www.huffingtonpost.com/robert-weissman/big-pharma-digs-in_b_99666.html.

Wheeler, C 2006, 'The public interest: we know it's important, but do we know what it means', in Australian Institute of Administrative Law *AIAL Forum no 48*, pp. 12–26, R Creyke & A Mantel (eds.), viewed 1 September 2013, http://www.aial.org.au/Publications/webdocuments/Forums/Forum48.pdf.

White, JM 2012, 'The communicative action of journalists and public information officers', *Journalism Practice,* vol. 6, no. 4, pp. 563–80. DOI: 10.1080/17512786.2011.644899.

Yankey, J & Willem, C 2005, 'Strategic alliances', in RD Herman and Associates (eds.), *The Josey Bass handbook of nonprofit leadership & management*, 2nd edn, Wiley, San Francisco, pp. 254–75.

4 Communication and Media in the Public Interest

To understand communication is to understand much more.
(Peters 1999 in Craig 2005, p. 662)

Introduction

Former International Communication Association (ICA) President Robert Craig (2005, p. 662) describes our interrogation of communication as a meta-discourse which is 'what we do when we reflexively talk about talk for some pragmatic purpose.' He suggests that communication provides the opportunity to participate, critically and constructively, in the formation of public culture and contribute more broadly to important political and social debates.

> Public interest in our discipline is rooted in popular beliefs that communication is important, faulty communication is to blame for many human problems, and better communication can make a better world.
> (Craig 2005, p. 662)

Craig (2005, p. 662) calls for a critical approach to communication, noting how theory must inform our understanding of 'public metadiscourse—how we talk about how we talk—in the public interest' (2005, p. 666). Accordingly, what follows in this chapter is an analysis and critique of a wide range of communication and media theories and structures—from speech-making and traditional print media to online knowledge management and the collaborative and participatory model of Wikipedia. It draws on a mix of theoretical, critical and functional perspectives, examining explicit and implicit ramifications for public interest communication, concluding with a list of checks and balances to maximize public interest outcomes.

This chapter draws from critical and political economy theories in examining the role of the public interest. In his examination of media and communication, social media theorist Christian Fuchs (2014) explains the logic of applying both these approaches: 'If one wants to understand power then one needs to analyze both ideology and political economy' (Fuchs 2014, p. 97). As such, the political economy of media and communication examines the *production* and *distribution* of commodities and advertising, while critical theory addresses the *ideological dimensions* of media and communication through the dissemination of ideas within political and economic structures (Fuchs 2014, p. 21; Murdock & Golding 1974). Accordingly, Fuchs suggests a two-fold approach to, first, couple critical insights from these theories in order to consider the potentials and limits for a just society, while at the same time moving new knowledge forward. In much the same way, this chapter provides points of entry for the public interest within different structures, forms and contexts of communication and media, identifying where the public interest may exist, be at risk or compete with self-interest.

Speech Acts

When Australian Prime Minister Paul Keating delivered his now-famous 'Redfern Park' speech (1992), in celebration of the Year of the World's Indigenous People his words had a profound effect on the Australian people. His monologue, which addressed Australia's record of human rights against its indigenous population, included some stark admissions:

> We took the traditional lands and smashed the traditional way of life.
> We brought the diseases. The alcohol.
> We committed the murders.
> We took the children from their mothers.
> We practised discrimination and exclusion.
> It was our ignorance and our prejudice (Keating 1992).

His speech was to have a ripple-on effect within the Australian community for many years and remains one of the best-known pieces of political rhetoric the country has ever seen. It foregrounded future developments including the Commonwealth Native Title Act (1993), the Australian Human Rights Commission's *Bringing them Home* report into the country's 'Stolen Generations' of Indigenous children (1997) and the subsequent 'Apology' speech delivered by the next Labor Prime Minister, Kevin Rudd, more than a decade later (2008), in which the government apologized to the Stolen Generations on behalf of the Australian public (Australian Government 2008).

As communication acts, both speeches placed an intensely important issue of social justice onto the public agenda. The 'Apology' speech was called 'an act of true reconciliation' and a 'noble step' by Indigenous leader Mick Dodson (2008). Outside parliament house, watching the apology on one giant screen, the symbolism of the event was articulated in the comment from an Indigenous onlooker: 'I felt like the chain had finally broke from us' (in Welch 2008). At the same time, scholars have criticized both speeches for not delivering outcomes: the Redfern Park speech, for 'producing a phenomenon of pseudo-social justice through aural osmosis' (Birch 2004, p. 142); the 'Apology' speech as empty rhetoric, 'all talk, no action' (Fredericks 2010). Thus, while both speeches continue to resonate within the public consciousness and history records, attracting praise and appreciation for what they did, they also generated derision and contempt for what they *did not* do in terms of making change happen.

Liebersoln, Neuman and Beckerman (2004) suggest that speeches of apologia are quite common within democratic societies. So, does this make them an easy fix, based on the notion that 'words are cheap'? Or can we look to speeches as illustrations of overt acts of public interest communication? While these speeches arguably fell short of being change agents, as speech acts—rather than policy statements—both held significant public interest by placing the issues of colonization, marginalization and domination of the Indigenous Australian peoples onto the public agenda, thus playing a part in consciousness-raising for social change. Liebersoln and colleagues' (2004) study of political speeches of apologia provide some useful insights into how we might determine what constitutes public interest speech-making. Part of any such evaluation includes a balance of self-interest in the motivation or context of the speech. They argue that certain elements must be present, or absent, if apology speeches are to be taken seriously, considered within specific socio-semiotic and cultural-political contexts. Issues such as where is the speech delivered, its timing, its audience and the context for delivery must all be considered.

Crucially, they argue that 'cultural rhetorical resources' must be considered. These they define as the 'general rhetorical patterns that organize the communication process of a given group through a mediating textual form embedded in the symbolic realm of a given culture' (Liebersoln, Neuman & Bekerman 2004, p. 927). Such an approach enables the reading of a speech within a specific cultural context. Different cultures provide different rhetorical resources for public apologia speeches and 'one must pay close attention to the way an apologizer draws on historical, social and political contexts' (2004, p. 921). In analyzing two speeches—one by former United States President Bill Clinton and one by former Israeli Prime Minister Ehud Barak—they consider elements such as the following:

- The motivation of the speech (is it for obvious political gain, positioned for example, near an election, or alternately intended to atone for wrongdoing?);
- Whether it is delivered unreservedly (without equivocation or justification);
- Whether it is delivered at a culturally appropriate time (considering the audience's cultural beliefs and calendar); and
- Whether it is delivered at an appropriate location (is there a power-differential between the apologizer and the audience?).

Such analysis provides us with a schema for interrogating speeches of apologia, or political speeches in general, in turn providing some criteria to assist in analyzing them for public versus self-interest potential. If they are intended to truly atone for injustice, and thus eschew the insincerity often associated with political rhetoric, certain speeches have the potential to stand out as exemplars of public interest communication. Of course, compelling, powerful, even hypnotic speeches that call for social change can also represent *the antithesis* of public interest, as evidenced by Adolf Hitler's speeches which invoked Christianity in the ethnic cleansing of the Jews (Baynes 1942). Clearly, in such instances, motivation is a key factor, thus reinforcing the idea that the public interest must be considered in context and on a case-by-case basis.

Communicative Action and Discourse

The theory of communicative action can be instructive in analyzing speech acts, such as the Redfern and Sorry speeches, and other forms of communication, and in identifying whether or not they may be classed as public interest communication. Habermas (1984, 1998) argues that the complexity of social interaction locates three basic validity claims which are potentially at stake in any speech act used for cooperative purposes, that is, one that constitutes communicative action. These three validity claims are the following:

- the speech act is sincere (non-deceptive),
- it is socially and culturally appropriate or right (in time and place), and
- it is factually true (or more broadly: representationally adequate) (Bohman & Rehg 2011).

As such, speech acts can be criticized for failing on any one, or more, of these claims, so fully successful speech acts must satisfy the demands connected with all three basic validity claims, which Habermas equates with sincerity, rightness, and truth (or validity). Habermas's validity claims, therefore, reflect the criteria raised by Liebersoln and colleagues (2004) and these might collectively be applied in determining communication claims to the public interest; that is, if they are deficient in any of the validity claims, can they be said to be in the public interest?

Habermas provides a way of making such judgments. He argues that 'to recognize the validity of such claims is to presume that good reasons could be given to justify them in the face of criticism' (Bohman & Rehg 2011, n.p.). To achieve this, he proposes a 'reflective form' of communicative action which applies his theory of 'argumentation or discourse' (Bohman & Rehg 2011, n.p.). Habermas distinguishes three aspects of argument-making practices:

- argument-as-product,
- argument-as-procedure, and
- argument-as-process,

which he loosely aligns with logic, dialectic and rhetoric. They are summarized in Table 4.1.

Table 4.1 Habermas's three elements of argument-making

Product	Logic	Arguments are products based on sets of reasons that support conclusions based on intrinsic properties. The logical strength of such arguments depends on how well one has taken into account all the relevant information and possible objections. E.g. public speech.
Procedure	Dialectic	Arguments and counterarguments are pitted against each other in critical discussion in competition for the better argument. E.g. public debate.
Process	Rhetoric	Robust critical testing of competing arguments depends on the rhetorical quality of the persuasive process. A rhetorically adequate process identifies four presuppositions: (i) no one capable of making a relevant contribution has been intentionally excluded, (ii) participants have equal voice, (iii) they are internally free to speak their honest opinion without deception or self-deception, and (iv) there are no sources of coercion built into the process and procedures of discourse. E.g. consultation process.

Pragmatic analysis of argumentation. Adapted from Bohman & Rehg 2011 Habermas's three elements of argument-making

When a speech act is challenged, it may shift reflexively from ordinary speech to discourse, which is described as 'processes of argumentation and dialogue in which the claims implicit in the speech act are tested for their rational justifiability as true, correct or authentic. Thus the rationality of communicative action is tied to the rationality of discourse' (Bohman & Rehg 2011, n.p.). Habermas chooses to use the term 'validity claim' rather than empirical truth, recognizing a spectrum of 'validity claims' that also includes, at the least, claims to moral rightness, ethical goodness or authenticity, personal sincerity and aesthetic value (Bohman & Rehg 2011, n.p.).

Fuchs (2014) argues that Habermas's notions of communication *can* be critical, but are not necessarily so, whereas those who critique exploitation and domination are by their nature *always* critical. As such, Habermas's approach to discourse is communication-focused rather than power-focused. In contrast are Foucault (1980) and Fairclough (1992, 2001), who find power at the *center* of discourse. And, importantly, while discourse regimes not only govern what is said, they can also exclude or prohibit certain language, controlling 'what can be known' (Malpas & Wake 2006, p. 175). Public relations plays a significant role in the development of discourses, by translating information and developing 'what can be known' in government, political, economic, social and cultural contexts. The political speeches previously analyzed are illustrative of this. Dutta and Pal (2011, p. 196) call these 'public relations practices that manufacture, reproduce, and circulate symbolic representations and interpretive frames that carry out … agendas.' Discourse, thus, must have a purpose in seeking to achieve agendas.

Controlling discourses are often examined in the context of power struggles with subaltern groups within the wider society. Cottle (2000) argues of the need to recognize the historically variant forms that marginalization and racism can assume within discourses, narratives and media representations and how these are produced within and through state, institutional and everyday practices, as evidenced and supported elsewhere in the literature (see, for example, Weedon 2004; Dutta 2011; Dutta & Pal 2011; Johnston 2016).

For example, in her analysis of asylum seekers, Johnston (2016) examines competing discourses and the difficulties of countering the powerful and deeply ingrained hegemonic discourses of fear and exclusion. We can contrast this with parallel projects elsewhere; in Scotland, for instance, where the *Asylum Positive Images Project*, developed collaboratively, was aimed at opening communication channels and reversing negative stereotyping through media education (Oxfam 2007). The public interest potential for such projects can bring together many industries and sectors to deal with a social problem—in this case, government, media, police, advocacy groups, non-profits and educational organizations. Such initiatives provide a learning environment for the news media to assist in better understanding complex issues, ideally translating into public interest communication that is more balanced, accurate and ultimately more productive. As such, the simple act of developing media guides, particularly on complex or misunderstood issues, can represent a public interest benefit by opening rather than restricting channels of communication. In the following snapshot, media guides on a range of social and health issues are summarized to illustrate their role in public interest communication.

Snapshot

Media Guides

Forward Together: Ideas for Working with Asylum Seekers, Refugees, the Media and Communities (Oxfam Scotland, 2007)

This document builds upon Scotland's Asylum Positive Images Project that began in 2003 and undertook activities that targeted the media portrayal of asylum seekers (via content and framing) to create positive public attitudes toward asylum. Oxfam has worked in partnership with around 20 organizations including government, police, media, volunteer and community-based groups on this project. Initiatives include the *Fair Play Journalists Guide* (in its third edition in 2008) designed to challenge racism, informing public

(Continued)

perceptions of asylum to assist asylum seekers to settle safely in Scotland. This guide includes information on the asylum process and support, relevant legislation, who's who in the asylum process and key contacts. Exceptional and accurate reporting on the asylum seeker issue is recognized via the Refugee Week Scottish Media Awards, while journalism students are targeted via university lectures about reporting on this ethical issue. It also includes media training for asylum seekers to assist their understanding of media and engaging journalists as well as community outreach activities to reach the wider society as outlined in the *Forward Together* guide (Oxfam 2007).

A Way with Words and Images: Suggestions for the Portrayal of People with Disabilities (Employment and Social Development Canada, 2006, with Updated Website 2013)

The Canadian government produced this 18-page document in 2006 (updated in 2013) to promote the fair and accurate portrayal of people with disabilities. It recommends substitute terms for expressions such as 'birth defect' and 'congenital defect.' It provides interviewing tips: 'Before the interview, ask yourself: Am I reporting on this piece because it involves a person with a disability or because the issue and related circumstances are relevant to the general population?' There is advice for media behavior during interviews. 'When talking with a person with a disability, speak directly to him or her, rather than through a companion, interpreter, or intervener.' These guidelines make media aware that often human interest story lines dominate, rather than in-depth coverage of issues important to people with disabilities, such as lack of access to facilities, employment and poverty. Appropriate images are also covered with advice such as 'use images that show people with disabilities participating in society. Do not use images that isolate or call special attention to people with disabilities unless they are appropriate to the subject matter' (Canadian Government 2006, 2013).

It's not OK: Guidelines for Reporting Domestic/Family Violence (New Zealand Government 2007)

The New Zealand government launched the 'It's not OK' campaign in 2007 to change attitudes and behavior that tolerate any kind of family violence. Its messages are 'Family violence is not OK' but 'It is OK to ask for help.' Two media resources were produced to help convey the campaign messages— *Guidelines for Reporters* and the *Media Manual* for community agencies to use when engaging with the media about family violence. The *Guidelines for Reporters* highlights that media tend not to reflect the prevalence and severity of family violence and often perpetuate commonly held but untrue beliefs about domestic violence. It lists six common myths about domestic violence, including that it is an unpredictable, private tragedy; it is caused by substance abuse, stress, poverty, or a failed marriage; the victim is to blame; domestic violence is not as serious as other assaults/murders. Moreover, it suggests journalists include recent statistics and expert sources (provided) as well as tips for reporting, such as 'identify the murder/incident as domestic violence; place it in the context of local and national statistics and recent events; provide information about the nature of domestic violence; use experts; name family violence as a crime' (New Zealand Government 2007).

Media guides, such as these, actively seek to manage discourse about issues of social importance. In providing the media with these tools, public relations practitioners also assist in developing positive source-media relations, linking Habermas's concept of 'lifeworld' through shared language and understanding.

The Source-Media Relationship and Lifeworld

The news media have perennially cited the public interest as part of their *raison d'etre*. So how does public relations' relationship with the media translate into public interest practice? Because the news media still represent one of public relations' principle access points to the public, we can find it useful to consider the source-media relationship and the power structures which surround it, once again drawing on the work of Habermas. The concept of the 'lifeworld' is well known to many public relations scholars and is useful in better understanding relationships—in this case the source-media relationship—which can ultimately either translate into public interest communication or become hijacked by special interests. The lifeworld is based on 'institutionally bound' speech acts centered on rules, norms, language and conventions that presuppose a certain level of knowledge (Habermas 1998, p. 283). Such knowledge is drawn from a common frame of reference—a lifeworld—which is specific to certain institutions or sectors within societies. Where complex issues can take journalists beyond their level of expertise (and, by association, their lifeworld), the public relations source can level the playing field of knowledge by providing information or reference materials such as those in the previous snapshot. We commonly also see this in the interpretive role of public relations in science, health and legal communication, which translates complex material for general or media understanding, as previously discussed and critiqued in chapter 3.

Habermas views lifeworld as a shared linguistic context or background for communication practice. If a lifeworld is shared, that is, if social and cultural understandings are common and understood, there is a greater likelihood of communicative action, ideal speech and consensus. Cook (in Habermas 1998, p. 16) notes that the 'background knowledge of the lifeworld forms the indispensable context for the communicative use of language; indeed without it, meaning of any kind would be impossible.' Likewise, McCarthy (1981, p. 282) notes that lifeworld must be considered in the context of understanding speech. He refers to a 'double structure' of ordinary language. In it, if a speaker and listener are to reach an understanding, they must communicate simultaneously at two levels: the first, the level of inter-subjectivity on which speaker and listener establish the relations that permit them to come to an understanding with one another, and the second, the level of experiences about which they want to reach an understanding in the communicative function determined by the first part of the structure. In source-media relationships, such a double structure must exist with both a mutual understanding of a subject and a desire to want to learn or impart information about it. If either of these steps breaks down, then the communication will be flawed and may result in incorrect reportage that misquotes a source, withholds information or obfuscates the facts.

Journalism and public relations are governed by certain rules, norms and conventions. Knowledge of each other's lifeworld suggests that many of these are shared: for example, the concepts of on and off the record, tip-offs, deadlines and embargos. Others are known but not shared: for example, interviewing tricks in journalism or staying 'on message' in public relations, essentially part of the unwritten media and public relations contract. As Franklin (2003) points out, if either party breaks one of these rules or conventions, it can trigger either confrontation or conflict. However, as Shin (2006, p. 32) notes:

> ... source-reporter conflict is not necessarily deleterious to the news process or to societal interests. It is inherent in the relationship and is healthy to some degree since the source-reporter relationship embodies both destructive and constructive aspects of conflict.

These conflicts, driven by differing motivations and objectives, will, by necessity, incorporate different public interest priorities. While Franklin (2003) is highly critical of how information (via the media) and the 'propagandist' (via the source) are destined to routinely collide, he also concedes that the two have mutually adapted to each other's needs and are driven by a 'strategic complementarity of interests' (Franklin 2003, p. 47); that is, they work best when they complement each other for strategic purposes. Thus, their exchange relationship, while often asymmetrical, is symbiotic: for example, politicians and their press agents rely on the media to position themselves and to gauge public opinion, while the media need information from politicians and press agents to effectively cover political stories (Franklin 2003, p. 47). This forms the very basis of agenda-setting and agenda-building theories, which center on informing, managing and shaping public discourse as part of the *sine qua non* that the media and source (public relations) have traditionally shared. In truth, the often paradoxical source-media relationship is both functional and dysfunctional, as illustrated in 40 years of metaphors to describe the relationship:

- a strategic ritual (Tuchman 1972),
- a dance (Gans 1979),
- a tug of war (Gans 1979),
- a parent–child relationship (Tiffen 1989),
- a shared snake-pit (Hoggart 2002 in Franklin 2003),
- a poacher and gamekeeper (Johnston 2013).

Following Cancel, Cameron, Sallot and Mitrook (1997), Shin positions the media-source relationship along a continuum, which she describes as stretching from 'pure advocacy to pure accommodation' (2006, p. 8) and though the relationship will vary along this continuum, and often include conflict, each nevertheless benefits from the other. But does this mean the public interest is served in the relationship? The answer is both yes and no. Critical scholarship would suggest that problems arise in the potential for the media to become an extension of an organization or public position— whether government, corporate, interest group or other—and complicit in its agency. Moreover, while well-resourced organizations, such as political parties and large corporate entities, can achieve benefits from this model, others which have less access or active agency will be denied the same benefits. Political communication, for example, often finds cozy relationships existing between media, politicians and political minders. This may take the form of what have been called 'journo-politicos' (Franklin 2003, p. 51), representing not only a closeness between sources and journalists but also a degree of 'cross-over' between the two in terms of their jobs and career histories. It follows that a less critical approach by the news media can thus result in a deficit in public interest simply by a lack of critique and investigation.

Political economy concerns exist about the over-reliance on official 'experts' and sources in the news, the lack of context in much news report-ing, the prominence of the commercial motivations of media organizations, and the concentration of news ownership that leads to a lack of diversity in news coverage and approach. Thus, in public interest terms, questions arise across two key issues: first, the source-media relationship and the transfer of information within this space, across both public and private spheres, as already discussed; and second, in the political economy of the media and communication organizations as the dominant and powerful public spheres which select, prioritize and spin news and information as they see fit. Dutta (2011, p. 269) explains how:

> ... the concept of media power not only attends to the processes by which powerful actors within social systems use the media to serve their agendas, but also foregrounds the powerful role of media as the catalyst of social action in contemporary complex societies.

Like many other media scholars (Hamilton 2004; McChesney 2008; Forde 2011), Couldry and Curran (2003, p. 3) have expressed concerns that 'media power itself is part of what power watchers need to watch.' Likewise, Habermas (1974, 1989) argues how the mass media, which began as the embodiment of a new public sphere, particularly with the rise of the penny presses of the early 1800s, became the mouthpiece for business and the bureaucracy. Not surprisingly, this power comes at the expense of weaker voices and minority interests. As Cottle (2000, p. 2) notes:

> The media occupy a key site and perform a crucial role in the pub-lic representation of unequal social relations and the play of cultural

power. It is in and through representations ... that members of the media audience are variously invited to construct a sense of who 'we' are in relation to who 'we' are not, whether as 'us' or 'them', 'insider' and 'outsider' ... By such means, the social interests mobilized across society are marked out from each other.

Within predominantly white societies and Western dominant cultures, economic forces prioritize 'middle ground' white opinion and interests since this is where the largest market and profits are found, thereby marginalizing minority interests, voices and opinions (Cottle 2000, p. 20). This argument is supported by Moloney (2006) who sees the media as complicit in publishing the news based on parties who 'wrangle and horse-trade for advantage' (2006, p. 86). When this is examined within the scope of news media needing to create and report news on a relentless basis, with 'conflict' as one of its key news drivers or news values, the dominant news is often that which accommodates these interests.

Potential sites for the public interest see *alternative* media as having emerged in response to capitalism and media imperialism (Hamilton 2004), as a 'statement against dominant media practices, content and context' (Forde 2011, p. 45). Described as encompassing community, grassroots, radical, citizens and independent media (Forde 2011, p. 3), this space is also seen as inclusive of oppositional, participatory and collaborative media practices (Deuze 2006) as part of civil society and pluralist voices. Forde notes a consistency in alternative media: 'to give a voice to the voiceless, to fill the gaps left by mainstream media, to empower ordinary people to participate in democracy, and in many instances, to educate people with information they cannot access elsewhere' (2011, p. 45). It is also a site for the dissolution of the traditional audience-producer barrier, which is often internet based. Though alternative media's capacity for serious empowerment and presenting counter public spheres is questionable, those who research in this space remain cautiously optimistic of the benefits it provides (Cottle 2000; Downing 2003; Deuze 2006; Forde 2011). As such, the alternative media can provide an entry point for the public interest in providing agency for those denied access to mainstream media.

Internet and Social Media

Broadly speaking, the rise in information and communication technologies (ICTs) raised hopes for 'participatory production' and 'democratization,' especially for those without access to the dominant media. However, the realization of this potential represents major points of contestation within media scholarship. In analyzing this debate, we find a complex environment for claims of public interest communication. On the one hand, the rise in ICTs has broadly provided the capacity for a newly available democratic space for participation and production and, hence, by association, the dispersing of power (Jenkins 2008; Bruns 2008). Some see this as bringing the promise of symmetrical participation (Shirky 2008) and a reinvigo-rated public sphere through enabling access to the masses (Moore 2010). Within this context, the capacity for public interest is clear; ICTs are seen as enabling and connecting 'produsers' or 'prosumers' (Bruns 2008), no longer just consumers of media but active participants who take part in public discourse. Others see this as allowing the co-creation of 'subaltern narra-tives in global spaces that challenge neoliberal hegemony' (Dutta 2011, p. 277). For minority groups the internet thus provides 'instantaneous flows of information and ideas as well as the ritual exchange of symbols and images, thereby serving to construct and affirm imagined—and now increasingly—virtual communities' (Cottle 2000, p. 4). This includes new communication opportunities for embattled and sometimes dispersed ethnic minorities, in helping to keep alive memories and myths of home-lands plus collective hopes for the future (Cottle 2000) and providing a repository for language and culture in diasporic communities (Byrne & Johnston 2015). Social media are also credited for their importance in protest and revolutions, summed up in the following often-cited quote from an un-named Egyptian activist during the Arab Spring:

> *We use Facebook to schedule the protests,*
> *Twitter to coordinate, and*
> *YouTube to tell the world.*

On the other hand, however, the capacity for Web 1.0 or 2.0 to *truly* enable this kind of change is seriously questioned. In the case of the Arab Spring, Fuchs refutes the role of social media as enabling revolution, arguing that the media are not responsible for change, *people* are. 'There are no Twitter-, Facebook- or YouTube-Revolutions. Only *people* who live under certain social conditions and organize collectively can make rebellions and revolutions' (Fuchs 2014, p. 102, my emphasis). Indeed, research has found that interpersonal commu-nication, traditional media and telecommunications were more important information sources and communication tools in the Egyptian revolution than social media and the internet (Fuchs 2014, p. 85). In their analysis of the Arab Spring, Chebib and Sohail (2011, p. 143) explain, 'For any mass movement to take place, a space for communication is needed. A few decades ago, this used to happen in bookshops and underground newspapers' offices. Today, online spaces have been added to the regular ones on the ground.' Thus, social media are *one tool* for revolution, protest and crisis management (rather than necessarily *the primary tool*, albeit an important one).

In critiquing social media and the internet, political economists translate their concerns for traditional media into these newer spaces. McChesney observes how new networks combine with market economics to 'point more toward monopoly' (McChesney 2008, p. 19). Fuchs and others (see, for example, McChesney 2008; Couldrey & Curran 2003; Picard 2014) challenge the internet's capacity for equal and fair participation within the so-called democratized spaces. Fuchs criticizes the 'corporate coloniza- tion of social media' (2014, p. 102), arguing that they do not 'constitute a public sphere or participatory democratic space' but are instead based on a 'false social media reality that neglects the role of capitalism' (Fuchs 2014, p. 102). It is an issue that has divided scholars and brings into question the public interest capabilities of more recent ICTs.

> Out of sheer naiveté and wishful thinking many proponents of and commentators on social media—including many of our colleagues in communication and media studies—have portrayed the Internet and its services as an empowering force, a democratizing institution, and a space free from the constraints that hobbled legacy media. These observers exhibit inadequate critical thought and analysis, venerate the technology, and tumble into the trap of technicism.
>
> (Picard 2014, p. 3)

The increasing commercialization of social media and the internet and the growing use by business interests and political elites see corporations and governments bypassing legacy media to promote private interests without even the pretense of constraint and, according to media analyst and politi- cal economist Robert Picard (2014), little attention to truth and accuracy. Picard's warnings lie first with the veneration of and uncritical approach to the newer media platforms and, second, with the limited capacity to imple- ment policies in any case. Nevertheless, he concedes that individuals and civil society organizations are able to use this new means of communication more often, and in more ways, than they were able to use legacy mass media in the past (Picard 2014, p. 4).

Key concerns among critics include how the audience is used as a commodity to sell to advertisers (Fuchs 2014, p. 107) and social media's role in facilitating 'concealed public relations' (Demetrious 2013, p. 144). Corporate web operators and third parties monitor and record personal data and online activity which are stored, merged and analyzed and ulti- mately used to influence the 'prosumers' themselves (Fuchs 2014) in a cycle of commodification. Fuchs cites Gandy's earlier research as it applies to social media, as a 'panoptic sorting of internet prosumers' (Gandy 1993 in Fuchs 2014, p. 109), which systematically *identifies* consumers interests, *classifies* them into consumer groups, *assesses* their interests and *targets* them accordingly. Demetrious adds how the 'confluence of purposes that form social media create ideal conditions for hidden relations of self-inter- est within a powerful discursive forum characterised by a culture of dis- traction and self-gratification' (2013, p. 144). Ultimately, what transpires is an environment of heightened self-interest, reduced transparency, and standardized co-optation from business, government and other organiza- tional powers which collectively threaten to undermine the public interest benefits that were earlier promised.

Online Knowledge

At the same time, notions of 'democratization' and 'participation' on the internet are also caught up in the commercialization of the knowledge economy. Scholarly journals and periodicals—now almost entirely online—have attracted extensive criticism for their increasing costs, effectively pricing many out of the market (Darnton 2009, 2014; McKiernan 2014). In the United States, for instance, subscriptions to scientific journals have increased at astronomical rates since going online: the average price of a year's subscription to a chemistry journal in 1970 was $33; in 2014 it had risen to $4,044 (Darnton 2014). Historian and director of the Harvard University Library, Robert Darnton is highly critical of the way the online economy has hijacked information and knowledge, through the limits that are placed on access to information by those who create it, arguing the public interest suffers as a consequence. While he accepts that information does not come free, he questions the (lack of) balance that is currently in place. 'No one can ignore the economic realities that underlie the new information age, but who would argue that we have reached the right balance between commercialization and democratization?' (Darnton 2014, p. 8). The loser, he points out, in 'the scramble to gain market share in cyberspace,' is the public interest (Darnton 2014, p. 8) as research libraries, hospitals, small-scale laboratories and data-driven enterprises are forced to cancel subscriptions to scientific journals (Darnton 2009, 2014).

The irony of this situation should not go unnoticed. The scholars who conduct the research and publish in academic journals are employed by the very institutions which have been most affected by the cost increases, a situation Darnton (2009, p. 106) calls 'a contradiction at the heart of academic life.' Some university libraries have stood their ground in protest over the price increases. The University of California, for example, organized a boycott when it was advised of a 400 percent increase in 67 journals—noting that the university's faculty had contributed 5,300 articles to those journals during the previous six years (Darnton 2014). Alternate models have been developed to prioritize access to information in the public interest. For example, open-access journals have emerged all over the world, providing no-cost publishing or access, while digital repositories are also being established within university-owned repositories. The Faculty of Arts and Sciences at Harvard has developed the Digital Access to Scholarship at Harvard (DASH), which allows free access to anyone with some provisos. In 2014, DASH included 17,000 articles and had registered three million downloads (Darnton 2014). Also in response to limited access and large volumes of online literature, JSTOR has developed various access models including its 'register & read' database, which enables anyone to register and read-only a limited number of journals at any given time. In conjunction with various publishers, it also provides access to some archival collections for universities, schools and museums and reduces or waives fees for not-for-profits in developing countries (JSTOR 2012).

At the same time, Darnton acknowledges that publishers' interests must be looked after if scholars are to maintain the intense regime of publishing increasingly required within their sector, pointing out: 'It should be possible to enlist vested interests in a solution that will serve the public interest, not by appealing to altruism but rather by rethinking business plans in ways that will make the most of modern technology' (2014, p. 10). Darnton's proposals serve a dual approach for the public interest; they are as much about consciousness-raising in the academic community as they are about developing models for a more freely flowing system of communication and information to the wider community.

> In place of a close, privileged, and costly system, it will help open up a world of learning to everyone who wants to learn [in] a digital commonwealth, in which ideas would flow freely in all directions.
>
> (Darnton 2009, p. 106)

This somewhat idealistic statement might well be describing the actual online space of Wikipedia. The world's most popular encyclopedia, and the sixth most visited website globally (Alexa 2014), Wikipedia sits in stark contrast to the relatively closed-access world of scholarly journals. Clearly serving a very different purpose to academic publishing, it is nevertheless a major part of the knowledge economy and one which has found many intersections with public relations, as outlined in the following snapshot. Identified by Fuchs as the 'only successful WWW platform thus far that is not based on a capital accumulation model' (2014, p. 48), Wikipedia was envisioned by its founder Jimmy Wales in the following way:

> Imagine a world in which every single person on the planet is given free access to the sum of all human knowledge ... It is my intention to get a copy of Wikipedia to every single person on the planet in their own language.
>
> (Wales 2004)

Scholarly interest in Wikipedia has ranged from its collaborative environment (Bruns 2008; Elliott 2006; Viegas, Wattenberg, Kriss & van Ham 2007; Fuchs 2014) to its historical development (Kittur, Pendleton & Mytkowiz 2006; Bruns 2008) and its value to information technology (Mihalcea 2007; Milne & Witten 2013). Yet despite garnering a great deal of interest from within the academy, there remains little critical scholarship that has examined its application to and intersections with specific sectors or industries or its capacity to influence commercial, political or government agendas. Following Byrne and Johnston's (2015) research into Wikipedia as a tool for public diplomacy, this chapter will examine the intersections between public relations, Wikipedia and the public interest. First, however, it is important to develop a clear understanding of the Wikipedia philosophy, described by Bruns as 'unfinished artefacts in a continuing process' (Bruns 2008, p. 110).

In principle, and by many estimates, Wikipedia must be classed as a public interest resource, created by many people, for many more people. Wikipedia's characteristic 'ad hoc,' collaborative nature has earned it the title of a 'folksonomy,' due to its development by internal users or 'folk' (as compared to experts), and its structure which is inherently highly fluid and organic in nature (as opposed to a taxonomy based on rigid structures). Noruzi (2006, p. 199) defines a folksonomy as 'an Internet-based information retrieval methodology consisting of collaboratively generated, open-ended labels that categorize content such as web resources, online photographs, and web links.' Bruns (2008) explains that the concept of the folksonomy centers on 'folk intelligence,' based on a perpetually emerging, continuously changing collective that eschews the idea of the expert as knowing best, instead drawing on individuals' collective knowledge to establish primacy. As such, the value of folksonomies may be seen in both enabling and encouraging the encounter of and engagement between differing views on how to structure knowledge (Shirky 2008, p. 194; Bruns 2008). Wikipedia is further described as a 'stigmergic collaboration,' defined as a system that 'self-organizes due to the collective input of large numbers of individuals' (Elliott 2006, n.p.).

Though characterized as a minimal-rule environment, Wikipedia has nevertheless evolved to include certain 'rules of engagement' with its democratized ethos containing key policies and procedures. Its own documents outline how 'respected editors [must] also respect the anarchic "accept all comers" approach to this collaborative endeavour' (in Bruns 2008, p. 109). In short, Wikipedia's philosophy is based on the following rules:

- Neutral point of view: content must be written so as to represent significant views fairly, proportionately and without bias.
- Verifiability: material must be attributed to a reliable, published source. This means that people reading and editing the encyclopedia can check that information with that source.
- No original research: no original thought or new analysis must be used. All material must be attributable to a reliable, published source.
- No vested interests: although anyone can contribute to Wikipedia, it has strict rules on self-promotion and conflicts of interest. It further states, 'Where advancing outside interests is more important to an editor than advancing the aims of Wikipedia, that editor stands in a conflict of interest' (Wikipedia 2014a; 2014b).

Thus, the issue of 'interest' in Wikipedia is evident in its rejection of conflicts—both self-interest and conflicting interests. As the following snapshot illustrates, Wikipedia has seen the best of stigmergic collaborations and folksonomies, as well as flagrant defiance of Wikipedia principles and a co-optation of the space and conflict of interest, the latter resulting in a unified correction by public relations professionals for the public interest.

Snapshot

Wikipedia and Public Relations

Byrne and Johnston's (2015) examination of the role of Wikipedia as a tool for public diplomacy found that, following 2009, many villages, towns and even countries globally realized the value that a high-ranking presence in Wikipedia could produce. The authors examined several examples of the development of Wikipedia pages and the use of crowdsourcing and other tactics to drive online traffic to certain destinations, thereby enhancing search engine optimization (SEO). What began as a 'social experiment' and a competition to create a Wikipedia profile for a small museum in Derby, northern England, snowballed into the creation of Wikipedia's first 'online town' of Monmouth in Wales, a formula that was soon emulated to create Praguepedia, Joburgpedia, Freopedia, Bremenpedia, Umepedia and other destinations (Byrne & Johnston, 2015).

For the creation of what became known as the Wikitown of 'Monmouth-media,' more than 550 Wikipedia articles, 1,000 images, and 1,000 quick response or QR codes (called QRpedia) were developed, achieving 250 news stories across 30 countries in just a few weeks (Byrne & Johnston 2015). As such, the Monmouthmedia project resulted in massive publicity and was heralded a major success for the town and its development team of Wikimedia[1] United Kingdom and the Monmouthshire County Council (Wikipedia 2012a). However, it was not without criticism from the Wikipedia community which saw the development as contrived and inconsistent with the Wikipedia principles. 'What seems to have happened … is that this simple idea got co-opted in two ways. WP [Wikipedia] became a focus instead of a tool, and people saw that they could advance their own goals through this project' (Murphy 2012, n.p.). It was, however, to be the development of Gibraltar in the south of Spain—'Gibraltarpedia'—that brought the issue under close scrutiny for its governance practices amid claims of conflicts of interest (Wikipedia 2012b; Blue 2012; Murphy 2012). What followed was an independent inquiry into Wikimedia UK, which recommended a major overhaul of governance practices, including a new management structure (Lombard 2013; Byrne & Johnston 2015).

The inquiry, and the media reporting of the issue, blamed public relations, at least in part, summed up in 2012 in the following two headlines:

- 'Corruption in Wikiland? Paid PR scandal erupts at Wikipedia' (Blue 2012, n.p.);
- 'A stealth PR campaign for Gibraltar proves existential crisis for Wikipedia' (Stern 2012, n.p.).

The headlines were emblematic of a rash of reports that questioned overt and covert public relations activity behind Wikipedia page development more generally. One US public relations company, 'Untrikiwiki,' advertised:

WE HAVE THE EXPERTISE NEEDED to navigate the complex maze surrounding 'conflict of interest' editing on Wikipedia. With more than eight years of experience, over 10,000 edits, and countless community connections we offer holistic Wikipedia services.

(Orlowski 2012, n.p.)

Meanwhile, Wikipedia condemned the black hat practice of paid advocacy editing and 'sockpuppeting' on Wikipedia, including more than 300 accounts believed to be fakes, or 'sockpuppets' (using a false identity to post self-serving information) (Sebastian 2014, n.p.). Untrikiwiki was subsequently reported to have committed to a more ethical approach to its Wikipedia consulting work (Orlowski 2012).

At the same time, the Chartered Institute of Public Relations (CIPR) in the United Kingdom responded to the issue by developing its first edition of *Wikipedia: Best Practice Guidelines for Public Relations Professionals*, subsequently updated in 2014. The guide states it is:

> intended to provide clear and detailed advice on how PR professionals should engage with the Wikipedia community. It also aims to highlight best practice and equip public relations professionals with the advice needed to navigate the grey areas of Wikipedia engagement and with an understanding of how to protect an organisation's or client's reputation openly and transparently (Chartered Institute of Public Relations 2014).

Guidelines developer Phillip Sheldrake positioned it as a healing tool, noting the 'poor reputation PR starts with in the eyes of Wikipedians. We have trampled on their community somewhat over the years after all' (Sheldrake 2012, n.p.). The guidelines endorse the principles and independence of Wikipedia and, as such, serve a public interest both for the public relations industry and for Wikipedia itself.

Likewise in the United States, the relationship between Wikipedia and the public relations industry had reached a low point when, in 2014, following a brokered meeting between PR members and Wikipedia editors, 11 leading public relations organizations delivered a statement intended to repair the poor relationship (Sebastian 2014). The statement, published on Wikipedia, by the following leading public relations companies, committed to abiding by Wikipedia editing principles (Sebastian 2014, n.p.). The participating organizations included:

- Edelman
- Ogilvy & Mather
- Fleishman Hillard
- Burson-Marsteller
- Ketchum
- Porter Novelli
- Peppercomm
- MDC Partners
- Voce Communications
- Allison & Partners
- Beutler Ink (Sebastian 2014 n.p.)

(Continued)

It noted the importance of working *within* Wikipedia's terms, publicizing ethical positions relating to transparency and better understanding the fundamental policies of Wikipedia and other Wikimedia projects. It read, in part:

> On behalf of our firms, we recognize Wikipedia's unique and important role as a public knowledge resource. We also acknowledge that the prior actions of some in our industry have led to a challenging relationship with the community of Wikipedia editors. Our firms believe that it is in the best interest of our industry, and Wikipedia users at large, that Wikipedia fulfill its mission of developing an accurate and objective online encyclopedia. Therefore, it is wise for communications professionals to follow Wikipedia policies as part of ethical engagement practices.
> ...
> We also seek opportunities for a productive and transparent dialogue with Wikipedia editors, inasmuch as we can provide accurate, up-to-date, and verifiable information that helps Wikipedia better achieve its goals.
>
> (Sebastian 2014, n.p.; Wikipedia 2014c, n.p.)

These intersections between public relations and Wikipedia illustrate the complexity of working in the Wikipedia space; they are also illustrative of much broader internet communication issues. Fuchs (2014, p. 84) notes 'the media—social media, the internet and all other media—are contradictory because we live in a contradictory society.' Indeed, the level of contradictions and complexities challenges any simplistic response to what and who might lay claim to the public interest. Instead, like the Wikipedia principle of constant updates, public interest communication needs both constant review and diligent attention if it is to stay relevant, accurate and transparent.

Conclusion

Critical and political economy theories have provided frameworks for examining communication and media used within self-interest, conflicting interests and public interest contexts. As Horkeimer notes, critical theory 'never simply aims at an increase of knowledge as such' (Horkeimer in Fuchs 2014, p. 24); rather, it analyzes 'the tensions between potentiality and actuality, what man (sic) and things could be and what they are in fact' (Marcuse in Fuchs 2014, p. 24). Moreover, this approach is consistent with Craig's statement at the start of this chapter that 'public interest in our discipline is rooted in popular beliefs that communication is important, faulty communication is to blame for many human problems, and better communication can make a better world' (2005, p. 662).

Accordingly, the chapter has drawn together concepts, snapshots and illustrations which have put this statement to the test and, in so doing, has challenged how we can apply the public interest while also identifying interests in communication and media practice and scholarship.

For communication to be in the public interest there must be checks and balances within systems, plus the capacity to critique and the will to improve. Thus, the public interest can be enhanced in the following ways:

- using communication and media to raise issues of social, political and cultural significance;
- educating media workers about complex social, political and health issues;
- assisting with accuracy in interpreting complex information such as scientific, financial or legal material;
- developing open and trust-based relationships with individual media that can facilitate accurate reporting;
- enabling alternative forms of media and communication to provide agency and access to less powerful publics, such as minority groups;
- remaining diligent about the potential for powerful voices to hijack and dominate media and communication spaces; and,
- working transparently as communications practitioners, respecting the non-commercial nature of some communication platforms.

Through such checks and balances, communication and working with the media can be identified not just as outcomes but as part of the public interest process as well.

Note

1. Wikimedia is the parent of Wikipedia.

References

Alexa 2014, *The top 500 sites on the web*. Available from http://www.alexa.com/topsites.

Australian Government 2008, *Apology to Australia's Indigenous peoples,* Audio, video and transcript, viewed 1 June 2014, http://australia.gov.au/about-australia/our-country/our-people/apology-to-australias-indigenous-peoples.

Australian Human Rights Commission, 1997, *Bringing them home: the 'Stolen Children' Report,* viewed 1 June 2014, https://www.humanrights.gov.au/our-work/aboriginal-and-torres-strait-islander-social-justice/publications/bringing-them-home-stolen.

Baynes, NH 1942, *The speeches of Adolf Hitler, April 1922-August 1939 Volumes I & II,* Oxford University Press, London.

Birch, T 2004, 'The first white man born: contesting the "stolen generations" narrative in Australia' in *Imagining Australia: literature and culture in the New World,* J Ryan & C Wallace-Crabbe (eds.), Harvard University Press, Cambridge, pp. 137–57.

Blue, V 2012, 'Corruption in Wikiland? Paid PR scandal erupts at Wikipedia,' C/Net, viewed 1 June 2014, http://www.cnet.com/au/news/corruption-in-wikiland-paid-pr-scandal-erupts-at-wikipedia/.

Bohman, J & Rehg, W 2011, 'Jürgen Habermas', in EN Zalta (ed.), *The Stanford encyclopedia of philosophy*, viewed 30 June 2014, http://plato.stanford.edu/archives/win2011/entries/habermas/.

Bruns, A 2008, *Blogs, Wikipedia, Second life and beyond: from production to produsage*, Peter Lang, New York.

Byrne, C & Johnston, J 2015 in press, 'Wikipedia as both medium and model of public diplomacy collaboration', *The Hague Journal of Public Diplomacy*.

Canadian Government, 2006, *A way with words: suggestions for the portrayal of people with disabilities*, viewed 30 June 2014, http://www.esdc.gc.ca/eng/disability/arc/way_with_words.pdf.

Canadian Government, 2013, *A way with words: suggestions for the portrayal of people with disabilities*, viewed 30 June 2014, http://www.esdc.gc.ca/eng/disability/arc/words_images.shtml.

Cancel, AE, Cameron, GT, Sallot, L & Mitrook, MA 1997, 'It depends: a contingency theory of accommodation in public relations', *Journal of Public Relations Research*, vol. 9, no. 1, pp. 31–63.

Chartered Institute of Public Relations 2014, *Wikipedia and public relations*, viewed 29 June 2014, http://www.cipr.co.uk/content/policy-resources/best-practice-guides-toolkits/wikipedia-and-public-relations.

Chebib, NK & Sohail, RM 2000, 'The reasons social media contributed to the 2011 Egyptian revolution', *International Journal of Business Research and Management*, vol. 2, no. 3, pp. 139–62.

Commonwealth Native Title Act, 1993, Australian Government, viewed 1 February 2015, http://www.austlii.edu.au/au/legis/cth/consol_act/nta1993147/.

Cottle, S 2000, 'Media research and ethnic minorities: mapping the field', in S Cottle (ed.), *Ethnic minorities and the media: changing cultural boundaries*, Open Universities Press, Buckingham, pp. 1–31, viewed 21 June 2014, http://www.mheducation.co.uk/openup/chapters/0335202705.pdf.

Couldry N & Curran, J 2003, 'The paradox of media power', in N Couldry & J Curran (eds.), *Contesting media power: alternative media in a networked world*, Rowman & Littlefield, Lanham, MD, pp. 3–15.

Craig, RT 2005, 'How we talk about how we talk: Communication theory and the public interest', *Journal of Communication*, vol. 55, no. 4, pp. 659–67.

Darnton, R 2009, *The case for books: past, present and future*, Public Affairs, New York.

Darnton, R 2014, 'A world digital library is coming true!' *The New York Review of Books*, vol. LXI, no. 9, May-June, pp. 8–12.

Demetrious, K 2013, *Public relations, activism and social change: speaking up*, Routledge, London.

Deuze, M 2006, 'Ethnic media, community media and participatory culture', *Journalism*, vol. 7, no. 3, pp. 262–80.

Dodson, M 2008, 'Finally their voices will be heard', *Sydney Morning Herald*, 13 February, viewed 1 August 2014, http://www.smh.com.au/news/national/finally-their-voices-will-be-heard/2008/02/12/1202760301415.html.

Downing, J 2003, 'The independent media', in N Couldry & J Curran (eds.), *Contesting media power: alternative media in a networked world*, Rowman & Littlefield, Lanham, MD, pp. 243–58.

Dutta, M 2011, *Communicating social change*, Routledge, New York.

Dutta, M & Pal, M 2011, 'Public relations and marginalisation in a global context: a postcolonial critique', in N Bardham & K Weaver (eds.), *Public relations in a global cultural context*, Routledge, New York, pp. 195–226.

Elliott, M 2006, 'Stigmergic collaboration: the evolution of group work', *MC Journal*, vol. 9, no. 2, May, viewed 15 August 2014, http://journal.media-culture.org.au/0605/03-elliott.php.

Fairclough, N 1992, *Discourse and social change*, Polity Press, Oxford.

Fairclough, N 2001, 'The dialectics of discourse', *Textus*, vol. 14, no. 2, pp. 231–42.

Forde, S 2011, *Challenging the news: The journalism of alternative and community media*, Palgrave Macmillan, Basingstoke, Hampshire.

Foucault, M 1980, *Power/knowledge: selected interviews and other writings 1972–1977*, Pantheon, New York.

Franklin, B 2003, 'A good day to bury bad news? Journalists, sources and the packaging of politics', in S Cottle (ed.), *News, public relations and power*, Sage, Thousand Oaks, CA, pp. 45–62.

Fredericks, B 2010, 'We've had the Redfern speech and the apology: what next?' *Outskirts: Feminisms Along the Edge,* vol. 23, viewed 10 August 2014, http://www.outskirts.arts.uwa.edu.au/volumes/volume-23/fredericks.

Fuchs, C 2014, *Social media: a critical introduction*, Sage, London.

Gans, H 1979, *Deciding what's news: a study of CBS Evening News, NBC Nightly News, Newsweek and Time*, Pantheon Press, London.

Habermas J 1974, 'The public sphere: an encyclopaedia article', *New German Critique*, vol. 1, no. 3, first published 1964, pp. 49–55.

Habermas, J 1984, *The theory of communication action,* Beacon Press, Boston.

Habermas, J 1989, *The structural transformation of the public sphere: an inquiry into a category of bourgeois society*, MIT Press, Cambridge, MA.

Habermas, J 1998, *On the pragmatics of communication,* MIT Press, Cambridge, MA.

Hamilton, J 2004, *All the news that's fit to sell: how the market transforms information into news,* Princeton University Pres, Princeton, NJ.

Jenkins, H 2008, *Convergence culture*, New York University Press, New York.

Johnston, J 2013, *Media relations: issues and strategies*, Allen & Unwin, Sydney.

Johnston, J 2016, 'Public relations, postcolonialism and the other', in J L'Etang, D McKie, N Snow, & J Xifra (eds.), *Critical perspectives of public relations, the Routledge handbook of critical public relations*, Routledge, London, pp. 130–42.

JSTOR, 2012, *JSTOR in 2012: Annual summary*, viewed 9 September 2015, about. jstor.org/sites/default/files/misc/JSTOR-Annual-Summary_2012_v6.pdf.

Keating, P 1992, *Redfern Speech*, viewed 2 February 2015, https://antar.org.au/sites/default/files/paul_keating_speech_transcript.pdf.

Kittur, A, Chi, EH, Pendleton, BA, Suh, B & Mytkowicz, T 2007, 'Power of the few vs. wisdom of the crowd: Wikipedia and the rise of the bourgeoisie'. Paper presented at *25th annual ACM conference of Human Factors on Computing Systems*, 28 April–3 May, San Jose, CA, viewed 15 August 2014, http://www-users.cs.umn.edu/~echi/papers/2007-CHI/2007-05-altCHI-Power-Wikipedia.pdf.

Liebersohn, YZ, Neuman, Y & Bekerman, Z 2004, 'Oh baby, it's hard for me to say I'm sorry: public apologetic speech and cultural rhetorical resources', *Journal of Pragmatics*, vol. 36, pp. 921–44.

Lombard, D 2013, 'Review urges major overhaul of governance at Wikimedia UK', *Third Sector,* February, viewed 20 July 2014, http://www.thirdsector.co.uk/

review-urges-major-overhaul-governance-wikimedia-uk/governance/article/
1170282.

Malpas, S & Wake P (2006), 'Names and terms', in S Malpas & P Wake (eds.), *The Routledge companion to critical theory*, Routledge, London, pp. 141–269.

McCarthy, T 1981, *The critical theory of Jurgen Habermas*, MIT Press, Cambridge, MA.

McChesney, R 2008, *The political economy of the media: enduring issues, emerging dilemmas*, Monthly Review Press, New York.

McKiernan, E 2014, 'University research: if you believe in openness, stand up for it', *Guardian Online* 22 August, viewed 20 July 2014, http://www.theguardian.com/higher-education-network/blog/2014/aug/22/university-research-publish-open-access-journal.

Mihalcea, R 2007, 'Using Wikipedia for automatic word sense disambiguation', *Proceedings of National American Association for Computer Linguistics HLT*, pp. 196–203.

Milne, D & Witten, I 2013, 'An open-source toolkit for mining Wikipedia', *Artificial Intelligence*, vol. 194, September, pp. 222–39.

Moloney, K 2006, *Rethinking public relations,* Routledge, London.

Moore, R 2010, 'Encountering Australian journalism', in M Deitz (ed.), *Watch this space, the future of Australian journalism,* Cambridge University Press, Melbourne, pp. vii–x.

Murdock, G & Golding, P 1974, 'For a political economy of mass communications', in P Golding & G Murdock (eds.), *Political economy of the media,* Edward Elgar, Cheltenham, pp. 3–32.

Murphy, D 2012, 'Monmouth: where it all started to go wrong', Wikipediocracy, viewed 1 September 2014, http://wikipediocracy.com/forum/viewtopic.php?f=8&t=926.

New Zealand Government 2007, *It's not OK/ are you OK*, viewed 20 June 2014, http://www.areyouok.org.nz/family_violence.php.

Noruzi, A 2006, 'Folksonomies: (un)controlled vocabulary?' *Knowledge Organization*, vol. 33, no. 4, pp. 199–203.

Orlowski, A 2012, 'Conflict-of-interest scandal could imperil Wikimedia charity status: "A positive Wikipedia article is invaluable SEO"', *The Register*, viewed 1 July 2015 http://www.theregister.co.uk/2012/09/20/wikimedia_uk_scandal/.

Oxfam 2007, *Forward together: ideas for working with asylum seekers, refugees, the media and communities,* viewed 18 June 2014, http://www.epim.info/wp-content/uploads/2011/01/Forward-Together-Ideas-for-working-with-asylum-seekers-refugees-the-media-and-communities.pdf.

Picard, RG 2014, 'The humanisation of media? Social media and the reformation of communication', Keynote speech at the *Australia & New Zealand Communication Association 2014 Conference*, Melbourne, 9 July.

Postman, J 2009, *SocialCorp: social media goes corporate.* New Riders, Berkley.

Sebastian, M 2014, 'Top PR firms promise they won't edit clients' Wikipedia entries on the sly', *Advertising Age* 10 June, viewed 1 July 2014, http://adage.com/article/digital/top-pr-firms-edit-wikipedia-sly/293634/.

Sheldrake, P 2012, *Version one of Wikipedia guidance for PR practitioners,* viewed 20 June 2014, http://www.philipsheldrake.com/2012/06/version-1-of-wikipedia-guidance-for-pr-practitioners/.

Shin, JH 2006, 'Conflict, contingency and continuum: a conceptual model of the source–reporter relationship between public relations professionals and journalists,'

Paper presented at the *International Communication Association Conference*, Dresden, Germany.

Shirky, C 2008, *Here comes everybody: the power of organizing without organizations*, Penguin, London.

Stern, MJ 2012, 'A stealth PR campaign for Gibraltar proves existential crisis for Wikipedia', *Future Tense*, 20 September, viewed 20 June 2014, n09/20/roger_bamkin_gibraltor_s_repeated_appearance_on_did_you_know_provkes_existential_crisis_for_wikipedia_.html.

Tiffen, R 1989, *News and power*, Allen & Unwin, Sydney.

Tuchman, G 1972, 'Objectivity as strategic ritual: an examination of newsmen's notions of objectivity', *American Journal of Sociology*, vol. 77, no. 4, pp. 660–79.

Viegas, F, Wattenberg, M, Kriss, J & van Ham, F 2007, 'Talk before you type: coordination in Wikipedia', *System Sciences, 40th Annual Hawaii International Conference on System Sciences,* viewed 30 July 2014, http://ieeexplore.ieee.org/xpl/login.jsp?tp=&arnumber=4076527&url=http%3A%2F%2Fieeexplore.ieee.org%2Fxpls%2Fabs_all.jsp%3Farnumber%3D4076527.

Wales, J 2004, *Wikipedia founder Jimmy Wales responds*, 28 July, viewed 18 August 2014, http://slashdot.org/story/04/07/28/1351230/wikipedia-founder-jimmy-wales-responds.

Weedon, C 2004, *Identity and culture: narratives of difference and belonging*, McGraw Hill, New York.

Welch, D 2008, 'Kevin Rudd says sorry', *Sydney Morning Herald* 13 February, viewed 18 June 2014, http://intranet.cbhslewisham.nsw.edu.au:82/sor/supdocs/The%20day%20the%20PM%20apologised.pdf.

Wikipedia 2012a, 'Wikipedia/GLAM/Monmouthmedia', *Wikipedia* (wiki article), viewed 20 September 2014, http://en.wikipedia.org/wiki/Wikipedia:GLAM/MonmouthpediA.

Wikipedia 2012b, 'UK chapter rocked by Gibraltar scandal', *The Signpost Wikipedia* (wiki article), September 24, 2012, viewed 20 September 2014, http://en.wikipedia.org/wiki/Wikipedia:Wikipedia_Signpost/2012-09-24/News_and_notes.

Wikipedia 2014a, 'Wikipedia: core content policies', *Wikipedia* (wiki article), viewed 19 September 2014, http://en.wikipedia.org/wiki/Wikipedia:Core_content_policies.

Wikipedia 2014b, 'Wikipedia: conflict of interest', *Wikipedia* (wiki article), viewed 20 September 2014, http://en.wikipedia.org/wiki/Wikipedia:Conflict_of_Interest.

Wikipedia 2014c 'Wikipedia: statement on Wikipedia from participating communications firms', *Wikipedia* (wiki article), viewed 21 September 2014, https://en.wikipedia.org/wiki/Wikipedia:Statement_on_Wikipedia_from_participating_communications_firms#Statement_on_Wikipedia_from_participating_communications_firms.

5 Culture and Public Interest
Community Voices, Social Inclusion and Participation

> *... there is not one aspect of human life that is not touched and altered*
> *by culture.*
> (Hall 1981, pp. 16–17)

Introduction

This chapter draws on a broad tapestry of culture to inform our under-standing of the public interest as it intersects with global and local public relations. It brings together a collection of theories, methods and paradigms providing challenges, insights and opportunities for reflexivity about how culture can be used to inform public relations scholarship and practice in this interface. As with the public interest, culture is a contested concept and definitions proliferate. In 1963 Kroeber and Kluckholn found more than 160 definitions from a variety of disciplines. More than half a century later the figure had doubled when Baldwin, Faulkner, Hecht and Lindsley (2006) listed 313 definitions in *Redefining Culture: Perspectives Across the Discipline*. In the book's foreword Rosaldo (2006) noted that culture had 'migrated to different fields of study' (2006, p. xi) citing French structuralism, sociobiology, cognitive anthropology, the ethnography of speaking, cultural materialism, neo-Marxism, neo-evolutionism, neo-functionalism, practice theory, the anthropology of experience, subaltern studies and interpretive anthropology, feminism, anti-imperialism, Indigenous rights and gay libera-tion through the 1960s and 1970s. During the ensuing 'culture wars' of the 1980s and beyond, it evolved yet again with a broad acceptance that culture is always changing (Rosaldo 2006, p. xii) and in this way, it finds common ground with the public interest because it is time and context specific. The study of culture has also 'migrated' to public relations, with a solid body of literature examining it from societal and organizational perspectives (see, for example, Sriramesh & White 1992; Hodges 2006; Sriramesh & Verčič 2012; Waymer 2012; Edwards & Hodges 2011).

Hall (1981) argues how, on the one hand, culture is so deeply ingrained in humans we cannot put it aside yet it also exists at various physical and external levels, such as in geography and artifacts. Culture provides the meaning for communication behaviors, the rules and norms that govern when and how these behaviors should be used, plus the clues on how messages are structured and interpreted (Valintini 2007). At the same time, culture is not static, giving us a 'moral direction rather than a moral destination' (Rodriguez 2002, p. 7) bound up with power (Foucault 1984; Spivak 1988; Dutta 2011) and fundamentally part of globalization (Bardhan & Weaver 2011; Curtain & Gaither 2007). As the two following definitions from leading public relations and communication authorities illustrate, culture, like the public interest, is understood as a process. Curtin and Gaither (2007, p. 35) note it to be the following:

> The process by which meaning is produced, circulated, consumed, commodified and endlessly reproduced and negotiated in society.

While Dutta (2011, p. 11) uses Geertz's (1994) definition:

> … the communicative process by which shared meanings, beliefs, and practices get produced.

This chapter is heavily informed by critical theory, most notably the cultural writing of Paulo Freire in the *Pedagogy of the Oppressed* (2005 [1970]). Freire called for a praxis in learning, combining '*reflection* and *action*' to be directed at structures to be transformed (Freire 1970, p. 126 his italics). His postcolonial work, plus that of others such as Said (1978, 1981, 1993) and Spivak (1988), and communication literature on culture and subalternity (Dutta 2011; Curtin & Gaither 2007; Bardhan & Weaver 2011; Dutta, Ban & Pal 2012) inform the chapter, providing fundamental and central themes. These include the need for praxis to facilitate change; the links between culture, communication and power; the importance of bottom-up participation in cultural understanding; and the role of pedagogy in moving toward participatory models of transformational culture. With all this in mind, this chapter continues its interrogation into how the public interest holds potential for public relations theory, practice and criticism and, importantly, in the role played by pedagogy as part of the process. It begins by a brief analysis of the important work at the intersection of culture and the public interest: the dedicated stream of 'public interest anthropology.'

Public Interest Anthropology

The field of anthropology may appear a somewhat unlikely stable-mate for public relations. Yet, latterly, public relations scholar Jacquie L'Etang (2010, 2011, 2012) has embraced the combination, arguing that anthropology, and its research through ethnography, can offer public relations a strong line of inquiry. Habermas's work, popular within public relations scholarship and central to many of the themes in this book, examines social and cultural anthropology through his advocacy of dialogue and moral responsibility and concepts such as lifeworld and communicative action, discussed elsewhere in the book. As such, a foundation exists for further examination of anthropology in our interrogation of culture and public relations, given its development as 'a dialectical process between research and experience with other cultures' (Sanday & Jannowitz 2004, p. 64). It is the specialized field of 'public interest anthropology' that particularly provides compelling inclusion in this book. Sanday and Jannowitz (2004, p. 64) note that public interest anthropology 'grows out of a long legacy in anthropology of shaping public sensitivity to the role of culture in human affairs.' They note how public interest anthropology represents a late twentieth-century trend in anthropology, seen in efforts to:

- confront the political as part of the research process in the interest of correcting the disorders of our times;
- develop theory by working directly with publics in their interest rather than applying theory to work for publics; and
- communicate the public implications of research to multiple audiences in the interest of change (Sanday & Jannowitz 2004).

Accordingly, they note that public interest anthropology addresses '*macro-social* issues related to equality of educational opportunity, social justice, health and nutrition, human rights, and social wellbeing' (2004, p. 65), which see synergies with descriptions of public interest law and public interest groups, discussed elsewhere in the book.

Perhaps not as neatly or automatically associated with the public interest as the law and the media, anthropology takes a conciliatory and inductive social position by considering multiple perspectives in its practice. Rather than definitive 'rights' and 'wrongs,' it accepts that there will be different approaches to the same issue, and it is at these intersections that the public interest, or multiple public interests, can be examined and integrated. By using inductive rather than deductive reasoning, it accommodates the idea of multiple or pluralistic interests where many factors need to be considered in decision making. Johnston, Paley, Sabloff and Sanday (1997) note that where interests may conflict—and they often do—the public interest anthropologist may need to take a 'hands off' approach, stand back and consider many cultural turns, effectively applying a disinterested approach. Their explanation resonates for any industry or discipline—public relations included—faced with multiple perspectives when considering public interest process and outcomes and the need to see things 'from the other's point of view' (Johnston et al. 1997, p. 1). As they point out,

> ... it is essential for the public interest anthropologist to articulate in relation to whom interest is defined and to understand the ramifications of competing interests with respect to a specific problem and course of action. This is not to say that the anthropologist will serve all interests, but that serving one interest often implies considering another.
>
> (Johnston et al. 1997, p. 3)

In illustrating their point, they cite the example of the genital mutilation of women in Africa, where 'traditional cultural interests' compete with modernized approaches to sexuality and marriage, as well as health risks (1997, p. 4). While not endorsing genital mutilation, they are mindful that, for some, sociocultural norms of the rite of passage, ritual, continuity of tradition and nationalism also represent a public interest. They emphasise how, as public interest anthropologists, they do not have the answers to such complex and often polarizing issues. Instead it is important to enter into such arenas fully informed and to look *within* communities for answers. The issue of female genital mutilation (FGM) is examined in the following snapshot, written from a participant point of view.

Public interest anthropology falls into two discreet categories: (1) the organizational, scientific method, which sets out to solve practical problems through planning and action, where researchers are seen as experts, generating new scientific knowledge; and (2) the alternative method, influenced by Edward Freire, Marxism, feminism and postcolonial thinking, where communities are viewed not as objects but as *subjects* of their own experience and inquiry, and researchers are seen as catalysts of change that emanate from within the community (Lamphere 2004). Lamphere (2004, p. 436) suggests the second view represents a 'sea change' for public interest anthropology by shifting the emphasis of the discipline to a collaborative approach, with local communities in public outreach programmes, moving away from Western-dominated notions of science to be more inclusive of localized knowledge, illustrating new levels of communication. This approach reflects a common theme within this chapter of social inclusion and participation—a field we will explore in some depth, incorporating Freire's postcolonial pedagogy which forms a central pillar of the chapter. In short, public interest anthropology can bring much to the study of how the public interest coalesces with culture, providing a critical literature that can alert the scholar to the possibilities of the public interest within other fields, including the human, social and critical field of public relations.

Snapshot
The Cultural Challenge of FGM

Introduction

This snapshot is told by Jamilatou (Jamila) Saidy, an educated Mandinka woman, who works as a consumer affairs manager with the national utilities company in the West African country of The Gambia. After working in this role for eight years, Jamila chose to combine her work with an advocacy role, campaigning against the practice of female genital mutilation (FGM). Jamila now combines her formal role across many regions in The Gambia as a consumer affairs manager, while also advocating for the abolition of FGM,

(Continued)

working on behalf of a non-government organization. As her following story illustrates, Jamila's local knowledge, religious awareness, cultural understanding and firsthand experience uniquely positioned her to take up advocacy work against FGM.

Figure 5.1 Jamilatou Saidy, quietly working to create dialogue on the cultural practice of female genital mutilation with her fellow women, men and children in The Gambia. Photograph by Kelly Chen

Jamila's Job

My job as a consumer affairs manager for the Public Utilities Regulatory Authority (PURA) of The Gambia is to travel the country every year on a sensitization campaign to educate consumers about their rights and obligations relating to the use of utility services, including telephony land line and mobile communication, water, electricity and sewage. PURA is (technically) independent of the government, funded principally by the World Bank.

The Gambia, as a country, has eight administrative regions: Banjul, Kanifing, Brikama, Janjanbureh, Kuntaur, Mansakonko, Kerewan and Basse. In some of these regions, due to dilapidated roads, it is difficult to access some of the remote villages which are accessed using donkey carts or foot, for up to five kilometres. Communities are informed of our visits through audio recordings sent to their local radio stations, however the country has only one national radio called The Radio Gambia which has an extensive coverage in the city but has poor reception in certain parts of the country, so many regions have local radio stations, which are supported by NGOs or commercial sources. The heads of the villages are also informed through their National Assembly representatives or Members of Parliament (MPs) when sensitization will take place at their respective locations. The villagers gather in their community hall or centre, known as 'bantabas' and, as tradition dictates, the head of the village is always given cola nuts at these meetings as a show of respect. The meetings are aimed at educating and advising the villagers about their rights and responsibilities in all utilities, including how to manage mobile phones without electricity, which sometimes calls for charging through battery set-ups which we assist in setting up.

Jamila's Culture

My culture as a Mandinka, which forms 40 percent of the ethnic society of The Gambia, has a traditional belief that a girl-child becomes a real woman after undergoing 'cutting' or female genital mutilation (FGM). Cultural belief has it that FGM is a religious obligation for Muslim women for preservation of purity, virginity, family honour and assurance of marriageability. Parents continue with the ancestral belief that conducting FGM on a girl-child will prepare her for the process of getting married, in order to make her 'clean enough for marriage' for fear that 'no man will marry an uncut woman—known by the derogatory term of Solima.' In societies where it is practiced, girls and young women believe if they do not respect the social rule they will suffer consequences such as marginalization and loss of status. However, in recent years, FGM has been found to have dire health consequences for the girl. Immediate complications and consequences are shock from bleeding and pain and stress resulting from cutting very sensitive and delicate area of the genitalia without the use of anaesthetic. Long-term consequences are extremely painful menstruation due to the build-up of urine and blood in the uterus leading to inflammation of the bladder and internal sexual organs, difficulty in childbirth which in instances of long and obstructed labour may lead to foetal death and brain damage of the infant, and, in cases of infibulation, acute and chronic pelvic infection leading to infertility and/or tubal pregnancy, accumulation of blood and blood clots in the uterus and/or vagina (African-Women.org, 2009).

The NGO: GAMCOTRAP

As a literate woman who understands the teachings of the Holy Quran, I conducted research having found out that FGM is not a religious obligation and cannot be justified by promoting unauthentic hadith (tradition) to inflict harm on the girl-child and woman. I developed an interest in a Non-Governmental Organisation called The Gambia Committee on Traditional Practices (GAMCOTRAP) which provides information and education to communities and professional bodies through advocacy, training and information campaigns, sensitization and social mobilization affecting the health of women and children. The GAMCOTRAP has taken the responsibility to conduct awareness campaigns all over the country, in both print and electronic media and through word of mouth. Every educated person, especially women, are tasked by the GAMCOTRAP to educate our own local societies and beyond about the dangers of this mal-practice. I saw my consumer affairs role as an opportunity to talk to women of all ages about FGM. In many instances, they are scared to discuss this issue due to their belief in the traditions which exist in Janjanbureh, Kuntaur, Mansakonko, Kerewan and Basse, where it is most practiced. As a victim of this mal-practice, once you begin to identify yourself with their pain, the tension is diluted and they begin to comprehend.

(Continued)

FGM: The Campaign

The principle aim of the campaign is to create and raise awareness among women and girls about the preservation of beneficial practices as well as the elimination of harmful traditional practices. Protecting the rights of children by involving them in decision-making processes is important. Furthermore, it is important to promote and create dialogue and develop respect for different opinions, identifying and promoting the status of the girl-child and women, using international and national instruments that address discrimination and violence against them. There remains social, political and religious resistance to the elimination of FGM but many individuals including high profile Gambian people, including some men, as well as many NGOs, have lent support to the campaign. In addition, the country's leader, His Excellency Sheikh Professor Alhaji Dr. Yahya Abdul-Azziz Jemus Junkung Jammeh, has empowered Gambian women; his vice president is a woman and other women hold positions of power. This is conducive to a culture of change for women.

Part of the process lies in helping the women who perform the cutting into alternate forms of employment, such as working in small industries like the textile industry. For many of them cutting has been their only source of income and their only job, so by finding them alternative employment, they become less resistant to change. Ultimately, the local communities are the ones who can work through these changes. On the day that the knives and blades are surrendered, the whole village celebrates. They call it a celebration day.

Contributed by Jamilatu Saidy—Mandinka woman, mother of three, consumer affairs manager and advocate against FGM.

Jamila's work thus combines an institutional position in consumer affairs with an activist role about which she feels passionate. Yet, in addition to actively spreading a message, she sees her role as opening dialogue and facilitating, by engaging with men, women and children at a personal, grassroots and collectivist level. Jamila's work, with people of The Gambia, in both her formal and activist roles, is illustrative of many of the themes and theories that we will now examine within the chapter.

Freire and Cultural Hegemony

While Paolo Freire's seminal work *The Pedagogy of the Oppressed* (1970) is widely cited in examinations of culture, pedagogy and power (for example, see Lamphere 2004; Nyland 2006; Somekh 2008; Dutta 2011), it has remained largely outside public relations critique. Freire's work is a multi-layered critique of capitalism, competing interests and social change which examines the binary of the oppressed and oppressor in modern societies, within the context of hegemonic systems and cultural exchange. Described at once as a postmodernist, a social democrat, a postcolonial scholar, a Marxist and an objective idealist (Gibson n.d.), Freire argued that the best education practices center on dialogue, inclusion and problem-posing as a way of enabling students to learn from within rather than from external dominant pedagogies. Accordingly, students—indeed, all people—are always in the 'process of becoming' (Freire 2005, p. 82).

Out of Freire's education critique emerged a wider interrogation of politics and society, one which focused on broader issues of hegemonic power, cultural control and issues of equality, centering on interest politics in the modern world. He argued that 'since oppressors and oppressed are antithetical, what serves the interests of one group disserves the interests of the others' (Freire 2005, p. 143). At the same time, he saw a way through the dialectic in the process of cultural synthesis, drawing a distinction between what he called 'cultural invasion' by oppressive hegemonic powers and 'cultural synthesis' which seeks to preserve existing culture.

> Cultural invasion ... always involves a parochial view of reality, a static perception of the world, and the imposition of one world view upon another. It implies the "superiority" of the invader and the "inferiority" of those who are invaded, as well as the imposition of values by the former ... for cultural invasion to succeed, it is essential that those invaded become convinced of their intrinsic inferiority.
>
> (Freire 2005, p. 151)

On the other hand:

> Cultural synthesis does not deny the differences between the two views; indeed, it is based on these differences. It *does* deny the *invasion* of one *by* the other, but affirms the undeniable *support* each gives *to* the other.
>
> (Freire 2005, p. 179, his italics)

For Freire, dialogical practice was the means by which such cultural synthesis could be achieved. His explanation of this holds many similarities to the ideas that underpin Habermas's concepts of ideal speech, discussed elsewhere in the book. Freire argues that dialogue, as essential communication, must underlie any cooperation—and that cooperation can only be achieved through communication (2005, p. 166). Freire's theory of 'antidialogical action,' essentially based on the shutting down of dialogue, involves a subject who conquers another person and transforms that person into a 'thing' or an 'it' (Freire 2005, p. 165). In much the same way, postcolonialist scholar Edward Said's explanation of those who are seen as apart from, or outside, the dominant culture are known as the 'Other.' Those who have experienced such exclusion have found Freire's work transformative.

Mercedo, in writing the introduction to the anniversary edition of Freire's seminal text, recalls (2005, p. 10):

> Reading *Pedagogy of the Oppressed* gave me a language to critically understand the tensions, contradictions, fears, doubts, hopes, and 'deferred' dreams that are part and parcel of living a borrowed and colonized cultural existence … This offered to me—and all of those who experience subordination through an imposed assimilation policy—a path through which we come to understand what it means to come to cultural voice.

Mercedo's illustration thus epitomizes Freire's 'outsider' or 'oppressed,' which may be transformed through inclusion, both in educational contexts and within society more broadly. Accordingly, Freire's philosophy has a capacity to raise public interest for and in the struggle and rights of minorities in developing and maintaining their cultural voice. At the same time, through these ideas of cultural synthesis, cultural voice and dialogical action, public relations can take a responsive position that supports rather than invades cross-cultural activity. Freire's philosophy of education can also extend the call from public relations scholars to expand the pedagogical perspectives beyond those of dominant, Western cultures and be more inclusive of and responsive to a wider range of cultures and pedagogies. Increasingly public relations scholars have called for the integration of postcolonial theory, co-creational learning and international insights (Bardhan & Weaver 2011; Edwards & Hodges 2011; Fitch & Surma 2006; Fitch 2013; Fitch & Desai 2012; Sison 2013; Hodges 2006, 2013). Hodges (2013) has suggested a 'transformational curriculum' where, like Freire's co-creation of pedagogy, students and teachers co-create knowledge, using cultural imagination in multi-cultural settings.

Moreover, the field of postcoloniality has quite recently been embraced within public relations scholarship, gaining the attention of scholars as a means of critical reflection on the role of cultural communication and hegemonic power within the global environment (McKie & Munshi 2007; Dutta & Pal 2011; Curtin & Gaither 2012). For public relations, the postcolonial critique suggests working with cultural groups as participants, not in co-opting, but in learning from them. This provides the greatest interface for the public interest, with the inclusion of those from within the culture actively participating and driving their own agendas and outcomes, consistent with central themes throughout this book.

A Culture-Centered Approach

The idea that culture is best known by members within a community is thus outlined within postcolonial scholarship. Consistent with this view is the 'culture-centered' approach espoused by Dutta (2011, p. 10) in which he

argues that within different communities 'cultural members actively participate in defining problems and developing solutions.' This theory eschews
any top-down approach, instead suggesting a shift to enable an alternative
discursive and structural engagement with subaltern or minority cultural
communities (Dutta 2011). Dutta's culture-centered approach is found in
'the interaction between culture, structure, and agency that contributes to
the co-construction of meaning by cultural members of the community'
(2011, p. 11) logically following from Freire and postcolonial theory, linking the public interest through cultural inclusion and participation.

Along with colleagues Ban and Pal, Dutta is highly critical of what he
sees as public relations' top-down tendency, arguing instead for a reversal of
the communication flow by turning the focus to subaltern voices. They specifically address interest politics by explaining how this would broaden the
'understanding of public relations as a communicative form that advocates
not only organisational interest but also people's interest' (Dutta, Ban & Pal
2012, p. 10). In placing the emphasis on cultural context and human agency,
they argue that the public interest and true participatory democracy can be
served (2012).

Dutta points to how the culture-centered approach is founded on two
'key concepts of structural transformation and participatory communication' (Dutta 2011, p. 57) and can thus be divided into a dynamic relationship
between the symbolic and the material. The symbolic refers to communication and meaning-making, while the material refers to economic structures
and resources (Dutta 2011, p. 62). While he suggests that the emphasis of
cultural studies to communication can result in a loss of direction away
from material domains or structural changes, structural transformations
can be shaped by participation from within the local communities. In particular, he calls for 'alternative cultural stories' and 'culture jamming' (Dutta
2011, pp. 284–85) to be developed from internal cultural vantage points.
These locally situated voices sit in contrast to the grand narratives of development told by the state and the corporations in their dominant discourses
and are instead found in poems, songs, dances, plays, art, and other cultural
articulations and symbols which emerge from a cultural knowledge base. As
such, the re-telling of stories from local cultural viewpoints can offer a point
for structural transformation.

Research from Foxwell-Norton, Forde and Meadows (2013) into Indigenous Australians illustrates Dutta's point. Their study of First Nation
Australians locates the importance of storytelling and listening as central
to culture. 'Storytelling is a sacred act shared from the heart that relives/
recounts their history and culture. It is their story—stories—that bring
back life' (Dunbar 2008 cited in Foxwell-Norton, Forde & Meadows 2013,
p. 157). Stories and the use of oral history are thus core to Indigenous
cultural and intellectual traditions, often associated with how Indigenous
people reclaim their past, give testimony to injustices and identify their connections to the land. Foxwell-Norton and colleagues illustrate this point

by providing two contrasting passages on the worldview associated with 'ownership' of the land: one of belonging, the other of possessing. The first is from Oodgeroo, a Gorenpul woman from Minjerribah/North Stradbroke Island, a First Nation Australian, activist and poet (in Foxwell-Norton et al. 2013, p. 150):

> We cannot own the land.
> We are but the custodians of the land.
> – Oodgeroo (Kath Walker)

The second is from Englishman and Enlightenment philosopher John Locke ('Of Property'), from whom we find early ideas of individual property ownership (Locke 1689 in Foxwell-Norton et al. 2013, p. 150):

> And hence subduing or cultivating the earth, and having dominion, we see are joined together. The one gave title to the other. So that God, by commanding to subdue, gave authority so far to appropriate: and the condition of human life, which requires labour and materials to work on, necessarily introduces private possessions.

Finally, Foxwell-Norton and colleagues identify the importance of listening to their participants as being critical to elevating Indigenous voices, stories and pictures. Their research incorporates a participatory action approach, a method that is inclusive of the 'owners' of the culture, as we will now examine.

Participatory Action Research

The ideas that underpin participatory action research resonate throughout this chapter—from Freire in the 1970s to Dutta more than 40 years later. The approach tells us that clearer and deeper sociocultural understandings are drawn from *within* communities. But this approach has roots in the much earlier work of educational philosopher John Dewey, whose ideas on the public interest and cooperative communities from the early twentieth century were examined in chapter 2.

Somekh (2008) explains how participatory action research (which she, like some others, call simply action research) is not a single method but has been influenced by several strands of development including teaching-led research inquiry and community-led understanding, grounded in the values and actions of participant communities. 'As such, it is a fluid methodology that adapts to fit different contexts' (Somekh 2008, p. 6). A common element is its suitability for research within fields of social justice and cultural and political environments where collaborations between participants, within the research environment, and external facilitators or researchers are combined (Somekh 2008, p. 6). Accordingly, it provides for 'insider knowledge' while also, importantly, giving communities knowledge through feedback and the power to resist institutional practices. Participatory action research can generate knowledge about the interrelationship between human behavior and specific sociocultural situations rather than generalizable truths, providing narrative accounts and rich descriptions as well as analysis (Somekh 2008). Kemmis and McTaggart (2005) draw connections between participatory action research and Habermas's ideas of communicative action. It also corresponds to Freire's ideas of how education can be changed by either external political and systemic means, or by those who are being educated *within* the system.

The Third Culture

For Freire, liberation for the subaltern is 'not a gift, not a self-achievement, but a mutual process' (1970 contents page). By extension, the idea of the third culture provides a normative model that 'promises shared cultural growth over cultural imperialism' (Bardhan 2011, p. 91). The third culture thus presents an entry point for outsiders or interlopers to enable and enhance cultural understanding. First suggested as a way of understanding children who grew up overseas and straddled life between two worlds, existing as a sociological understanding of how people can serve as bridges between cultures and co-create and co-construct meaning (Useem, Donoghue & Useem 1963; Kent & Taylor 2011), the concept was later introduced to intercultural communication theory by Fred Casmir (1978), who argued that cooperation and mutuality were important for 'third culture building' (Casmir 1993, p. 419). Far from new to the public relations literature, the third culture is used as a way of explaining the role of public relations as 'cultural interpreter' or 'cultural broker' (Grunig et al. 1995; Wakefield 1996; Bardhan 2011, p. 88; Holtshausen 2011, p. 153; Edwards & Hodges, 2011; Edwards 2012).

Bardhan (2011) points out that the third culture provides an important shift from the social scientific cultural interpreter-translator model of intercultural communication to a more interpretive approach. This shift means that unlike many intercultural communication models that focus on how individuals adapt to cultural differences, third-culture building centers on a co-creational model of people coming together to negotiate differences. In his later development of the theory, Casmir argued that third culture goes beyond understanding the cultural 'Other' by requiring a kind of mutuality, personal commitment and openness to change in a 'symbolic interaction and not just a transfer' (Bardhan 2011, p. 91). Many elements must be considered in the dynamic, including the following:

- The need for listening;
- A genuine willingness to adjust;
- An acceptance that meanings may be negotiated;
- An understanding that contexts change; and
- A need for 'relational empathy' (see Broome 1991).

Public relations scholars (Kent & Taylor 2011; Curtain & Gaither 2007) and cultural theorists (Kluckhohn & Strodtbeck 1961; Hall 2000a, 2000b) suggest that understanding *time* and *context* can also assist in developing dialogic relationships and co-creating cultural meaning. In particular, Hall's (2000a) concepts of monochronic and polychronic time, or M-time and P-time, as well as his high-context culture (HCC) and low-context culture (LCC) (2000b) provide cultural indices which assist in understanding. While they should be read as 'procedural shorthand' (Curtin & Gaither 2005, p. 105) that can deprive insights into 'the rich and messy lived experience that forms the texture of daily work and living' (L'Etang 2011, p. 221), they are nevertheless useful in sorting our thoughts and understanding. Suffice to say, while indices can provide cultural roadmaps, they are best used as one of a range of tools considered within a broader understanding of culture's complexity and are never absolute.

Hall explains how cultural groups have different perceptions of time. For example, Anglo-Americans tend to focus on time control through schedules and time units, thus being on M-time. Alternately Latin, Arab and Asian cultures are more likely to be P-timers, prioritizing involvement of people and completion of transactions above adherence to schedules (Hall 2000a). Consider also the difference that comes from temporal orientations to the fast pace of big city life, the more moderate pace of country life, or the idea of 'island' time which suits the holiday-maker, light-heartedly described in the *Urban Dictionary* as:

> The time vacuum created by the ocean's presence. Similar to 'stoner's time', everything moves nice and slow. This carefree aura even has the ability to travel with islanders and can engulf you in their presence. (http://www.urbandictionary.com/define.php?term=island+time)

Likewise, Hall's ideas of high-context culture (HCC) and low-context culture (LCC) provide a useful tool for understanding cultures. Hall identifies how high-context cultures (HCC), such as those in the Middle East, Asia, Africa, and South America, may be more likely to place an emphasis on interpersonal, relationally based communication which is intuitive and contemplative. These cultures are often collectivist, prioritizing group harmony and consensus over individual achievement. Messages are received through means other than words; non-verbal and paraverbal cues such as tone of voice, facial expression, gestures and posture, proxemics and social standing all provide communication cues. Politeness and 'face' are of utmost importance in these contexts. Low-context cultures (LCC), such as those of North America, Australasia, and much of Western Europe, are more literal, direct, linear, individualistic, and action-oriented. Facts may take precedence over intuition, and communicators are expected to be direct, concise, open and to the point in their explanations (Hall 2000b). A distinguishing generalization is that HCCs tend to value group harmony over individualism, while LCCs are more likely to favor individualism (Curtain & Gaither 2007, p. 61). If we recall elsewhere, many of the differences resonate with public interest theories which distinguish between communitarianism, pluralism, individuality and so on, thus reinforcing the links between culture and the public interest. Consider the following examples which have been developed by public relations scholars and practitioners; one is based in Vietnam and the other in Estonia. Practitioner Tuong-Minh Ly-Le (2014) has identified cultural elements of practice in her home country of Vietnam relating to traditional Vietnamese and Western values, interpersonal communication styles, proxemics, media, cultural and business standards, public perceptions of public relations, and public relations standards. For Ly-Le, the differences must be taken into consideration in her public relations client practice. Vietnamese born, but educated in various Eastern and Western cultures, Ly-Le uses third-culture knowledge in her role as cultural intermediary and public relations practitioner (see Table 5.1).

Likewise, scholars have identified the blending of Eastern and Western cultures and traditions in newly emerging democracies, such as Estonia, which occupy a dialectic between cultural relativism and ethnocentrism (Curtain & Gaither 2012). Curtain and Gaither discuss the development of public relations in Estonia, following the collapse of the Soviet empire. 'Culture, language and history are among the Estonian hallmarks that bind its citizens and positioned it precariously as both part of the USSR but different from other Society republics' (2012, p. 223). Fundamental to its transformation has been technology—particularly the internet—seen as 'indispensable as electricity in Estonia' (Curtain & Gaither 2012, p. 223). Changes have resulted in the growth of a third-cultural Estonian public relations practice, containing both Western elements and Eastern traditions. Estonia's embracing the internet empowers public participation, thus creating a strong space for public relations, yet the newly wired country must also manage resistance to change, non-universal access to the internet and apathy on issues of e-democracy. Curtain and Gaither suggest this represents a third culture for public relations, working in a space between two cultures.

So, what happens when an organization ignores the cultural context in which it moves? Hall (2000b) argues of the inextricable link between context and cultural meaning, so it follows that without understanding context, meaning is lost. For Kent and Taylor (2011) context provides 'meaning and behavioral cues' that guide actions and reactions in intercultural encounters. A well-known illustration of a contextual cultural misfit lies in the development of Euro-Disney in Paris in 1992. Disney used its traditional American model in the set-up and operations of its Paris theme park, ignoring cultural differences such as culinary practices, French holiday choices and uniforms (Bardhan 2011; Casmir 1993). Its lack of cultural awareness, consultation and much-reported culturally imperialistic attitude were seen to be responsible for both reputational and financial problems. In correcting its mistakes, it paid closer attention to the 'contextual cultural values' of the French as well as micro-level communications to achieve a third-culture

Table 5.1 PR in cultural contexts: A comparison between traditional Vietnamese and Western cultural and communication approaches as applied to contemporary PR practice

	Traditional Vietnamese	Western
Values base	Traditional/established style of practice using a collectivist approach based on Confucianism, practiced by governments and long-established firms. Qualitative Outputs.	Individualism and consumerism. Individualism increasingly adopted by Gen Y practitioners. Quantifiable expectation – return on investment.
Interpersonal communication styles	Storytelling part of business and cultural models. Face-to-face preferred – as Vietnam is a high-context culture, it is hard to read between-the-lines.	Physical meetings but increasingly use virtual meetings (teleconference) and online (email). Low-context culture means literal communication may be perceived as blunt or not suitably nuanced.
Proxemics	Close distance preferred, as it shows sincerity and hospitality. Roundtable approach, intimate settings.	Generally avoid personal space intrusion. Spacious settings preferred.
Other cultural/ business considerations	Traditional organizational strategy: hierarchical, one-way information flow, centralized decision-maker.	Relational organization strategy: two-way information flow, decentralized decision-maker.
Media	Poorly paid, less respected (except for the leading, national media), social media makes large impact as it is perceived to provide more objective news.	Well paid, traditionally agenda setting, but increasingly challenged by social media.
Public perception of PR – service	Equivalent to or a mix of marketing, advertising and social media.	Reputation management.
PR standards	Standards from practitioners heavily influenced by journalism standards.	Agency and/or PR professional organization's standards.

Table developed by PR practitioner Tuong-Minh Ly-Le (2014)

approach (Bardhan 2011, p. 89; Casmir 1993). Among its changes, Disney employed more people with local knowledge (Bardhan 2011). Contextual sensitivity can thus provide a foundation for public interest public relations that accommodates local communities, embracing local people and considering their culture as central pillars in development of campaigns, strategies and tactics. More than two decades after Disney set up, the US-based

Guggenheim Foundation proposed to develop its fifth museum in Helsinki, Finland. The proposal also ran into both financial and cultural obstacles, which resulted in Guggenheim having to reassess its original approach to the project. The following snapshot outlines the cultural elements of the Guggenheim Museum's proposed development in Helsinki.

Snapshot
Guggenheim and the Finnish Experience

Background

The first Guggenheim Museum was opened in New York in 1939, followed by Venice in 1949, Bilbao in 1997, Abu Dhabi, proposed for opening in 2017, with a fifth proposal for the Finnish capital of Helsinki. Guggenheim's development in Bilbao, Spain, generated what became known as the 'Bilbao Effect' due to the impact the museum had on the region's prosperity and its global cache. Within three years of opening, $110 million had been spent in the city and, by 2013, more than one million people had visited Bilbao's 'gleaming metallic structure' (Edelson 2015, n.p.). The museum's success reportedly resulted in the Guggenheim Foundation annually receiving 'about a dozen requests from cities seeking a franchise for the halo effect of the Bilbao museum' (Carvajal 2014, n.p.).

The first Guggenheim proposal for Helsinki was submitted in January 2011 but was controversially rejected due to construction costs and proposed licensing fees, with critics questioning the overall terms of the development deal between the Guggenheim Foundation and the city of Helsinki. In addition to the costs, criticism lay with the lack of community consultation that underpinned the project. A survey of Helsinki residents at the time found 75 percent were opposed to the project with the *New York Times* reporting how 'the backlash against the project surprised the Guggenheim Foundation's top executives' (Carvajal 2014, n.p.). Among the issues raised was the potential cultural misfit of the U.S. organization for the Finnish capital, with the city divided between the city's conservatives, many of whom wanted 'to be Guggenheimed' and left-wingers and Greens who did not (Merrick 2014, n.p.). The proposal was further marred when claims of a conflict of interest by a director of the Helsinki Art Museum, supporting the Guggenheim proposal, were confirmed by the Finnish Parliamentary Ombudsman. In questioning the objectivity and impartiality of the director, the Ombudsman reported: 'The project prompted strong opposition and support, for which reason it was the focus of major public interest' (Parliamentary Ombudsman of Finland 2013).

Guggenheim's Response: 2013

In 2013, following the rejection of the first plan, the Guggenheim Foundation launched a second bid. The revised proposal noted how the organization had taken into consideration lessons from the original bid, including concerns by the public, the artists' community and the Helsinki

(Continued)

Art Museum's board of directors. In addition, Guggenheim reported that it had engaged Finnish public relations company the Miltton Group to coordinate the public affairs, media, and private-funding aspects of the project and 'to help ensure that Finnish cultural values would be incorporated into the proposal' (Guggenheim 2013, p. 11). Moreover, it announced it would hold a series of forums called 'Guggenheim Helsinki Live' which would include panel discussions. These public programs would provide a local presence for one-on-one conversations and informational exchanges on the proposed ideas for the new museum. The company stated, 'The Guggenheim is interested in hearing from all sectors of Finnish society and looks forward to the opportunity to interact more closely with the public' (2013, p. 7). As the siting of the proposed museum for Helsinki's South Harbor had proven a major obstacle in the first iteration of the proposal, Guggenheim also took a major international step in launching a massive global architectural competition to design the proposed museum building, drawing 1,715 submissions, and finally announcing the French winner in June 2015.

The Counter-Response: 2014

The architectural competition, which achieved widespread positive media coverage, also received criticism (see, for example, Capps 2015) and spawned a counter-competition, driven by independent arts organizations and members of the international architectural community, intent on gaining local backing and keeping the new museum separate from an international organization. In 2014, the 'Next Helsinki' competition was launched, seeking rival proposals for the Guggenheim's £105 million proposal, and receiving more than 200 entries from around the world (Fulcher 2015).

Project organizers described the competition as driven out of a sense of 'outrage at the march of the homogenizing multi-national brand culture emblematized by the imperial Guggenheim franchise' (Sorkin 2014, n.p.). The response focused heavily on Helsinki's sense of place, setting, form and culture, questioning 'why a city so indelibly fixed in the urban firmament, so superb, would want to surrender such a fabulous site to some starchitect (sic) supermarket' (Sorkin 2014, n.p.). The polemic that came from the chair of the International Jury of the Next Helsinki, Michael Sorkin, questioned 'whether a big foreign institution was the most logical way to prompt the arts to flourish at the community level' (Sorkin 2014, n.p.).

> We certainly hope to leverage the idea that there's a big community discussion going on about the place of the arts in urban development. However, there's also something a little sad about thinking about Helsinki, one of the great cities of the world, as a backwater that needs an institutional boost.
>
> (Sorkin in Edelson 2015, n.p.)

The Public Interest Process

At the time of publication the future of proposals for the Guggenheim Museum for Helsinki and the alternative 'Next Helsinki' remained undecided. What is clear, however, is that the public interest was served by the museum proposal achieving a high level of public attention, consultation and local inclusion, resulting in greater collaboration with local residents and the arts community, international support by an international jury, and a listening approach that appears to have been limited in the original 2011 proposal. The degree of reflexivity that resulted thus arguably provided a third-culture sensitivity, increased cultural competency and a greater involvement by the affected community, thus achieving a public interest outcome in the process regardless of which proposal is ultimately accepted.

Public relations must be cognizant of difference or resistance and be accommodating to this resistance within any proposal or period of transition. Questions need to be asked: What if the existing culture/community does not want change? Or exchange? Accordingly, Casmir points to the limitations of the third culture which may not be appropriate for all situations; indeed, the model is described as 'more advisory than explanatory' (Bardhan 2011, p. 91). Public relations scholars are in general agreement that there is a need for understanding and openness to other cultures, but this must also include a true acceptance of difference and cosmopolitanism, in which individual difference can transcend the collective. A capacity for cultural competency and an understanding of its limitations can thus also be instructive.

Cultural Competency

Cultural competency calls for understanding and empathy across cultures, incorporating cultural awareness, knowledge acquisition, skill development and inductive learning (Nyland 2006). The concept has gained traction in the past several decades as individuals, institutions and industry accept the need to proactively address marginalization of and ignorance about other cultures that have developed out of dominant expansionist cultures and taken for granted worldviews. In particular it has been identified as a key area for many professions—notably there is a significant literature from the medical and health professions—and it is central to educational pedagogies, as examined in this chapter (Nyland 2006; McClaren 1994; Freire 2005 [1970]). Nyland points to its complexity, advocating a 'critical multicultural' approach both within the classroom and by the professions (or industry) which requires a deeper and fuller understanding than simple competency. As such, he argues critical competency and multiculturalism include the following features:

- socio-historical construct of race, and its intersections with class, gender, nation, sexuality and capitalism;
- pedagogical conditions in which students interrogate conditions of Otherness;

- challenge to the idea of the social sciences as an apolitical, trans-historical practice removed from the power struggles of history; and
- historical and social construction of whiteness (Nyland 2006).

A lack of cross-cultural competence was found to be a central theme in the *Royal Commission of Inquiry into Aboriginal Deaths in Custody* in Australia, which identified high levels of ignorance and cultural insensitivity among professionals and service providers, reflecting Nyland's critical approach. The report found Indigenous Australians had been subject to service delivery frameworks which were not only ineffectual but also inconsistent with Indigenous cultural norms and needs. The Commission determined that:

> Along with many other Australians, [professionals] are generally poorly informed about Aboriginal people, their cultural differences, their specific socio-economic circumstances, and their recent history within Australian society. As a result, unrealistic expectations, culturally inappropriate care and treatment, poor communication and intolerance ... can be the consequences (Royal Commission of Inquiry into Aboriginal Deaths in Custody 1991 in Universities Australia 2011, p. 40).

The Royal Commission recommended cultural competency should be included in the training of professionals, suggesting the following:

- all employees of government departments and agencies ... be trained to understand and appreciate the traditions and culture of contemporary Aboriginal society
- such training programs should be developed in negotiation with local Aboriginal communities and organisations; and
- such training should, whenever possible, be provided by Aboriginal adult education providers with appropriate input from local communities (Royal Commission of Inquiry into Aboriginal Deaths in Custody 1991, cited in Universities Australia 2011 p. 40).

Yet trying to apply cultural competency measures comes with its own limitations. Critics argue cultural competency models used by health professions can simply reinforce stereotypes, resulting in failure to capture the diverse and changing nature of culture and identity and, ultimately, pathologizing ethnicity (Lee & Farrell 2006). 'Rather than using trait-based cultural competency models, practitioners need to adopt a more dynamic, interactive view of culture and communication and pay attention to important cues that could help improve the delivery of medical care' (Lee & Farrell 2006, p. 4).

Smith (1999) argues that cultural competence first requires deconstruction and negotiation of *our own* identities and positions and the accompanying power and privilege that we bring to working with marginalized people. Others have problematized cultural competency as a form of 'liberal multiculturalism' which 'tends to exoticize others in a nativistic retreat that locates difference in a primeval past of cultural authenticity' (Perry 2002 in Nyland 2006, p. 196). Postcolonial scholar Gayatri Spivak (1988) speaks to this issue—in particular, of a paternalistic approach to understanding culture—highly critical of European postmodern scholars whose 'networks of power/desire/interest [were] … so heterogeneous that their reduction to a coherent narrative is counterproductive' (1988, p. 272). Other scholars, meanwhile, have also been highly critical. In an article titled 'The Myth of Cultural Competence,' which examines social work contexts, Dean (2001) questions how any person can become competent when culture and individual cultural identity are continually changing. Rather than accepting that anyone can become competent in the culture of another, she proposes an alternative model based on a *lack* of competence in cross-cultural matters with a focus back on the subject.

> With "lack of competence" as the focus, a different view of practicing across cultures emerges. The client is the "expert" and the clinician is in a position of seeking knowledge and trying to understand what life is like for the client. There is no thought of competence—instead one thinks of gaining understanding (always partial) of a phenomenon that is evolving and changing.
>
> (Dean 2001, p. 623)

As such, Dean brings the issue of cultural competency full circle within this chapter, placing the onus on the external person to adapt (in her case, the client and the clinician). Likewise, public relations examples have shown how practitioners must champion cultural competency at several levels: first, in their own interfaces with people, as in the examples of Guggenheim and Disney, which call for cultural sensitivity, understanding and knowledge as well as the need to work within that culture; and second, as facilitators and interpreters for *other industries* (such as the sciences and law) that rely on public relations practitioners' communication expertise in channelling information to the wider community. In achieving this status, without resorting to reductionism or stereotyping, public relations activity can pass through a virtual public interest culture funnel.

Conclusion

It is wisely suggested by French anthropologist Raymond Carroll (1990) that even before embarking on the journey into the culture of others, we must first become aware of our own culture, our own cultural presuppositions, of the implicit premises that inform our own interpretations and of our verities. In his book *Cultural Misunderstandings: The French American Experience,* he suggests that 'Only after taking this step, which is the most difficult one, can I begin to understand the cultural presuppositions of another' (1990, p. 4). This is good advice for any industry, and for public relations, with its focus on planning, listening and research, it makes simple, good sense. Among public relations scholars there is clear consensus that activity within a global context must be culturally sensitive to be successful (Sriramesh & Verčič 2001; Zaharna 2001; Valentini 2007; Bardhan 2011). Public relations must be *responsive to* culture rather than try to *manage* culture. In following a culture-centered approach, it can be responsive to societal and organizational cultures through, among other things, listening and learning.

This chapter has drawn on a range of established paradigms and theories for viewing culture and its place within a globalized world, heavily informed by critical theory, postcolonialism, participatory action research, public interest anthropology, as well as theories of the third culture and cultural competency. Each has contributed to the broader patchwork of culture, public relations and the public interest. Public relations can take much from the ideas and theories generated within public interest anthropology. Sanday and Jannowitz (2004, p. 65) note that public interest anthropology bridges the applied and academic fields of anthropology; it achieves this by grounding theory, research, and knowledge production in the interest of solving social issues. They argue that 'civic engagement without multicultural awareness renders the former null and void' (2004, p. 65); thus the two must be examined together. For Sanday and Jannowitz (2004) public interest anthropology centers on a service model approach: a combination of service learning, civic engagement, multicultural sensitivity and critical thinking, achieved through theoretical and practical understanding of multiculturalism, and a commitment to 'problem solving in the interest of building a community-oriented moral order based on equal rights' (2004, p. 64). There is no reason why public relations cannot follow suit in adopting such a service model approach.

Finally, public interest anthropology has been successfully brought into the classrooms of universities and schools in order to achieve certain ends—a move that is consistent with Freire's educational philosophy, participatory action research and culture-centered approaches that underpin pedagogical and curriculum change. For contemporary public relations scholars, these represent models and ideas to embrace and explore. Freire's critique called for pedagogy to be inclusive of the student and the local community. He argued the following:

> In cultural synthesis, the actors who come from "another world" ... do not come to *teach* or to *transmit* or to *give* anything, but rather to learn, with the people, about the peoples (sic) world.
>
> (Freire 2005 [1970], p. 178 his italics)

If public relations scholars and practitioners see such perspectives as opportunities instead of challenges, the field can advance its claim to the public interest through deeper cultural sensitivity, competency and understanding.

References

African-Women.org, 2009, *Consequences of FGM*, viewed 30 June 2013, http://www. african-women.org/FGM/consequences.php

Baldwin, J, Faulkner, S, Hecht, M & Lindsley, C 2006, *Redefining culture: perspectives across the disciplines*, Laurence Erlbaum, Mahwah, NJ.

Bardhan, N 2011, 'Culture, communication, and third culture building in public relations within global flux', in N Bardhan & K Weaver (eds.), *Public relations in global cultural contexts*, Routledge, New York, pp. 77–107.

Bardhan, N & Weaver, K (eds.) 2011, *Public relations in global cultural contexts*, Routledge, New York.

Broome, BJ 1991, 'Building shared meaning: implications of a relational approach to empathy for teaching intercultural communication', *Communication Education*, vol. 40, pp. 235–49.

Capps, K 2015, 'Here are the top 6 designs for the Guggenheim Helsinki, and they're all a bad idea', *Citylab*, viewed 1 July 2015, http://www.citylab.com/ design/2014/12/here-are-the-top-6-designs-for-the-guggenheim-helsinki-and-theyre-all-a-bad-idea/383312/.

Carroll, R 1990, *Cultural misunderstandings: the French American experience*, University of Chicago Press, Chicago.

Carvajal, D 2014, 'Helsinki divided on plan for a Guggenheim Satellite', The New York Times, viewed 1 July 2015, http://www.nytimes.com/2014/07/15/arts/ design/helsinki-divided-on-plan-for-a-guggenheim-satellite.html?_r=0

Casmir, FL 1978, 'A multicultural perspective on human condition', in FL Casmir (ed.), *Intercultural and international communication*, University Press of America, Washington DC, pp. 241–57.

Casmir, F 1993, 'Third-culture building: a paradigm shift for international and inter-cultural communication', *Communication yearbook*, vol. 16, pp. 407–28.

Chib, A 2013, 'The promise and peril of mHealth in developing countries', *Mobile Media & Communication*, January, vol. 1, no. 1, pp. 69–75. DOI: 10.1177/ 2050157912459502 http://www.readcube.com/articles/10.1177/205015791245 9502.

Curtin, PA & Gaither, TK 2007, *International public relations: negotiating culture, identity and power*, Sage, Thousand Oaks, CA.

Curtin, PA & Gaither, TK 2012, *Globalization and public relations in postcolonial nations*, Cambria Press, Amherst, NY.

Curtin, P A and T K Gaither 2005, 'Privileging identity, difference, and power: the Circuit of Culture as a basis for public relations theory,' *Journal of Public Relations Research*, vol. 17 no. 2, pp. 91–116

Dean, R 2001, 'The myth of cross-cultural competence', *Journal of Contemporary Human Services*, vol. 82, no. 6, pp. 623–30.

Dewey, J 1927, *The public and its problems*, H. Holt & Co., New York.

Dutta, M 2011, *Communicating social change*, Routledge, New York.

Dutta, M, Ban, Z & Pal, M 2012, 'Engaging worldviews, cultures, and structures through dialogue: the culture-centered approach to public relations', *Prism*, vol. 9, no. 2, pp. 1–10.

Dutta, M & Pal M 2011, 'Public relations and marginalisation in a global context: A postcolonial critique' in N Bardham & K Weaver (eds.), *Public relations in a Global Cultural Context*, Routledge, New York, pp. 195–226.

Edelson, Z 2015, '"We mean to be provocateurs": Michael Sorkin on the Next Helsinki Competition', *Metropolis,* 22 January, viewed 1 July 2015, http://www.metropolismag.com/Point-of-View/January-2015/We-Mean-to-Be-Provocateurs-Michael-Sorkin-on-the-Next-Helsinki-Competition/.

Edwards, L 2012, 'Exploring the role of public relations as a cultural intermediary. occupation', *Cultural Sociology*, vol. 6, no. 4, pp. 438–54.

Edwards, L & Hodges, C (eds.) 2011, *Public relations, society & culture: theoretical and empirical explorations,* Routledge, Abingdon.

Fitch, K 2013, 'A disciplinary perspective: the internationalization of Australian public relations education', *Journal of Studies in International Education*, vol. 17, no. 2, pp. 136–47.

Fitch, K & Desai, R 2012, 'Developing global practitioners: addressing industry expectations of intercultural competence in public relations graduates in Singapore and Perth', *Journal of International Communication*, vol. 18, no. 1, pp. 63–78.

Fitch, K & Surma, A 2006, 'The challenges of international education: developing a public relations unit for the Asian region', *Journal of University Teaching and Learning Practice*, vol. 3, no. 2, pp. 104–13.

Foucault, M 1984, *The history of sexuality, vol 1: an introduction*, trans. R Hurley, Penguin, Harmondsworth.

Foxwell-Norton, K, Forde, S & Meadows, M 2013, 'Land, listening and voice: investigating community and media representations of the Queensland struggle for land rights and equality', *Media International Australia,* no. 149, November, pp. 150–61.

Freire, P 2005, *The pedagogy of the oppressed*, trans. MB Ramos, Continuum, New York, original work published 1970.

Fulcher, 2015, 'Guggenheim Helsinki rival contest nets more than 200 entries', *Architect's Journal,* 13 April, viewed 1 July, http://www.architectsjournal.co.uk/news/daily-news/guggenheim-helsinki-rival-contest-nets-more-than-200-entries/8681143.article.

Geertz, C 1994, Readings in the Philosophy of Social Science, MIT Press, Cambridge MA.

Gibson, R n.d., *Paolo Freire and revolutionary pedagogy for social justice*, San Diego State University, viewed 1 May 2013, http://richgibson.com/freirecriticaledu.htm.

Guggenheim 2013, *Guggenheim Helsinki revised proposal 2013,* The Solomon R. Guggenheim Foundation, New York, pp. 1–37.

Grunig, J, Grunig L, Sriramesh, K, Huang, Y & Lyra, A 1995, 'Models of public relations in an international setting', *Journal of Public Relations*, vol. 7, no. 3, p. 163–86.

Hall, E 1981, *Beyond culture,* Anchor Books, Garden City, NY.

Hall, E 2000a, 'Monochronic and polychronic time', in LA Samavoar & RE Porter (eds.), *Intercultural communication: a reader,* 9th edn, Wadsworth, Belmont, CA, pp. 380–86.

Hall, E 2000b, 'Context and meaning', in LA Samavoar & RE Porter (eds.), *Intercultural communication: a reader*, 9th edn, Wadsworth, Belmont, CA, pp. 34–42.

Harkavy, I, Puckett, J & Romer, D 2000, 'Action research: bridging service and research', *Michigan Journal of Community Service Learning*, special issue, pp. 113–18.

Hodges, C 2006, 'PRP culture: a framework for exploring public relations as cultural intermediaries', *Journal of Communication Management*, vol. 10, no. 1, pp. 80–93.

Hodges, C 2013, 'Cultural imagination in public relations education', *Public Relations Inquiry*, vol. 2, no. 1, pp. 27–50.

Holtshausen, D 2011, 'The need for a postmodern turn in global public relations,' in N Bardhan & CK Weaver (eds.), *Public relations in global cultural contexts: multi-paradigmatic perspectives*, Routledge, New York, pp. 140–66.

Johnston, F, Paley, J, Sabloff, P & Sanday, P 1997, *Public interest anthropology: planning seminar, a program for research, teaching and action*, University of Pennsylvania, Philadelphia.

Kemmis, S & McTaggart, R 2005, 'Participatory action research: communicative action and the public sphere', in NK Denzin & YS Lincoln (eds.), *The Sage handbook of qualitative research*, 3rd edn, Sage, Thousand Oaks, CA, pp. 559–605.

Kent, M & Taylor, M 2011, 'How intercultural communication theory informs public relations practice in global settings', in N Bardhan & K Weaver (eds.), *Public relations in global cultural contexts*, Routledge, New York.

Kluckhohn, FR & Strodtbeck, FL 1961, *Variations in value orientations,* Row, Petersen, Evanston, IL.

Kroeber, AL & Kluckhohn, C 1963, *Culture: a critical review of concepts and definitions*, Vintage Books, New York, originally published 1952 as vol. 47, no. 1, *Papers of the Peabody Museum of American Archeology and Ethnology,* Harvard University.

Lamphere, L 2004, 'The convergence of applied, practicing, and public anthropology in the 21st century', *Human Organization*, vol. 63, no. 4, pp. 431–43.

L'Etang, J 2010, 'Making it real: anthropological reflections on public relations, diplomacy and rhetoric', in R Heath (ed.), *The Sage handbook on public relations,* Sage, Los Angeles, pp. 145–62.

L'Etang, J 2011, 'Imagining public relations anthropology', in L Edwards & C Hodges (eds.), *Public relations, society and culture: theoretical and empirical explorations*, Routledge, Abingdon, pp. 15–33.

L'Etang, J 2012, 'Thinking about public relations and culture: anthropological insights and ethnographic frames', in K Sriramesh & D Verčič (eds.), *Culture and public relations: links and implications*, Routledge, New York, pp. 218–37.

Lee, SA & Farrel, M 2006, 'Is cultural competency a backdoor to racism?' *Anthropological News: Rethinking Race and Human Variation*, special edition, American Anthropological Association, February-March.

Ly-Le, T 2014, personal communication, March.

McClaren, P 1994, 'White terror and oppositional agency: towards a critical multiculturalism', in DT Goldberg (ed.), *Multiculturalism: a critical reader,* Blackwell, Cambridge, MA, pp. 45–74.

McKie, D & Munshi, D 2007, *Reconfiguring public relations: ecology, equity and enterprise*, Routledge, New York.

Mercado, D 2005, 'Introduction to the anniversary edition', in P Freire, *The pedagogy of the oppressed*, trans. MB Ramos, Continuum, New York, pp. 11–29, original work published 1970.

Merrick, J 2014, 'Guggenheim Helsinki: shortlisted designs for the controversial art museum go on show', *The Independent*, 2 December, viewed I July 2015, http://www.independent.co.uk/arts-entertainment/architecture/guggenheim-helsinki-shortlisted-designs-for-the-controversial-art-museum-go-on-show-9898911.html.

Parliamentary Ombudsman of Finland, 2013, 'Helsinki art museum's directors impartiality was jeopardised in preparatory work for Guggenheim project: rebukes from deputy- ombudsman,' Press release, 23 July, viewed 10 April, http://www.oikeusasiamies.fi/Resource.phx/eoa/english/pressreleases/pressreleases.htx?templateId=5.htx&id=992.

Nyland, D 2006, 'Critical multiculturalism, whiteness, and social work: towards a more radical view of cultural competence', *Journal of Progressive Human Services*, vol. 17, no. 2, pp. 27–42. DOI: 10.1300/J059v17n02_03.

Rodriguez, A 2002, 'Culture to culturing: re-imagining our understanding of intercultural communication', *Journal of Intercultural Communication*, vol. 5, viewed 10 February 2015, http://www.immi.se/intercultural/nr5/rodriguez.pdf.

Rosaldo, R 2006, 'Foreword: defining culture', in J Baldwin, S Faulkner, M Hecht & C Lindsley (eds.), *Redefining culture: perspectives across the discipline*, Laurence Erlbaum, Mahwah, NJ.

Said, E 1978, *Orientalism*, Pantheon, New York.

Said, E 1981, *Covering Islam: how the media and the experts determine how we see the rest of the world*, Pantheon, New York.

Said, E 1993, *Culture and imperialism*, Knopf/Random House, New York.

Sanday, PR & Jannowitz, C 2004, 'Public interest anthropology: a Boasian service-learning initiative', *Michigan Journal of Community Service Learning*, Summer, pp. 64–75.

Sison, M 2013, 'Representing Asian public relations in the Asian Century', Paper presented at *Barcelona International Public Relations Conference*, July, Barcelona, Spain.

Smith, LT 1999, *Decolonizing methodologies: research and Indigenous peoples*, University of Otago Press, Dunedin, New Zealand.

Somekh, B 2008, 'Action research', in L Given (ed.), *The Sage encyclopedia of research methodologies*, vol. 2, pp. 4–6.

Sorkin, M 2013, *Visions for the Next Helsinki: celebrating the plurality of good ideas*, viewed http://www.nexthelsinki.org/.

Spivak, GC 1988, 'Can the subaltern speak', in C Nelson & L Grossberg (eds.), *Marxism and interpretation of culture*, Macmillan, Basingstoke, viewed 3 June 2014, http://www.uky.edu/~tmute2/geography_methods/readingPDFs/spivak.pdf.

Sriramesh, K & Verčič, D 2001, 'International public relations: a framework for future research', *Journal of Communication Management*, vol. 6, no. 2, pp. 103–07.

Sriramesh, K & Verčič, D (eds.) 2012, *Culture and public relations: links and implications*, Routledge, New York.

Sriramesh, K & White, J 1992, 'Social culture and public relations', in JE Grunig (ed.), *Excellence in public relations and communications management: contributions to effective organizations*, Lawrence Erlbaum Associates, Hillsdale, NJ, pp. 597–616.

Universities Australia 2011, *National best practice framework for Indigenous cultural competency in Australian universities*, Canberra, Australian Capital Territory.

Useem, J, Donoghue, JD & Useem, RH 1963, 'Men in the middle of the third culture', *Human Organization*, vol. 22, no. 33, pp. 129–44.

Valentini, C 2007, 'Global versus cultural approaches in public relationship management. The case of the European Union', *Journal of Communication Management*, vol. 11, no. 2, pp. 117–33.

Wakefield, R 1996, 'Interdisciplinary theoretical foundations for international public relations', in H Culbertson & N Chen (eds.), *International public relations: a comparative analysis,* Lawrence Erlbaum Associates, Mahwah, NJ, pp. 17–30.

Waymer, D (ed.) 2012, *Culture, social class, and race in public relations: perspectives and applications*, Lexington Books, Lanham.

Zaharna, R 2001, 'In-awareness' approach to international public relations', *Public Relations Review,* vol. 27, no. 2, pp. 135–48.

6   Social Capital and Capacity Building
Connecting Communities in the Public Interest

The community, as a whole, will benefit from the cooperation of all its parts.
(Hanifan 1916, p. 131)

Introduction

Robert Putnam wrote in 1993 (para. 3) that 'everyone would be better off if everyone could cooperate.' His comment wasn't just a random idealistic statement. Rather, Putnam was referring to the findings of his now famous study of Italian society. A political scientist, Putnam sought to find the best predictor of government performance, ultimately identifying how 'strong traditions of civic engagement—voter turnout, newspaper readership, membership in choral societies and literary circles, Lions Clubs, and soccer clubs—are the hallmarks of a successful region' (Putnam 1993, para. 8). Further, Putnam argued that 'communities did not become civic simply because they were rich. The historical record strongly suggests precisely the opposite: They have become rich *because* they were civic' (Putnam 1993, para 12, my italics). Not without his critics, Putnam remains one of several leading voices on the importance of social capital, both for governments and the communities that create it. He concluded that 'social capital is a "public good"; that is, it is not the private property of those who benefit from it' but rather it is like other 'public goods' such as clean air and safe streets (1993, para. 18).

Importantly, Putnam, along with James Coleman and Pierre Bourdieu, arguably the three central theorists on the philosophy of social capital, all included reference, in varying degrees, to the importance of the public interest in social capital (for Bourdieu see Goldberg 2013; Bourdieu 1986; Coleman 1981; Putnam 1993). For Coleman, the public interest was central to his philosophy of education, as evidenced in his article *Private Schools, Public Schools and the Public Interest* (1981) in which he argues for the overriding public interest 'in helping all children, particularly those of the disadvantaged, receive a better education' (1981, p. 29). All three identified how public benefits associate with social capital and, conversely, how it is not in the public interest to have poor levels or inequitable access to social capital. Why is this important, or relevant, for public relations? Heuristically, the answer lies in the common ground they all share: through the benefits that relationships, shared values and mutual interests can bring to individuals and communities. So, while social capital provides important insights for better understanding the public interest, there is much that the field of social capital can also bring to the study of public relations, as evidenced in the works of public relations scholars (Ihlen 2005; Kennan & Hazelton 2005; Hazelton, Harrison-Rexwode & Kennan 2007; Verhoeven 2008; Fitch 2009; Saffer, Taylor & Yang 2013).

This chapter explores how communities use social capital, how this, in turn, can build community capacity, and how this impacts on the public interest. Recognizing that communities are far from simple entities, the chapter examines the participatory, bottom-up approach that is most likely to provide successful outcomes, plus the importance of letting communities drive their own agendas. Such approaches show how, for example, indigenous grassroots associations can be as important to growth as physical investment or appropriate technology (Putnam 1993). 'Conversely, government interventions that neglect or undermine this social infrastructure can go seriously awry' (Putnam 1993, para. 19).

The chapter begins with a broad examination of *all* of the capitals—industrial, financial, intellectual, human, social, artistic, cultural and natural—flagging how scholars are increasingly calling for capital to be understood for its overlapping capabilities and intersections rather than as siloed concepts that work in isolation. So, while the chapter is intended to use social capital as a foundation for advancing our knowledge of the public interest as it may apply to public relations, it also picks up on patterns of thought that see social capital as interwoven with other capitals.

Forms of Capital

Capital is multi-faceted but, according to Pierre Bourdieu, different forms of capital should be viewed interchangeably (1986). In his essay on *The Forms of Capital* (1986) Bourdieu argued that traditional understandings of capital—as purely economic—ignore other forms of capital, notably social, cultural and artistic, in what is effectively an appropriation of one into the other, since all 'capital is accumulated labor' (Bourdieu 1986, p. 241). (This excludes the more recent understanding of natural capital). Bourdieu's analysis of social and cultural capital challenges economic theory to be more inclusive of all capital and through this he draws a connection to the interest-focus that exists within economic capital. His critical account of capital argued that by 'reducing the universe of exchanges to mercantile exchange, which is objectively and subjectively oriented toward the maximization of profit, i.e., (economically) *self-interested,* it has implicitly defined the other forms of exchange as noneconomic, and therefore *disinterested*' (1986, p. 2 his italics). He explains, 'Interest in the restricted sense it is given in economic theory, cannot be produced without producing the negative counterpart, disinterestedness' (1986, p. 2). In other words, economic capital ignores other capital because it is not equated with money, notably profit. As such, Bourdieu's critique of capital and interest centers on power, social networks, culture and inequalities and is highly critical of both the economic model and the scientific monopoly of understanding capital. He argues that 'practices and assets thus salvaged from the "icy water of egoistical calculation" (and from science) are the virtual monopoly of the dominant class' (1986, p. 242). His alternative, in calling for everything from education to kinship, to habitus (the internalization of external wealth and culture), to social networks, as *part of the capital equation*, is to give each a more equitable 'interest value.'

The interconnectedness of capitals has been well argued across many disciplines. Community management scholar Jenny Onyx notes how 'various forms of capital are not independent, nor are they alternatives, although they are often treated as though they were. They are interconnected in complex ways, and likely to be complementary, rather than substitutive,' (2002, p. 47). In particular, arguments for ecological sustainability have seen calls for social and human capital to bridge the environment and economy and to revision the relationship between all the capitals (Onyx 2002; Dale 2001; Peirce 1999). While there is a growing body of literature from within fields of social theory, communities and sustainability, in which public relations has played an active part (see, for example, Ihlen, Bartlett & May 2011; Demetrious 2013), other fields have also stepped up. Most recently the field of accounting has examined the interconnectedness of capitals, going so far as to proffer a revised approach to capitalism (Moulier-Boutang 2012; Gleeson-White 2014), with some even offering a practical modeling on how to apply the public interest to the profession of accountancy (Institute of Chartered Accountants in England and Wales 2012). Such industry frameworks are examined in the book's final chapter.

In her work *Six Capitals: The Revolution Capitalism Has to Have—or How Accountants Can Change the World,* Jane Gleeson-White (2014) identifies how accountants can provide a bridge to understanding the importance of the non-mercantile capitals: intellectual, human, social and natural. In giving these equal standing to financial and industrial capitals, she challenges her own profession of accountants, and also economists, to think beyond traditional business paradigms that calculate value based on money or gross domestic product (GDP) to a model inclusive of all capital. Like anthropology, media, law and politics examined elsewhere, accountancy now joins the list of disciplines that seek a revised and broader public interest approach to decision making. 'Because accounting is the primary language of corporations, the accounting revolution also acts as a psychological intervention by requesting the corporation to speak differently,' she explains (2014, p. xxiv). Gleeson-White calls for a new political economy, derived from a new system of measuring and valuing, based not around regulation but around a changed approach to capital.

The political economy which was born with Adam Smith no longer offers us the possibility of understanding the reality which is being constructed before our eyes—namely the value, wealth and complexity of the world economic system—and it also does not enable us to deal with the challenges that await humanity, whether ecological or social.
(Moulier-Boutang 2012 cited in Gleeson-White 2014, p. 24)

She points out how each new wave of wealth creation over time—notably agricultural, industrial, information—has required a new form of accounting (Elliott 1992 in Gleeson-White 2014, p. 1).

Gleeson-White (2014) attributes the concept of six capitals as they apply to her field of accountancy to the International Integrated Reporting Council (IIRC), a coalition made up of regulators, shareholders, accounting professionals and others from 25 countries which developed the concept of 'integrated reporting' in 2013. As such, what has gained the attention of accountants and regulators is the idea that the six capitals represent a holistic way of reporting business output, integrating reporting of financial and manufactured capital (already covered well in financial reports), social and natural capital (covered to a lesser extent in sustainability reports) and human and intellectual capital (not yet well reported in financial reporting). Through developing this new integrated reporting model which accommodates non-financial assets, it affirms the corporate social responsibility (CSR) approach that has become a fundamental tenet for much public relations practice and scholarship in integrating social capital (see, for example, Heath & Ni 2008; Ihlen, Bartlett & May 2011). And, in proposing the concept of 'cognitive capitalism,' which calls for a review of measuring and valuing, this approach is intended to enable very different conversations to those based on the formerly siloed financial and non-financial paradigms, as value-drivers found in technology, brand recognition, knowledge accumulation, and networks and partnerships now also register in financial reporting systems (Moulier-Boutang 2012; Gleeson-White 2014). The public interest is thus fundamental to the review of non-traditional capitals—intellectual, human, social/relational and natural—with the need to incorporate them into the value chain.

Though Gleeson-White (2014) and Bourdieu (1986) make their claims from different disciplines (accounting and critical sociology, respectively), theoretical positions (normative and critical, respectively), and time frames, almost 30 years apart, they each call for a holistic, non-economic understanding and counting of capital. Indeed, Bourdieu's argument is reflective of growing contemporary moves to 'endeavor to grasp capital and profit in all their forms and to establish the laws whereby the different types of capital (or power, which amounts to the same thing) change into one another' (Bourdieu 1986, p. 243).

For public relations, this paradigmatic turn calls for a revised interface with other disciplines that are increasingly thinking beyond traditional scientific and economic models. From normative and functionalist perspectives, key roles for public relations include communicating this thinking through reporting, for example, in annual reports, plus interpreting how the six capitals can apply within organizational day-to-day operations. Those already embracing CSR may find the shift equally encouraging and logical in its approach. Not only does the shift raise issues and challenges for the political economy but it also supports critical theory in challenging the inequalities and hegemonies of capitalism.

Social Capital

It is therefore not surprising that Bourdieu specifically argues that 'social capital is never completely independent of other forms of capital' (1986, p. 251). Nevertheless, social capital's relational focus and the interest within and for publics or communities give it an axiomatic fit with relationship management and building and will be the chapter's primary concern. Narayan's (1999b, p. 3) report on social capital for the World Bank noted that, despite differences in approaches and definitions, the central and unique element shared in all social capital was its relational capacity which can exist only when shared. Indeed, it has been called by many the 'glue' that binds communities together (Eckstein 2001, p. 830; Chapman & Kirk 2001, p. 19; Brooks 2005, p. 10; Narayan 1999b, p. 1).

Not surprisingly, public relations scholars have jumped on board and found logical synonymies between the two fields (Ihlen 2005; Kennan & Hazelton 2005; Fitch 2009; Heath 2014). For Ihlen (2005) social capital, coupled with the symbolic capital that comes with reputation, is at the heart of public relations. He positions social capital within an organizational context, noting how it falls to public relations to incorporate social capital into organizational programs (Ihlen 2005, p. 494). This organizational context is further explored by Kennan and Hazelton (2005), who see it emerging through 'the rich, varied, and textured communicative exchanges that occur among various organizational actors who are embedded in various contexts' (2005, p. 322). Specifically, Kennan and Hazelton position the value of social capital to internal public relations at three levels: through organizational advantage, for example, in higher levels of productivity and improved ethical practice; through reduced transaction costs, for example, in minimizing points of conflict such as union or legal disputes; and through the expansion, social capital provides segues into other fields of capital, such as intellectual or human capital. Meanwhile, Verhoeven (2008) and Fitch (2009) view the idea of community through a social capital prism, focusing on the benefits that come with flexibility, openness and voluntary commitment. Other public relations scholars identify social capital's resonance in the online space, extending the relational approach to the multiple relationships that online space provides (Hazelton, Harrison-Rexwode & Kennan 2007; Saffer, Taylor & Yang 2013). As such, social capital holds significant potential for enhancing a wide range of public relations activity, including community engagement, relationship management and internal communication, and it is precisely because of these synergies that it holds significant public interest potential.

More broadly, Hjerppe and Taipale (2000, p. 3) note that social capital provides a conceptual basis for conversations between economists and social scientists in better understanding the interface between their fields, particularly as they apply to processes of development and growth. Thus, in better understanding social capital, public relations—both within and external to formal organizational and institutional contexts—can broaden its understandings of relationships, interest exchanges, networking and change-making and, in turn, also gain a stronger sense of its role within the broader capital framework.

Developing Social Capital

Like the public interest, social capital is conceptually complex. Best known from the works of sociologists Bourdieu and Coleman and political scientist Putnam, the theory has burgeoned in recent years as researchers have used it to find answers to a diverse range of issues across rural and urban town renewal (Brooks 2005; Chapman & Kirk 2001), general health and well-being (Harpham, Grant & Thomas 2002; Carpiano 2006), mental health (McKenzie, Whitley & Weich 2002; Gallagher 2009; Patel & Copeland 2011), politics and public policy (Putnam 1993, 1995, 2000; Fukuyama 2001; Knack 2002; Brooks 2005), poverty reduction (Narayan 1999a/b; Story, Taleb, Ahasan & Ali 2015), public relations (Kennan & Hazleton 2005; Ihlen 2005; Verhoeven 2008), housing (Kagan, Lawthorn, Knowles & Burton 2000; Chapman & Kirk 2001) and accounting (Gleeson-White 2014).

Though it is generally considered a contemporary concept, emerging out of the three principle theorists of the 1980s and 1990s, the term actually appeared a century ago when, in 1916, educationalist LJ Hanifan identified the importance social capital held for schools and education (Hanifan 1916, pp. 131–32). Hanifan was also to link to the importance of the public interest:

> The individual is helpless socially ... If he may come into contact with his neighbor, and they with other neighbors, there will be an accumulation of social capital, which may immediately satisfy his social needs and which may bear a social potentiality sufficient to the substantial improvement of living conditions in the whole community. First then, there must be an accumulation of community social capital.

Hanifan went on to conclude: 'The more the people do for themselves, the larger the community social capital will become, and the greater will be the dividends on the social investment' (Hanifan 1916, p. 138). Notably, he also found common ground with Bourdieu (1986), Coleman (1988, 1981) and

Putnam (1993) who also examined schools and education in explicating social capital.

While Bourdieu saw social capital as 'the aggregate of the actual or the potential resources which are linked to a possession of a durable network of ... relationships' (1986, p. 248), Putnam defined it as having 'features of social organization, such as networks, norms, and social trust that facilitates coordination and cooperation' (Putnam 1995, p. 67). Siisiäinen (2000) draws a useful distinction between the two, noting how Putnam's idea of social capital deals with *collective values* (principally trust and reciprocity) and *societal integration*, whereas Bourdieu's approach is offered from the point of view of actors engaged in *struggle in pursuit of individual goals and interests*. Carpiano (2006, p. 167) meanwhile distinguishes Putnam's favoring of *social cohesion and reciprocity* and Bourdieu's two-part characterization of *social networks and resources*. These concepts are further developed by distinguishing the two parts: *structural and cognitive*. Structural social capital is located in what people do to gain access to resources, measured by assessing individual actions and behaviors, as well as roles, rules, precedents, networks and institutions. Cognitive social capital, on the other hand, focuses on how people feel about their community, measured in attitudes and perceptions, such as trust, values, attitudes and beliefs that produce cooperative behavior (Knack 2002; Story, Taleb, Ahasan & Ali 2015; McKenzie, Whitley & Weich 2002).

Putnam's (2000) distinction between 'bonding' and 'bridging' forms of social capital provides further clarification. These terms are generally well understood as bonding capital, essentially *within* a group, and bridging capital, essentially *between* groups. Moreover, bonding refers to the networks and relationships of trust within communities often associated with ties of social class, ethnicity/race or social status, also associated with cognitive aspects of trust and reciprocity. Bridging refers to the networks and interrelationships between communities and external organizations and agencies, including those with power and resources. While bonding is sometimes associated with the idea of 'getting by' (through existing connections), bridging is seen to enable communities to 'get ahead' (by developing new connections) (Kagan, Lawthorn, Knowles & Burton 2000, p. 4).

Social Capital, Communities and the State

While social capital is known to be difficult to generate *through* public policy (Fukuyama 2001), governments nevertheless acknowledge the benefits in integrating social capital considerations to help ensure that policies, programs and regulations work *with* and *alongside* community-generated social capital (Narayan 1999; Productivity Commission 2003; Chapman & Kirk 2001; Kajanoj & Simpura 2000; Brooks 2005). Examples include local government land-care initiatives that incorporate the role of environmental groups, council allocation of space for homeless where charities also work to provide food and clothing and programs in schools that are assisted by parent-teacher associations. At the same time, while social capital is known to exist as complimentary to government programs and policies, it is also identified as a substitute for communities where governmental action and input is either absent or in short supply. In his report into social capital and poverty for the World Bank, Narayan (1999b, p. ii) explains:

> The nature of interaction between state and society is characterized as complementarity and substitution. When states are functional, the informal and formal work well together—for example, government support for community-based development. When states become dysfunctional, the informal institutions become a substitute and are reduced to serving a defensive or survival function.

Research shows that high levels of benefit come to communities where government-community partnerships are strong, especially where communities are enabled via social inclusion partnerships (SIPs) (Brooks 2000; Chapman & Kirk 2001). Moreover, governments 'involving communities in a committed and non-tokenistic way can bring a range of benefits' (Chapman & Kirk 2001, p. 3). Importantly, as Narayan (1999a) explains, social capital exists *with or without* state support but can hold its greatest public interest potential where the two work in cooperation. The following examples, drawn from international research, provide evidence of how social capital can assist in developing communities and either pressure or work with governments, while also showing how a *lack* of social capital, coupled with scarce or limited government support, can have negative consequences for communities and severely impact on the public interest and well-being. As such, public relations implications are scattered throughout these illustrations, for example, through relationship building, communication and community action.

Social Capital for Regional and Rural Renewal

Brooks (2005) examined two rural shires in New South Wales, Australia, in order to find out how social capital could be applied to rural renewal. The two shires, Corowa and Murray, were geographically and historically alike in terms of growth, income and age but had diverged in terms of economic and social development. Both shires were bordered on one side by the iconic Murray River, each with a town on the opposite side of the river in the neighboring state of Victoria. Data available from the Australian Bureau of Statistics (ABS) showed that Corowa shire had an average growth rate, while Murray shire was the fastest- growing shire in the state. Further ABS data about social and economic advantage and disadvantage showed that conditions in Corowa had remained unchanged over time, while they had improved over time in Murray. Brooks posited two theories of social capital, based on a pluralist and neoliberal model, and looked for social capital that was more or less indicative of these two categories. Accordingly, she ascribed each theory with a series of characteristics: the pluralist view was supported by ongoing involvement from the state in civic affairs, in part to ensure equity of access to all parties; the neoliberal view saw the minimization or the withdrawal of the state from the civil domain on the basis that this removed impediments to individual action.

Brooks explored the levels of social capital both within the communities and the approach of each local council (which notably is also made up of local community members). She found higher levels of perceived regional interaction and effectiveness between the Murray shire council and other levels of government, with the shire's general manager noted to be a motivator and instigator of vision. In addition, Murray shire residents were more inclusive of the neighboring Victorian community of Echuca, across the river. In general, Murray was found to have a higher level of interaction with external resources (bridging) beyond the immediate region, as well as a high level of 'bonding' with their local government. Overall, her findings located Corowa as adopting a more neoliberal approach and Murray a more pluralist one, concluding the neoliberal model 'does not recognise the influences on individual empowerment by the social and political environment in which services are delivered ... which posits it as being in the control of individuals' (2005, p. 14). In contrast, the pluralist approach sees the need for communities to be actively involved with government and other communities in order to achieve empowerment through long-term 'buy-ins' to policy initiatives. She concluded that long-term capacities, developed through social capital within a community, were consistent with a partnership approach between government and communities and that this may require a cultural shift by participants and a preparedness by government to devolve power to communities (Brooks 2005).

Social Capital and Urban Renewal

Kagan, Lawthorn, Knowles and Burton (2000) investigated the utility of social capital in a housing estate in a northwestern city in England. The 'overspill estate,' notionally called 'Meadowbank,' was indexed as one of the *most deprived* areas of England, situated next to one of the *most prosperous* towns in England. Thus, the researchers posited that the siting of the estate would have a severely diminished capacity to attract regeneration program money, otherwise linked to inner-city and poor rural areas. Compounding this, the estate fell between two government authorities, which resulted in tenants having limited political voice in the area. In addition, Meadowbank consisted of two parts, separated by a wooded valley known as 'the dip' which, over time, had filled with rubbish. The researchers noted this context had:

> a direct impact on the struggles of local people to become activists
> in order to endeavour to regenerate their area without substantial

regeneration moneys, and the difficulties they encountered in attempting to work in partnership with the local authorities'.

(Kagan et al. 2000, p. 4)

In response to the problems associated with the disadvantaged estate, a women's action group—the Women's Regeneration Group, later to become the Meadowbrook Community Association or MECA—was formed to stimulate public interest among residents in taking action to improve their quality of life. The group's initial focus rested on two issues: cleaning the dip of the tons of rubbish which had accumulated over years and resisting a move by the local council to hand over the control of housing in the estate to private landlords. MECA achieved an 18-month calendar of productive activities, including establishing media relations, raising funds, negotiating with council, procuring and renovating a community house, cleaning up the dip, and holding public meetings. It also suffered conflict, intimidation and a lack of support from other local community groups. Notably, social capital was found to be limited in Meadowbank from the outset due to perceptions by residents who had suffered years of neglect by authorities 'resulting in apathy and a disbelief in the possibility of change' (2000 p. 7). MECA's ultimate failure was attributed to a lack of an economic framework in which to support its activity, illustrating how 'the concept of social capital is insubstantial without a material base' (Cattell & Evans 1999 in Kagan et al. 2000, p. 55).

Ultimately, Meadowbank's social problems were too great for its level of social capital. Kagan and colleagues (2000, p. 7) developed the following five-point summary, based on Meadowbank's experience, which acts as a checklist for any social regeneration project:

- Social capital is necessary for local sustainable regeneration; otherwise it will lead to social disorganization and lack of cohesion;
- Community organizing in itself helps to develop trust and cooperation among members, equating to bonding capital;
- With obstruction and blocking from external agencies, it is difficult to develop bridging capital;
- In the absence of bridging capital, conditions arise for negative aspects of social capital to develop and trust and cooperation dissipate;
- The absence of bridging capital allows confrontational rather than consensual styles of community organizing to thrive.

Social Capital and Resourcing

What lessons can be taken from the illustrations? Meadowbank reinforces Bourdieu's idea of the power imbalance which lies at the core of social, cultural and human capital and that individuals are disadvantaged in the capital exchange where access to resources (possibly education, though this is not covered explicitly in the study) is limited, and furthermore, that social structures will be perpetuated by limiting the transmission of material capital (1986, p. 86) resulting in a cycle of poverty. This example shows how bonding social capital, seen in trust and reciprocity within a community, can exist with limited resources but this may not be sufficient to make change occur or to sustain long-term benefits.

Murray, Corowa and Meadowbank raise significant issues about social capital, not least of which are its limitations in the absence of resources and bridging networks. What is needed to make change for the public benefit and in the public interest is the internal *capacity* and *agency* to enable social capital to develop and grow *plus* external supports to sustain it. These examples point to the need for capacity building within communities to ensure their internal capabilities as well as their external support. Capacity building and a snapshot on regional renewal are examined later in the chapter.

Social Capital Within and Across Boundaries

In his analysis of the social capital in 50 American states, Stephen Knack (2002) found certain aspects of social capital were more likely to align with government performance than others. In particular, he found those associated with generalized reciprocity, such as social trust, volunteering and census response activities were associated with stronger government performance. Conversely, he found group membership did not necessarily correspond to having an impact on good government; rather, knowing the mechanisms to use and stay informed were more likely to impact on good government. Knack's (2002) research supports themes highlighted earlier in the book of associations between the public interest and government accountability, in this case, framed within a social capital context. Knack argued that: 'Making government more accountable to the broader public interest—i.e. preventing "state capture" by narrow interests—is arguably the most important means by which social capital influences government performance' (2002, p. 773). Knack's research is important for two reasons: first, it directly identifies the link between social capital and the public interest; and second, it raises questions about the generalizability of social capital indexes. While this latter point tends to stray beyond the scope of this chapter, it is worth pursuing this line of inquiry briefly because it includes important issues relating to culture and difference.

Knack argued that researchers such as Putnam before him should be 'cautious in constructing social capital indexes and mix(ing) indicators of social connectedness with indicators of generalized trust and reciprocity' (2002, p. 783). Other researchers have also noted the lack of universality that adheres to the development of indexes of social capital, especially across cultures (Narayan 1999b; Story et al. 2015). For example, while a Social Capital Assessment Tool was developed for the World Bank in 1999, it was found to be inadequate for research in rural and urban settings in Bangladesh some years later because each new cultural situation and time frame requires new validation (Story et al. 2015, p. 807). Social capital research elsewhere affirms the importance of looking carefully at socio-cultural difference. For instance, a study of Japanese bonding and bridging capital found how the comparative racial and ethnic homogeneity of Japanese society meant that bridging capital may more likely be based along gender and generational differences rather than racial or ethnic dimensions as found elsewhere (Iwase, Suzuki, Fujiwara, Takao, Doi & Kawachi, 2012). In contrast, ethnicity and race were highly heterogeneous in India and, hence, required the use of entirely different indexes (Varshney 2002).

Better understanding of social capital within specific socio-cultural contexts can thus provide beneficial outcomes for both research and practice. For example, Story and colleagues (2015) noted that since Bangladesh attracts great interest from NGOs, which aspire to improve health and well-being through community-based strategies, a clearer understanding of social capital in those communities could assist in directing the support. While critical scholars such as Dutta (2011) raise concerns over external agendas dominating local needs and voices, he also points to social capital's capacity to provide political power through the organizing process and, ultimately, in providing access to resources through community-based collective organizing and networking. Consider, for example, the way social capital has been used to assist in better understanding mental health and work through issues of social exclusion. Greater understanding of social capital has been identified as helping to resolve debates between 'psychosocial' and 'neo-materialist' explanations for health inequalities and prove a mediating factor between community, collective attributes of members and individual health (McKenzie et al. 2002). In recent years mental health campaigns have proliferated as governments and NGOs make efforts to improve overall health literacy, including promoting public understanding of mental health while breaking down barriers associated with social exclusion. With its recent incorporation into public health discourse, notions of mental illness sufferers as 'Other' are slowly being eroded. Organizations that champion support for mental health awareness and advocacy work do so from a wide variety of entry points: in lobbying government, in engaging with sufferers and families, in educating and in creating awareness in the media and the public. Social inclusion has been identified as one of the key priorities for reforming mental health governance (Gallagher 2009) with a key focus on reversing the social exclusion that has been experienced in the past (Patel & Copeland 2011; Gallagher 2009) and, importantly, by including families and those with a mental illness at the center of the process.

Though the mental health lobby is far from a homogenous one, the following brief snapshot illustrates how strong social capital foundations are being exploited through getting individuals to speak out and lobby on their own behalf. In this example, the National Alliance on Mental Health

(NAMI) in the United States has drawn on human and social capital to effect public interest changes in mental health support and policy development by using strategies of social inclusion, collaboration and capacity building (Patel & Copeland 2011) to achieve its goals.

Snapshot

National Alliance on Mental Illness (NAMI)

NAMI is one of America's largest grassroots mental health organizations. Its social capital includes strong bridging and bonding capacities, which are formed in the following ways:

> At policy-making tables in communities and all levels of government (bridging)
> At countless kitchen tables ... helping individuals and families (bonding)
> (NAMI 2015, n.p.)

In 2015, NAMI's approach to advocacy, with its capacity to 'cut through' the saturated lobbying space, was summed up in the following radio interview:

> Politicians are lobbied by so many competing interests, it's hard to get your concerns heard. A mental illness lobby group have decided to give their cause a competitive edge by teaching families how to lobby politicians directly, to successfully cut through and have their message heard.
> (Mitchell 2015, n.p.)

Examined from social and human capital perspectives, NAMI has been highly successful in bringing people with mental illness together to advocate for their cause while also linking to external publics, including legislators, policy makers and the media. One of NAMI's key strategies is to call on members of the community who have been affected by mental illness to tell their own story—and it teaches people how to do it and who must hear it. In its 2014 National Day of Action, 2,000 Americans converged on Capitol Hill in Washington, each armed with a story. NAMI urged that 'No one is more effective at delivering this message to the U.S. Congress than individuals and families with lived experience' (NAMI 2014, n.p.).

Social Capital's Dual Nature

Despite what is often presented as an overwhelming public good, social capital presents a dialectic. As Narayan (1999b, p. 8) points out, 'the same ties that bind also exclude.' Putnam reinforces this, noting 'social inequalities may be embedded in social capital. Norms and networks that serve some groups may obstruct others' (Putnam 1993, n.p.). Or, put another way, 'one person's civic engagement is another's rent-seeking' (Fukuyama

2001, p. 12). Although scholars have been quick to point to the importance of social capital in communities, either a lack of social capital or competing interests can see it divide internally (Bullen & Onyx 2000 cited in Chapman & Kirk 2001).

Where high levels of social capital do exist, people are more likely to:

- feel they are part of the community;
- feel useful and able to make a real contribution to the community;
- participate in local community networks and organizations;
- come together in times of crisis;
- welcome strangers; and
- participate as a group.

Conversely, where communities lack social capital and there are limited prospects for people to come together and work for the common good of that community, contributing factors may be found in the following:

- the lack of core building blocks—self-esteem, trust and communications skills;
- inadequate material well-being in the community;
- inadequate physical infrastructure such as places to meet, public spaces and access to basic equipment and resources like telephones and newspapers;
- the lack of opportunities to develop networks between people in a safe environment; and
- fear of discrimination (Bullen & Onyx 2000 cited in Chapman & Kirk 2001, p. 20).

The results see social capital as dividing the haves and the have-nots whereby social capital, or a lack of it, can impact on finding a job or being unemployed; assisting with the elderly or leaving the elderly to manage on their own; walking safely in the street at night or being afraid to leave the house; sharing knowledge with others or remaining educationally isolated. As such, the highest levels of social capital, as manifest in powerful, tightly knit social groups, may not only exclude but also can restrict the rights and freedoms of those involved in the community, most notably people with less power such as marginalized minorities (Fukuyama 2001; Narayan 1999b; Knack 2002). The results can see exclusion of those outside a group or excessively rigid boundaries within a group restricting individual freedoms. Moreover, social capital can also lie at the center of competing interests, as groups vie for finite resources with the most able and dynamic groups achieving at the expense of others. Community organizations possessing the knowledge and resources to deal with policies and procedures can gain advantage over less experienced or weaker groups (Chapman & Kirk 2001). In short, 'social and community capital in a neighbourhood is not as straightforward as one would think' (Chapman & Kirk 2001, p. 21).

One of the best-known expressions of social capital in action is volunteering. On the face of it, volunteering or volunteerism is viewed positively, working for the public interest, and known to public relations for its value-adding capacities in cause-related work, community organizations and fundraisers. Chapman and Kirk (2001, p. 35) note that voluntary organizations are a valuable part of the social economy, and many voluntary-sector organizations connect with excluded or marginalized groups. Volunteerism has been identified positively both as an individualist pursuit and a collectivist-grounded one (Eckstein 2001). Though figures vary, comparative data indicate volunteering in many Western democracies occurs consistently at around a third of the population (Australian Bureau of Statistics 2011; NCVCO 2012; Charities Aid Foundation 2010; United States Department of Labor 2015). For example, 38 percent of citizens in Australia volunteer, 39 percent in the United States, 35 percent in Canada and 29 percent in the United Kingdom (Charities Aid Foundation 2010).

However, the dialectical position presents when we consider how volunteering or volunteerism is identified in response to a lack of government support, dysfunction or even maleficence on the part of governments (Ganesh & McAllum 2009). Accordingly, social capital that volunteering brings can come from governments not doing their job, or doing it badly (Chapman & Kirk 2001; Knack 2002; Ganesh & McAllum 2009). Likewise, partnership agencies can overly rely on the voluntary sector to represent the views of the community, where they, like all organizations and individuals, will have their own agendas, funding targets and issues (Chapman & Kirk 2001, p. 38). The increase in volunteerism has been identified as a structural adjustment to reduced welfare seen as a way of neoliberal governments reducing expenditure on welfare and relying on unpaid labor (Ganesh & McAllum 2009). Critical scholars argue that political rhetoric effectively transfers responsibilities from the state to citizens and to the social networks of civil society (Ilmonen 2000, p. 144). As such, while volunteerism is often accepted as a noble pursuit, it is not without contradictions within the broader framework of social capital, how it sits as part of the public interest and how it is used as a public relations resource. Nevertheless, as the snapshot following indicates, coupled with capacity-building strategies and strong social capital, volunteerism's benefits to communities can be extensive.

Capacity Building and Communities-of-Interest

Onyx (2002) points out that 'What is implicit throughout most discussions of social capital is a sense of personal and collective efficacy, or personal agency' (Onyx 2002, p. 42). Where the focus on services and rights might place the individual in a *passive role,* the development of capacity building via improved social capital can make individuals *co-creators* of their collective future (Onyx 2002). Chapman and Kirk (2001) point out that in order to maximize the benefits of social capital some communities may require support to help gain necessary knowledge, skills and expertise and put them on an even footing with other communities. Public relations activity is often found at the enabling point of communities, either from within community groups or externally, such as via local government departments or agencies.

On a broad scale, the World Bank defines capacity building as an investment in people, institutions and practices that together can enable countries or communities to achieve their development objectives (World Bank 1997). Community capacity building more locally is a process of enabling 'local people to move from the status of objects manipulated by external forces and victims of social processes, to the status of subjects and active agents of change' (Albee cited in Chapman & Kirk 2001, p. 2). Thus, by extension capacity building will be strongest where social capital is highest. Communities-of-interest emerge as the physical embodiment of communities working within this space, with common interests, goals and purpose.

Community capacity building sees residents working together for social order and achieving goals through targeted mechanisms such as communications, leadership and training, policy-making and establishing networks for exchange (McGinty 2002). Capacity building is a bottom-up process reflecting local circumstances and local needs with the community itself. While *community development* requires input from outside experts, community capacity building places control within the community itself (McGinty 2002) requiring a shift in power relations away from traditional leaders and other professional stakeholders in favor of local communities steering their own course (Chapman & Kirk 2001). McGinty (2002) points out that while the demand for change emerges from civil society, other drivers, such as information technology, also play a part, with the growth in telecommunications making networking easier (McGinty 2002). This is illustrated in the social media use by communities in pursuing their goals and agendas, whereas in the past they relied on traditional media to position themselves and tell their stories.

Successful capacity building has been identified as providing the following benefits:

- communities have a direct perspective on issues facing them;
- community involvement helps to deliver programs which more accurately meet their needs;
- projects are more acceptable to the community with improvements lasting longer because communities own them;
- it helps to build community organizational skills making it easier to develop strong successor skills; and
- community involvement helps to revitalize local democracy (Chapman & Kirk 2001, p. 4).

The following snapshot illustrates how the social capital existing in a small town in regional Australia ultimately linked it to an international network of like-minded towns (communities-of-interest), achieving its goal of becoming a Booktown. As such, the story of Clunes provides a case study of successful bonding and bridging social capital, resulting in the community capacity building that renewed the town's future.

Snapshot

Clunes Booktown: Social Capital, Capacity Building and Rural Renewal

Community-Inspired Transformation

Clunes is a small rural town in central Victoria, Australia. In its heyday in the late nineteenth century, it was a booming gold-mining town, attracting miners and merchants from Europe, America and Asia. However, when the gold was depleted, the town fell into decline and throughout the twentieth century its number dwindled, the population falling to less than 1,000 residents by the beginning of the twenty-first century. Migration away from the town to cities and larger centers, plus a devastating ten-year drought, impacted harshly. Brady (2012, p. 2) notes how severe drought 'reinforces helplessness, a knowledge that the individual cannot act or make a difference.' She points out how the drought was a driving force behind a social change project for the town, which necessitated 'a willingness to dream, to imagine, and to act' (2012, p. 2). Action came in the form of a community-led rural renewal project that was to put Clunes on the international tourist map as one of 18 internally recognized Booktowns.

The fate of Clunes changed in 2007 when a group of four residents—all 'tree-changers' or rural lifestyle migrants—met to promote the idea of a town-focused renewal strategy based on cultural development in general and books in particular (Kennedy 2011). The four created the not-for-profit community organization 'Creative Clunes,' which set its sights on developing the town around the European concept of clustering together second-hand and antiquarian bookshops. Clunes's first Booktown event was a one-day festival to test the idea that books would generate tourism, intended as a branding exercise for Creative Clunes's broader cultural renewal objective (Kennedy 2011) with the ultimate aim of gaining membership into the International Organisation of Booktowns (IOB). The four residents brought together complementary core professional, governance and community skills, namely, marketing and media; government administration; community networks; logistical know-how; and writing, publishing and academic research. They used evidence-based cultural tourism research to spearhead their endeavor. Through the development of the Booktown concept, the principal objectives of the cultural renewal program were to accomplish the following:

- enhance the artistic and cultural life of the region;
- stimulate tourism; and
- build community capacity (Creative Clunes 2007; Creative Clunes & Kennedy 2013).

Ultimately Clunes was to realize 'its own place in the creative economy, through the adoption of a Booktown model and development of the town's cultural capital and built heritage assets' (Creative Clunes & Kennedy 2013, p. 1). 'In every sense ... Clunes becoming a booktown has been a community-building activity where *all* of the players have socially benefited' (Brady 2012, p. 14).

The Booktown Profile

The original Booktown was founded by Hay-on-Wye in Wales in the early 1960s. Its aim was to reverse the declining town's numbers by setting up first one bookshop, followed by others, resulting in Hay-on-Wye developing into a 'town of books' and a unique cultural, tourist destination (Seaton 1996). By the 1990s, the Booktown concept, as a means of providing a cultural tourism solution to overcoming the economic and developmental problems of rural areas, had been adopted by towns and villages in Europe, the United Kingdom and Asia, collectively forming the International Organisation of Booktowns (IOB).

The IOB defines a Booktown as 'a small rural town or village in which second-hand and antiquarian bookshops are concentrated' most having developed in villages of historic interest or scenic beauty. Clunes fitted the definition, eventually housing eight permanent bookshops, and attracting dozens of booksellers during its weekend festival in May. The town boasts both scenic beauty and history: situated on picturesque Creswick Creek in country Victoria, it also features an impressive collection of heritage buildings which has led to it being recognized as 'one of the most intact and original gold towns in Australia' (Arts Victoria cited in Creative Clunes & Kennedy 2013). Clunes is also close to regional centers and a 90-minute drive from the state capital, Melbourne, which in 2006 was named the second UNESCO City of Literature after Edinburgh (Brady 2012). This, coupled with a program of children's activities, writing workshops, visiting national and international writers, continues to generate media attention, more latterly supplemented by a social media strategy. As such, the town was well placed to aspire to a cultural hub and official International Booktown status.

Community Volunteers and Benefits

The strength in volunteer numbers was a huge asset to Clunes, with over 300 volunteers working hundreds of voluntary hours (Creative Clunes & Kennedy 2013). Brady explains how the volunteers trained the volunteers in setting up the crucial first full-time bookshop: 'We set up a computerised stock control system, trained ourselves, trained up to 50 volunteers and opened the shop seven days a week' (2012, p. 8). Overall, the endeavor resulted in significant developments and improvements for the town, including the following:

- hotel purchased and in restoration;
- 10 empty shops used in 2007 now have businesses;
- 6 retail/service businesses have further developed;
- 14 new retail businesses opened;

(Continued)

- restoration of heritage public buildings;
- town square (Collins Place) upgraded;
- ATM installed;
- real estate prices increasing;
- significant increase in accommodation options;
- railway station re-opened;
- Clunes Museum undergoing $3.23 million government-funded redevelopment;
- selection of Clunes in the 'Advancing Country Town' Program (Creative Clunes & Kennedy 2013, p. 17).

Overall, the Clunes community of 1,373 (Australian Bureau of Statistics 2011) attracts around 18,000 visitors annually to its Booktown weekend, with over 60 book-traders setting up shop for the popular public event (Brady 2012).

In summary, the 'group of volunteers [successfully] took on the rural renewal project of turning a quiet village of empty shops and public buildings into a booktown' (Brady 2012, p. 15). And, while they began with limited government support, Clunes now receives significant funding from various levels of government, arts organizations and commercial sponsors, ensuring its future, with the four original 'tree-changers' forming the consultative panel for its future development.

Conclusion

Social capital 'can be both cause and effect, so that its use can also generate effects that further increase its future availability' (Onyx 2002, p. 42). As such, examples throughout the chapter have highlighted Putnam's argument that communities become rich because they are civic rather than the reverse. But the chapter has also shown a social capital dialectic, amplified within Bourdieu's writing, of concerns for hegemonic conversion of capital, which see 'better disguised transmissions' (Bourdieu 1986, p. 16) privilege some over others. Unequal access to all forms of capital and their conversion, too much or too little social capital, are important for determining the public interest in any given context. Accordingly, the chapter does not hold social capital out as a panacea for social ills or any overarching greater public interest. Yet Knack (2002) rightly observes how the public interest may be served by the pressures which can be brought to bear by groups which 'own' their social capital, with potential benefits for the individual, the group or the cause. Fukuyama points out that, despite the negatives that can come from social capital, as outlined within this chapter, 'it is doubtless worse to have too little' social capital than too much (Fukuyama 2001, p. 12). For public relations purposes, in reconciling social capital with the public inter-est, the same must be said to apply.

Bourdieu and others, notably Gleeson-White, argue for a shift away from a money-dominated understanding of capital. Public relations has an inherent capacity to work outside the dollar value; in the organizational sense it does so, for instance, in increasingly refusing to equate advertising values with media coverage. In other words, public relations could be said to have already crossed the threshold of reducing all capital to a dollar value, through strategies for sustainability and relationships. Relationship building, as found in social capital, represents another non-dollar value which underpins the understanding of much organizational public relations activity. This is not a naïve argument of organizational public relations working for altruistic outcomes, beyond financial profit motives, nor of individual public relations practices as having no interest agenda. It simply means that public relations' currency is not always financial; rather it is inextricably connected with social and other capitals as well.

A clear potential, as well as a major challenge for public relations, is to enable the social capital *within* and *for* communities where it is in the public interest of advancing and enabling those communities. Where public relations is *part of the community*, as with advocacy roles, social capital can serve the interests from within; where public relations is *separate to the community* or *connected externally*, social capital as a form of self-actualization and advancement can provide a strong basis for partnerships. The chapter's two snapshots illustrate how social capital can work for communities—a geographical community in Clunes and a health-centered community via the mental illness lobby. Along with other examples throughout the chapter, they show how social capital can be utilized in capacity building within communities and in locating communities-of-interest where people have common goals. Likewise, communities lacking social capital, in particular bridging capital, as illustrated and discussed, are less likely to thrive, regenerate or grow.

References

Australian Bureau of Statistics (ABS) 2011, 'Census quick stats', viewed 1 March 2015, http://www.censusdata.abs.gov.au/census_services/getproduct/census/2011/quickstat/UCL221020?opendocument&navpos=220.

Bourdieu, P 1986, 'The forms of capital', in J Richardson (ed.), *Handbook of theory and research for the sociology of education*, Greenwood, New York, pp. 241–58.

Brady, T 2012, *Clunes Address*, World Booktown symposium, Paju Booksori, September.

Brooks, K 2005, 'Re-interpreting social capital—a political hijack or useful structural concept in community regeneration?', Paper presented at the *International Conference on Engaging Communities*, Brisbane, Australia, August 15–17.

Carpiano, R 2006, 'Toward a neighbourhood resource-based theory of social capital for health: can Bourdieu and sociology help?', *Social Science and Medicine*, no. 62, pp. 165–75.

Charities Aid Foundation 2010, *World Giving Index*, viewed 2 March 2015, https://www.cafonline.org/pdf/WorldGivingIndex28092010Print.pdf.

Chapman, M & Kirk, K 2001, *Lessons for community capacity building: a summary of research evidence*, Scottish Homes, Edinburgh, http://docs.scie-socialcareonline.org.uk/fulltext/scothomes30.pdf.

Coleman, JS 1981, 'Private schools, public schools, and the public interest', *National Affairs,* no. 64, http://www.nationalaffairs.com/public_interest/detail/private-schools-public-schools-and-the-public-interest.

Coleman, JS 1988, 'Social capital in the creation of human capital', *American Journal of Sociology, Supplement: Organizations and Institutions: Sociological and Economic Approaches to the Analysis of Social Structure*, no. 94, pp. S95–120.

Creative Clunes & Kennedy, M 2013, 'Tourism and the creative economy,' *OECD case study of Clunes Booktown Australia*, Community Planning and Development Program, La Trobe University, assisted by the Victorian Government Department of State Development, Business and Innovation, Melbourne, Australia.

Creative Clunes 2007, *Business Plan*, Creative ClunesInc, viewed 26 July 2013, http://www.booktown.clunes.org/documents/businessplan08.pdf

Dale, A 2001, *Sustainable development: a framework for governance*, University of British Columbia Press, Vancouver.

Demetrious, K 2013, *Public relations, activism and social change: speaking up,* Routledge, London.

Dutta, M 2011, *Communicating social change*, Routledge, New York.

Eckstein, S 2001, 'Community as gift-giving: collectivist roots of volunteerism', *American Sociological Review,* vol. 66, no. 6, pp. 829–51.

Fitch, K 2009, 'Communities and public relations', in J Johnston & C Zawawi (eds.), *Public relations: theory & practice*, 3rd edn, Allen & Unwin, Sydney, pp. 361–89.

Fukuyama, F 2001, 'Social capital, civil society and development', *Third World Quarterly,* vol. 22, no. 1, pp. 7–20.

Gallagher, K 2009, *Fourth National Mental Health Plan: an agenda for collaborative government action in mental health 2009–2014,* Commonwealth of Australia, viewed 30 March 2015, http://www.health.gov.au/internet/main/publishing.nsf/Content/9A5A0E8BDFC55D3BCA257BF0001C1B1C/$File/plan09v2.pdf.

Ganesh, S & McAllum, K 2009, 'Discourses of volunteerism', in C Beck (ed.), *Communication Yearbook 33*, Routledge, New York, pp. 343–83.

Gleeson-White, J 2014, *Six capitals: the revolution capitalism has to have,* Allen & Unwin, Sydney.

Goldberg, CA 2013, 'Struggle and solidarity: civic republican elements in Pierre Bourdieu's political sociology', *Theory of Sociology,* vol. 42, pp. 369–94. DOI 10.1007/s11186-013-9194-z.

Hanifan, LJ 1916, 'The rural school community center,' *Annals of the American Academy of Political and Social Science, New Possibilities in Education,* vol. 67, pp. 130–38.

Harpham, T & Thomas, E 2002, 'Measuring social capital theory within health surveys: key issues,' *Health Policy and Planning,* vol. 18, no. 1, pp. 106–11.

Hazelton, V, Harrison-Rexwode, J & Kennan, W 2007, 'New technologies in the formation of personal and public relations: social capital and social media', in S Duhé (ed.), *New media and public relations,* Peter Lang, New York, pp. 91–105.

Heath, R 2014, 'Terrorism, social capital, social construction, and constructive society?', *Public Relations Inquiry,* vol. 3, no. 2, pp. 227–44.

Heath, R & Ni, L 2008, *Corporate social responsibility*, Institute for Public Relations, viewed 9 June 2014, www.instituteforpr.org/corporate-social-responsibbility/.

Hjerppe, R & Taipale, V 2000, 'Foreword', in J Kajanoja & J Simpur (eds.), *Social capital: global and local perspectives*, Government Institute for Economic Research, Helsinki.

Ihlen, Ø 2005, 'The power of social capital: adapting Bourdieu to the study of public relations', *Public Relations Review*, vol. 31, pp. 492–96.

Ihlen, Ø, Bartlett, J & May, S 2011, in Ø Ihlen, J Bartlett & S May (eds.), 'Public relations and corporate social responsibility', in *The handbook of communication & social responsibility*, John Wiley & Sons, Hoboken, NJ. DOI: 10.1002/9781118083246.ch4.

Ilmonen, K 2000, 'Social capital: the concepts and its problems', in J Kajanoja & J Simpur (eds.), *Social capital: global and local perspectives*, Government Institute for Economic Research, Helsinki, pp. 141–67.

Institute of Chartered Accountants in England and Wales (ICAEW) 2012, *Acting in the public interest: A framework for analysis*, Market Foundations Initiative, file:///F:/Public%20interest%20PR/Chapter%208%20readings/Accountants%20 report%20public%20int%20rep%20web.pdf.

Iwase, T, Suzuki, E, Fujiwara, T, Takao, S, Doi, H & Kawachi, I 2012, 'Do bonding and bridging social capital have differential effects on self-rated health? A community based study in Japan', *Journal of Epidemiology and Community Health*, vol. 66, pp. 557–62. DOI: 10.1136/jech.2010.115592.

Kagan, C, Lawthom, R, Knowles, K & Burton, M 2000, 'Community activism, participation and social capital on a peripheral housing estate', Paper presented to European Community Psychology conference, Bergen, Norway.

Kajanoja, J & Simpura, J 2000 (eds.), *Social capital: global and local perspectives*, Government Institute for Economic Research, Helsinki.

Kennan, WR & Hazelton, V 2005, 'Internal public relations, social capital, and the role of effective organizational communication', in C Botan & V Hazelton (eds.), *Public relations theory II*, Lawrence Erlbaum, New York, pp. 311–38.

Kennedy, M 2011, 'Binding a sustainable future: book towns, themed place-branding and rural renewal. A case study of Clunes' Back to Booktown', in J Martin & T Budge (eds.), *The sustainability of Australia's country towns: renewal, renaissance, resilience*, VURRN Press, Ballarat, Vic, pp. 207–26.

Knack, S 2002, 'Social capital and the quality of government: evidence from the States', *American Journal of Political Science*, vol. 46, no. 4, pp. 772–85.

McGinty, S 2002, 'Community capacity building', Paper presented at the Annual Conference of the Australian Association for Research in Education, December, Brisbane, Australia, viewed 1 March 2015, http://files.eric.ed.gov/fulltext/ ED473884.pdf.

McKenzie, K, Whitley, R & Weich, S 2002, 'Editorial: social capital and mental health', *British Journal of Psychiatry*, vol. 181, pp. 280–83. DOI: 10.1192/ bjp.181.4.280.

Mitchell, N 2015, 'Being heard on mental health', *Life Matters,* Australian Broadcasting Corporation, viewed 6 May 2015, http://www.abc.net.au/radio/ programitem/pglR6WPbWV?play=true.

Moulier-Boutang, Y 2012, *Cognitive capitalism,* Polity, London.

NAMI 2014, 'Convention: National Day of Action 2014', viewed 6 May 2015, http://www2.nami.org/Template.cfm?Section=Convention&Template=/Content-Management/ContentDisplay.cfm&ContentID=164283.

NAMI 2015, '2015–2017 Strategic plan', viewed 6 May 2015, http://www.nami.org/getattachment/About-NAMI/Our-Structure/2015-2017NAMIStrategicPlan.pdf.

Narayan, D 1999a, 'Bonds and bridges: social capital and poverty', *Poverty Research Working Paper no. 2167,* World Bank, August, viewed 30 March 2015, https://play.google.com/books/reader?id=GhYLuMX2vLMC&printsec=frontcover&output=reader&hl=en&pg=GBS.PA1.w.1.0.0.

Narayan, D, 1999b, 'Bonds and bridges: social capital and poverty', World Bank, July, viewed 30 March 2015, http://info.worldbank.org/etools/docs/library/9747/narayan.pdf.

NCVCO 2012, 'How many people regularly volunteer in the UK?', *Civil Society Almanac,* viewed 29 March 2015, http://data.ncvo.org.uk/a/almanac12/how-many-people-regularly-volunteer-in-the-uk/.

Onyx, J 2002, 'The relationship between social capital and sustainable practices: revisiting "the Commons"', *Sustainability and Social Science Round Table Proceedings,* viewed 8 May 2015, http://www.minerals.csiro.au/sd/pubs/Onyx_Final.pdf.

Patel, V & Copeland, J 2011, 'The great push for mental health: why it matters for India', *Indian Journal of Medical Research,* vol. 134, no. 4, p. 407–09. http://www.ncbi.nlm.nih.gov/pmc/articles/PMC3237235/.

Pierce, J 1999, 'Making communities the strong link in sustainable development', in J. Pierce & A Dale (eds.), *Communities, development and sustainability across Canada.* University of British Columbia Press, Vancouver.

Productivity Commission 2003, *Social capital: reviewing the concept and its policy implications,* Commonwealth of Australia, Canberra.

Putnam, RD 1993, 'The prosperous community: social capital and public life', *The American Prospect,* vol. 13, Spring, viewed 20 March 2015, http://xroads.virginia.edu/~hyper/DETOC/assoc/13putn.html.

Putnam, RD 1995, 'Bowling alone: America's declining social capital', *Journal of Democracy,* vol. 6, no. 1, pp. 65–78. DOI: 10.1353/jod.1995.0002.

Putnam, RD 2000, *Bowling alone: the collapse and revival of American community,* Simon & Schuster, New York.

Saffer, AJ, Taylor, M & Yang, A 2013, 'Political public relations in advocacy: building online influence and social capital', *Public Relations Journal,* vol. 7, no. 4, pp. 1–35.

Seaton, AV 1999, 'Booktowns as tourism developments in peripheral areas,' *International Journal of Tourism Research,* no. 1, pp. 389–99.

Siisiäinen, M 2000, 'Two concepts of social capital: Bourdieu vs Putnam', *ISTR Fourth International Conference, The Third Sector: For What and for Whom?* University College, Dublin, viewed 25 March 2015, http://dlc.dlib.indiana.edu/dlc/bitstream/handle/10535/7661/siisiainen.pdf?sequence=1&isAllowed=y.

Story, WT, Taleb, F, Ahasan, SM & Ali, LA 2015, 'Validating the measurement of social capital in Bangladesh: a cognitive approach', *Qualitative Health Research,* vol. 25, no. 6, pp. 806–19. DOI: 10.1177/1049732315580106.

United States Department of Labor 2015, *Volunteering in the United States 2014,* Bureau of Labor Statistics, viewed 30 March 2015, http://www.bls.gov/news.release/volun.nr0.htm.

Varshney, A 2002, *Ethnic conflict and civic life: Hindus and Muslims in India*, Yale University Press, New Haven, CT.

Verhoeven, P 2008, 'Who's in and who's out? Studying the effects of communication management on social cohesion', *Journal of Communication Management*, vol. 2, no. 2, pp. 124–35.

World Bank 1997, *Partnerships for capacity building in Africa: a progress report*, World Bank, Washington, DC.

7 The Law, Social Change and the Public Interest

Legislators and policy makers recognise that the public interest will change over time and according to the circumstances of each situation.
(Carter & Bouris 2006, p. 4)

Introduction

From Plato in the fifth century BCE to Habermas today, 'every philosopher of any stature has felt compelled to comment on the law at some length.' This observation by socio-legal scholars Anthony Walsh and Craig Hemmens (2011, p. 10) confirms the priority that has been ascribed to the importance of law in society. The Platonic attention to the law was intended to 'regulate self-interested, contentious, and sometimes evil behaviour of mortals' (Walsh & Hemmens 2011, p. 11). As such, Plato proposed laws and legal institutions which managed the compromise between good and evil because justice was 'a middle point between the two' (Plato in Walsh & Hemmens 2001, p. 10). For Plato, like many other philosophers and leading theorists, the structural and discursive practices embodied within the law and argued within jurisprudence provided ways to better understand and manage the complex society in which he lived.

Modern democracies also place a high priority on the laws of the land. Steven Vago (2009) argues that mechanisms and structures of law have grown within Western society as these societies have become more complex, disconnected, pluralist and heterogeneous. He contrasts these with some traditional societies which continue to rely on custom as their primary source of governing, resolving disputes through conciliation or mediation by civic elders, community determinations or other moral authorities. Because traditional societies are often more homogeneous, social relations are more direct, interests are held in common and informal mechanisms for control are usually effective. Conversely, where societies have become more heterogeneous and 'common interests decrease in relation to special interests,' potential for conflict and dispute within these societies occurs (Vago 2009, p. 2). Habermas (1996, p. 113) considers the development of law within post-traditional societies as 'necessary to offset deficits arising from the collapse of traditional ethical life.' Galanter (1981), meanwhile, laments the loss of what he terms 'indigenous law' where laws might be dealt with at their source but instead are now managed within the formal structures of legislatures and courts. The momentum that follows is 'the more civilized man becomes, the greater man's need for law, and the more law he creates. Law is but a response to social needs' (Hoebel 1954, p. 292).

Within this complex and changing framework, the public interest can be increasingly difficult to determine, more splintered and, necessarily, more pluralist. What may be a consensus and common interest, thus representing the public interest in traditional societies, does not as easily translate into the complex, heterogeneous society. At the same time the law continues to hold up the public interest as the standard, while seemingly paradoxically, also conflating with self-interest. As Walsh and Hemmens note, 'the law is a mechanism by which diverse individual and community interests become so close as to being the same thing' (2011, p. 2). For our purposes, this chapter attempts to explicate this complicated and muddy notion of the law, balancing the interests of the individual with the public interest, or multiple public interests, while also acknowledging that there is no such thing as a 'definitive public interest.' As Australian constitutional lawyer Patrick Keyzer advises, 'The truth is that there can be no single version of the public interest' (2010, p. 91).

As such, under the law, interests often compete. In some cases the balance will be clear; in others, there will be implied competing interests—and both apply to the many instances that find public relations at the interface. For example, under the laws that apply to journalists and their sources in New Zealand, the public interest balance is spelled out. Section 68 of the *New Zealand Evidence Act* states that 'the public interest in the disclosure of evidence of the identity of the informant outweighs ... the public interest in the communication of facts and opinion to the public by the news media and ... the ability of the media to access sources of facts' (Evidence Act 2006 NZ, Section 68, para 2). Elsewhere, laws have been developed to support the public interest, but there is less clarity. For example, changes to British whistle-blower legislation in 2013, requiring whistle-blowers to ensure their claim is in the public interest, have been criticized for the lack of definition of what is in the public interest (Landau 2013, n.p.). Importantly for public relations, laws relating to many fields, such as employment, media activity and ownership, privacy, freedom of information, planning and the environment, are among the many areas where those in either organizational or activist roles might find themselves having to explain or justify their version of the public interest. The chapter uses the example of freedom of information laws as a field of law in which this may occur.

There are arguably three principle functions of law: social change, social control and dispute settlement (Vago 2009). This chapter focuses primarily on the first two: social change, due to its apposite relationship to the study of public interest and public relations; social control, because of it approximation with social order via formal and informal mechanisms. Both these fields, as we will see throughout the chapter, extend many of the themes that have emerged throughout the book. The relationship between social change and the law was succinctly expressed by American jurist and philosopher Oliver Wendell Holmes Jr, who noted, 'The law embodies the story of a nation's development through many centuries' (1881, p. 5 cited in Vago, p. 3). Indeed, legal systems stand in close relationship with interests, goals, norms, mores and values of their society and the political and economic climate with which they are interwoven (Hoebel 1954; Habermas 1996; Vago 2009; Walsh & Hemmens 2011). At the same time the association of public relations with social change is both logical and well documented (L'Etang 2008; Banks 1995; Ihlen, van Ruler & Fredricksson 2009; Demetrious 2013) as are its links to social order (Dozier & Lauzen 2000; Holtzhausen & Voto 2002). In this book, these connections are further explored through the work of Habermas, which examines the law through the lens of communication, social movements and civil society and via the dual nature that exists across positive and natural law, structures, morality and culture.

Essentially, there are three broad areas or themes through which the law and the public interest intersect with public relations that will be explored within this chapter. The first centers on how the public interest may be viewed as a shape-shifter and how it evolves and adapts to the social values of specific times and contexts. This is illustrated in Ireland's same-sex marriage referendum, examined in the chapter as a snapshot, which also identifies the public's role in spurring this referendum to fruition through the Irish Republic's Constitutional Convention. It is further reflected in the analysis of freedom of information (FoI) laws, which show how the public interest can move from abstraction to application and how public relations may be involved. The second is the social control and order represented in the courts as the forum for enforcing laws and the importance placed on open justice in representing the public interest to the citizenry. Developments within certain courts, including flexible Indigenous practices, are aptly illustrated through the work of the Australian Federal Court's moves to go 'on country' into remote Indigenous communities. The third intersection between the law, the public interest and public relations is in the functional role played by courts information officers (CIOs) in communicating and interpreting what goes on in courts and legal proceedings, both for the news media and, increasingly, directly to community groups, schools and other members of society via the courts' own media channels. These themes are overlaid with a theoretical explication of the law's relationship to social change and how public relations can play a part as both a function of the law (for example, via open justice) and within the parameters of legal structures (for example, via FoI).

Public Interest, Freedom of Information and Tips from the Law

As we already know from elsewhere in this book, the law has been debating the concept of the public interest and the common good for centuries.

Accordingly, we can borrow some legal reasoning in reviewing the public interest as a concept that has broader application, including for public relations. In their analysis of the public interest within the context of freedom of information (FoI) laws in Commonwealth countries, Carter and Bouris (2006) note that legislation *intentionally* does not define the public interest in order for it to be defined within the context to which it is applied. Indeed, law reform reviews in Australia and Canada have explicitly recommended that the public interest remain undefined (Carter & Bouris 2006, p. 4). Carter and Bouris (2006, p. 4) note the following:

> The public interest is an amorphous concept, which is typically not defined in access to information legislation. This flexibility is intentional. Legislators and policy makers recognise that the public interest will change over time and according to the circumstances of each situation.

FoI requests represent a field in which competing interests are often played out, with the public interest often in contestation. Carter and Bouris (2006) note how commercial exemptions have been found to be the most difficult type of exemption to override in the public interest, especially where timing of the release of information is important. For example, in one Irish case it was determined that despite a strong public interest, it would have been premature to release publically sought information. In contrast, in a case in Canada it was found that the only fair way to balance the public interest and corporate loss was to undertake some fact-finding within the company in question (Carter & Bouris 2006). While commercial interests of a public agency may favor release of information because of the need for accountability of public funds, in other circumstances public safety may override commercial interests (Carter & Bouris 2006). Importantly, public interest disclosure is likely to be strong where information would assist in public understanding of a current debate (Carter & Bouris 2006, p. 9). Thus, for example, in Canada the public debate surrounding Quebec's independence was seen to be an overriding public interest in disclosure. Carter and Bouris (2006) list dozens of examples across fields as diverse as accountability of funds to nursing home practices, to air and nuclear plant safety, to the fair treatment of a PhD candidate, indicating that public interest decisions cut across just about every conceivable field within society.

The vagaries of the public interest were tested in the Australian Federal Court judgment of *McKinnon v Secretary, Department of Treasury* (2005), an FoI case that includes 280 mentions of the public interest, in which Justice Tamberlin asserted (para. 12, his emphasis):

> The public interest is not one homogenous undivided concept. It will often be multi-faceted and the decision-maker will have to consider and evaluate the relative weight of these facets before reaching a final

conclusion as to where the public interest resides. This ultimate evaluation of the public interest will involve a determination of what are the relevant facets of the public interest that are competing and the comparative importance that ought to be given to them so that "the public interest" can be ascertained and served. In some circumstances, one or more considerations will be of such overriding significance that they will prevail over all others. In other circumstances, the competing considerations will be more finely balanced so that the outcome is not so clearly predictable. For example, in some contexts, interests such as public health, national security, anti-terrorism, defence or international obligations may be of overriding significance when compared with other considerations.

Briefly, the *McKinnon* case centered on an application from Australia's national daily newspaper, *The Australian*, seeking access to Federal Treasury documents concerning bracket creep in income tax and possible misuse of the First Home Owners Scheme grant. The case moved through several court channels, eventually ending in the High Court. Judith Bannister (2006, p. 962) points out this case was 'not about whether it is, or is not, in the public interest to know about how taxes are being collected and spent,' rather it was fundamentally about who decides what is 'in the public interest' and whether any scope exists for independent external review of that decision. What this instance highlighted is the importance of the context in which the public interest can be applied—in this case within a public service department. Accordingly, what this means for those in the role of facilitating or managing information—and public relations is certainly among those at the forefront of this—is how determinations of what is in the public interest are not necessarily abstract but are indeed quite concrete when decisions need to be made. As Carter and Bouris (2006, p. 3) point out, 'Deciding in which aspects and to what extent the public interest is relevant involves the exercise of judgment and discretion by the decision-maker.' This reality has implications for public relations within all sorts of interfaces—as communicators and advisers in industry, government and non-profits, as well as for individuals and interest groups. Whether seeking out information or having your own information sought by another (often the media), the priority placed on the public interest within the context of other interests will be of fundamental importance and, as such, an appreciation of the public interest both as a concept and a concrete application can only assist the involvement of public relations in the process.

Social Change and Social Order

As noted earlier, social change lies at the core of public relations (Banks 1995; L'Etang 2008; Dozier & Lauzen 2000; Ihlen, van Ruler & Fredricksson 2009; Demetrious 2013) and social order can be affected by social change.

While separate concepts, the two overlap, and the chapter explores their multifarious, separate but interlocking dimensions with the public interest and public relations firmly in sight. The concept of social change is defined by Walsh and Hemmens (2011, p. 282) as:

> any relatively enduring alteration in social relationships, behavior patterns, values, norms, and attitudes occurring over time ... every time society decides that the formerly unacceptable is acceptable or the formerly acceptable is now unacceptable it is engaging in social change.

Theories of social change and the law, as two concepts working together, focus on the cause-and-effect structure of the process. Legal thinking is divided over the question of whether laws change society or society changes laws (Vago 2009; Walsh & Hemmens 2011). On the one hand, it is argued the 'law is determined by the sense of justice and the moral sentiments of the population, and legislation can only achieve results by staying relatively close to the prevailing social norms' (Aubert in Vago 2009, p. 333). On the other hand, the law can be the vehicle through which a planned social evolution can be brought about (Vago 2009).

Vago (2009) finds a middle ground, suggesting more of a continuum or a series of chain reactions or, simply, the law serving as a conduit that guides the social reform that is already in progress (Walsh & Hemmens 2011, p. 285). In other words, there is a reciprocal relationship between law and social change. At the same time, social order is maintained through social controls, either informally or formally, which work through the internalization of group norms and mores, plus the application of external pressures (Clinard & Meier 2008; Vago 2009). Sociologists identify group norms of common practice and mores of right and wrong as being more effective in smaller communities and homogeneous societies with a tendency for more formal controls to emerge in more heterogeneous societies with competing sets of values, interests and ideologies (Vago 2009). It is important, therefore, to explicate and understand the interface between social change, social order and the law, which then provides a basis for further exploring the public interest and the interplay with public relations. Through its agency of social change movements or advancing certain interests, public relations is fundamentally and centrally, though often inadvertently, involved in understanding, using and even contributing to the legal process. Likewise, social controls, which bring about social order, exist with the cultural and structural systems within which public relations functions.

Habermas points to the complexity that exists within the law, proposing it has a dual character: first, as a system of knowledge (or set of public norms), and second, as a system of actions (or set of institutions) embedded in a social context (Rehg 1996, p. xxiv). As such, he combines theories proposed by Niklas Luhmann and John Rawls in explaining the embedded nature of the law across society. Thus, Luhmann's systems approach is too limited because it does not take account of inter-relationships with other sub-systems via 'empirically observed interdependencies' (Habermas 1996, p. 50). For Habermas the duality of the law must include interdependencies between the law, the political process, the public sphere and political culture, so he rejects Luhmann's notion that 'law can neither perceive nor deal with problems that burden society as a whole' (Habermas 1996, p. 51). As a consequence, Habermas looks beyond a systems-only approach, coupling it with the normative theory of justice proposed by Rawls in his *Theory of Justice* (1971), which embraces social stability and social norms. Rawls follows a social-contract model in developing the idea of a 'well-ordered' society, which makes possible just cooperation of free and equal citizens (Habermas 1996, p. 57). However, on its own this, too, provides an insufficient explanation for the role of the law in society because it does not consider how legal institutions implement and manage the complexity of competing interests and functions.

> The lesson of Habermas's reading of Rawls and Luhmann is this: if an account of modern law is to be neither sociologically empty nor normatively blind, then it must incorporate a dual perspective. The theorist of law can ignore neither the participants' own normative understanding of their legal system nor those external mechanisms and processes that are accessible to the sociological observer.
>
> (Rehg 1996, p. xxiii)

Habermas further sees a mutual accommodation between positive law (cultural sources of law which are socially constructed) and natural law (based on a universal set of moral standards) and it is this balance in which he finds the title for his exploration of the law in *Between Facts and Norms* (1996 book title):

> Rational natural law, having distinguished law from morality, took into consideration the tension *between facts and norms* built into positive law itself. This gave it from the start a more realistic focus than a morally oriented theory of political justice.
>
> (Habermas 1996, p. 65, my italics)

He suggests that 'moral legislation is *reflected* in juridical legislation, morality in legality, duties of virtue in legal duties, and so forth' (Habermas 1996, p. 106, his italics). While they have a complementary relationship, they should not be seen as imitations of each other, rather, 'norms of action *branch out* into moral and legal rules' (Habermas, 1996, p. 107, his italics). Therefore, 'as soon as rational collective will-formation aims at concrete legal programs, it must cross the boundaries of justice discourse and include problems of value (that depend on the clarification of collective identity) and the balancing of interests' (Habermas 1996, p. 154). Importantly, the law allows for members of civil society to function without domination from more powerful systems:

> The point is to protect areas of life that are functionally dependent on social integration through values, norms and consensus formation, to preserve them from falling prey to the systematic imperatives of economic and administrative subsystems growing with dynamics of their own, and to defend them from becoming converted over, through the steering mediums of the law, to a principle of association which is, for them, dysfunction.
>
> (Habermas 1984, p. 516)

Accordingly, the law should provide solutions for those who are less powerful within political structures—those within informal associations and ordinary citizens who work outside official political structures—which, in turn, place pressure and input into the formal, more powerful institutions (Grodnick 2005; Bohman & Rehg 2014, n.p.). Grodnick (2005) argues that while weak publics may be estranged from decision-making processes, they can be responsible for identifying social problems that are brought to the attention of society at large because, after all, 'weak publics are more aware of and sensitive to the affairs of society and the ordeals and hardships of individual members' (Grodnick 2005, p. 398).

This theory neatly places the idea of social change within the legal context. Yet, while this calls for power to begin at the bottom and filter its way up the institutionalized system (Grodnick 2005; Habermas 1984, 1996), the concept sits in contrast to Foucault's idea of law and power. Foucault's critique of law sees the law caught between the two poles of what he called 'bio-power'—discipline and government—with law simply a part of the continuum of power relations (Tadros 1998, p. 78). Foucault's criticism of law centered on what he saw as 'a system of rules [which] ... thus proceeds from domination to domination' (Foucault 1977 in Tadros 1998, p. 100). Tadros (1998, p. 93) notes how, for Foucault:

> ... legal theory has remained focused on the legitimacy of legislating on certain acts (pornography, civil disobedience, homosexuality, prostitution, and so on) the way in which law operates has shifted to the regulation of the lives. The modern regulatory aspect of law, then, ought not to be understood merely as 'power-conferring' but should be seen as intervening in the social construction and government of the modern subject.

Foucault saw power as operating 'through successive, trivial moments ... The succession of disciplinary forces ... results in a dominating form which both constructs the subject and subjects him to subtle forms of control' (in Tadros 1998, p. 78). While Foucault's writings are illuminating on the role of power in social systems, some argue that 'Foucault's historical analyses of the asylum, the prison, etc., succeed brilliantly at highlighting disturbing features, but … fail at the task of providing a coherent and plausible account of social order' (Simon 1994, p. 953). Habermas, alternately, presents a more holistic account of how social change and social law are affected, particularly within legislative contexts. He refers to problems within lawmaking as 'legitimation dilemmas' or 'legitimation crises' which can be identified 'when citizens do not support the actions of the state' (Grodnick 2005, p. 402). Grodnick suggests the importance of understanding Habermas's idea of 'crisis' is not the 'usual' type of crisis when a catastrophe occurs—one which is often associated with public relations' understanding of crisis management—rather, it is more subtle as something that undermines the political or legal system.

> A crisis occurs when law-making is estranged from the normative initiatives and the communicative will of the citizenry, and this provokes a political crisis that undermines the legitimacy of both systems … In a properly constituted state, the citizens are ensured that the formal system is acting legitimately and in accordance with the law that they authored.
>
> (Grodnick 2005, pp. 402–3)

Accordingly, if the system brakes down, less powerful publics should present a 'warning system' (Habermas 1996, p. 359) to dominant publics. In a normative context, dominant publics are thus compelled to consider these and be responsive. The snapshot, following, speaks to this issue, through the analysis of the Constitutional Convention in Ireland as emerging out of the civil dissatisfaction of the political system at the time.

The 'Squeaky Wheel'

The social order can thus be deconstructed and reconstructed through social movements bringing weight upon governments to legislate change (Dozier & Lauzen 2000; Walsh & Hemmens 2011). As such, social movements that work for the collective good are seen to be working in the public interest, though not necessarily without competing interests. Chief among the challenges for legislators therefore is how to preserve or advance law and change in the public interest without offending the cultural pluralism that makes up society, finding a balance between minority groups and the mainstream (Walsh & Hemmens 2011). In democratic societies social movements are not only tolerated but also are promoted and, as such, the 'squeaky wheel' approach is used to gain attention to a cause or interest (Walsh & Hemmens 2011, p. 285). But, though effective in democracies, the squeaky wheel approach to social change movements is often not tolerated in nondemocratic societies, which also preclude extra-legal tactics—often the stuff of public relations' activity—such as media and social media campaigns and protest rallies (Walsh & Hemmens 2011, p. 285).

While often embedded in decades of protest and lobbying, the citizenry can effect change, thus providing the impetus for new laws. Movements opposed to war, racial injustice, global warming, animal cruelty and child labor have, in varying degrees, been instrumental in initiating changed laws reflecting shifts in community values and attitudes. Take same-sex marriage, for instance. Between 2001 and 2015, 18 countries legalized same-sex marriage, with the first ceremony taking place in the Netherlands on 1 April 2001. Denmark was first to legalize civil partnerships for same-sex couples in 1989, moving to same-sex marriage in June 2012. The movement gained momentum in the United States over a space of only a few years: in 2013 six states plus the District of Columbia (or 11 percent of the population) had same-sex marriage laws; by 2015, 37 states plus the capital district (or nearly 72 percent of the population) had introduced same-sex marriage laws (Sedghi 2015). In May 2015, Ireland became the first country to vote for same-sex marriage by referendum, as examined in the following snapshot.

Snapshot

Ireland's Same-Sex Marriage Referendum

24 May 2015: 'Ireland has voted by a huge majority to legalise same-sex marriage, becoming the first country in the world to do so by popular vote in a move hailed as a social revolution and welcomed around the world.'

The quote from *The Guardian* (McDonald 2015, n.p.) summed up global elation following Ireland's 'Gay marriage referendum' in which legalized same-sex marriage was, for the first time, decided by popular vote. The historic world-first saw the Irish Republic's Fine Gael-Labour coalition put the question of marriage equality to the nation, with the proposal to unambiguously redefine marriage as between 'two persons.' The referendum ultimately saw the changed wording, for a revised Constitution, to include:

... marriage may be contracted in accordance with law by two persons without distinction as to their sex.

Ireland was to thus achieve an historic determination, becoming the first country in the world to expressly guarantee marriage equality in its Constitution via referendum (O'Mohoney 2014a, n.p.). A majority of 62 percent of Ireland voted in favor of gay marriage, ignoring the conservative 'No' line (McDonald 2015). The 'Yes' vote was described as 'a social revolution' by health minister Leo Varadkar, marking a milestone in Ireland's journey toward a more secular society (McDonald 2015, n.p.).

(Continued)

Ireland's Prime Minister (or Taoiseach) Enda Kenny told his country's gay community:

> In the privacy of the ballot box, the people made a public statement. With today's vote we have disclosed who we are. We are a generous, compassionate, bold and joyful people who say yes to inclusion, yes to generosity, yes to love, yes to gay marriage.
>
> (in McDonald 2015, n.p.)

The voter turnout of 61 percent was particularly high among younger citizens, the pro-reform vote energized by a social media campaign which urged Irish expatriates to 'be home to vote,' with #hometovote trending throughout the day (McDonald 2015, n.p.) and many of those within the diaspora returning for the occasion. Veteran Irish gay rights campaigner Senator David Norris, who was instrumental in lobbying the Irish government to decriminalize homosexuality in 1993, said he hoped the result would inspire other countries to follow, warning 'The battle is not over' for many homosexual people across the world (McDonald 2015, n.p.).

The Constitutional Convention

Ireland's same-sex marriage referendum was initiated by the country's Constitutional Convention, also called a citizen's assembly, which was established in 2013 'in partial response to public demands for institutional reform to address the governmental failings so starkly illustrated by the economic collapse of 2008' (Carolan 2013a, para. 2). Carolan notes how the Constitutional Convention offered the opportunity for a novel experiment in direct civic participation (Carolan 2013a). The Convention consisted of 66 members of the public, 33 elected representatives and an independent chair, described as a curious hybrid of 'ordinary citizens and experienced political representatives' (Carolan 2013a, para. 3). The mix of 'ordinary people' and politicians, originally criticized because of the potential for politicians to dominate, ultimately proved to be a highly successful formula which achieved international interest (Farrell 2015, n.p.)

The Convention investigated eight proposals, producing 38 recommendations including 18 referendums, on a wide range of topics, including the same-sex marriage referendum (Farrell 2015; Carolan 2013a). Following are the eight proposals:

- Reduction of the Presidential term of office to five years and the alignment with local and European elections;
- Reduction of the voting age to 17;
- Review of the Dáil electoral system;
- Irish citizens' right to vote at Irish Embassies in Presidential elections;
- Provisions for same-sex marriage;
- Amendment to the clause on the role of women in the home and encouraging greater participation of women in public life;
- Increasing the participation of women in politics; and
- Removal of the offence of Blasphemy from the Constitution (Carolan 2013a, para. 5).

During its deliberations, the Constitutional Convention took heed of opinion polls that suggested a substantial majority of Irish residents favored same-sex marriage (Carolan 2013a). Indeed, a 2012 Opinion Poll which found 66 percent supported the change was closely mirrored in the final result of 62 percent in 2015. Research Director for the Convention Professor David Farrell argued that it 'exceeded most observers' expectations' (Farrell 2015, n.p.) as a 'world first: a random selection of ordinary citizens sitting cheek by jowl with elected politicians, deliberating for a year on a range of constitutional issues, producing a large number of recommendations' (Farrell 2015, n.p.). Yet he, like others, held concerns over the broader questions of reform and the lack of government follow-through on other issues raised by the Convention (Carolan 2013b).

> This may be most relevant to the question of electoral reform where there is an obvious divergence between (a perhaps waning) public interest in reform of a political system that failed so spectacularly in the years leading up to 2008 and the self-interest of the politicians who are chosen by that system. If that is the case, the Convention may end up not as the innovative experiment in deliberative democracy that some may have hoped but as the final diversionary set piece in the political establishment's gentle deflation and eventual euthanisation of demands for substantial reform.
>
> (Carolan 2013b, para. 13)

And there were concerns that the conciliatory tone of the Convention had altered to become a battleground of interest-focused rhetoric prior to the referendum (Carolan 2013; O'Mohoney 2014a). Ultimately, however, the Irish Constitutional Convention did what no other citizen-led assembly had done: it successfully put a social movement onto its country's political agenda, exposed it to national debate, and let the people decide what they believed was in the public interest.

The Role of Courts

While the legal system in the broadest sense includes all legally regulated action systems (Habermas 1996), the principle place for the administration of criminal and civil justice are the courts, representing both symbolic and practical centers of the mediation between the state and society, and the individual and the individual. Walsh and Hemmens (2011) point out that courts, as formal forms of social control, usually exist in inverse proportions to the informal controls of family, school, church and community; that is, the higher the informal social controls the less need for formal controls. This chapter identifies and analyzes three key intersections between the courts, public interest and public relations. The first is the role of the courts in administering law and remaining open to public scrutiny through the principle of 'open justice'; the second is the communication function that has developed for and within the courts in facilitating access for the media and the public; the third is the role played by the courts in representing minorities and giving people 'voice.' Discussion of each of these intersections follows, concluding with a snapshot of courts going 'on country' in regional Australia in responding to cultural native title land claims.

Through remaining open, courts provide the opportunity for the public to monitor the due process of the law. As Habermas suggests, 'regulations demanding that certain proceedings be public ... for example those providing for open court hearings, are also related to ... public opinion' (Habermas 1974, p. 50). Effectively, then, as the courts provide the forum through which the public engages with the law, the public interest lies in the principle of open justice, which sees the legal process in action, transparent and subject to scrutiny. This utilitarian approach to transparency in courts is identified as a fundamental principle of a democratic system of law, summed up by Jeremy Bentham (1843, p. 310) in the often-cited quote: 'Publicity is the very soul of justice ... It keeps the judge himself, while trying, under trial.'

Somewhat paradoxically then, while courts (for the most part) are open to the public, most people do not attend courts. As a result, the media have taken up this role on behalf of the public, with a consequence that media practice—either through journalism or popular culture, such as film and television—tends to dominate public understanding of the juridical process. It has been argued that for most members of the public, who have never entered a court, the journalist's record of the courts is their principle window into the justice system (Tuchman 1978). This issue is a source of significant scholarly attention, most recently in light of how the news media increasingly focus on entertainment, drama and titillation from the courts (Ericson et al. 1987, 1998; Cohn & Dow 1998). Habermas (1989, p. 207) points to the risk therefore that lies with publicity through media coverage distorting perceptions of proceedings because:

> ... the trials in criminal court that are interesting enough to be documented and hawked in the mass media reverse the critical principle of publicity in an analogous manner; instead of serving the control of the jurisdictional process by the assembled citizens of the state, publicity increasingly serves the packaging of court proceedings for the mass culture of assembled consumers.

Partly in response to the high levels of media attention, courts in many Western democracies have, at various stages during the latter part of the twentieth century and into this century, appointed courts information officers (CIOs) to facilitate access, assist with accuracy and manage issues (Johnston 2008, 2011; Johnston & McGovern 2013). This role also sought to bridge what has at times been an uneasy tension between the courts and the media. The principle functions of the CIO include media liaison, community engagement, public education and judicial support. The adoption of CIOs into courts in Australia, the United States and elsewhere met with near universal support from journalists, the judiciary and other stakeholders (Parker 1998; Johnston 2005, 2008). In the United States they were seen as 'indispensable as a supplier of documentary information and answers to process questions' (quoted in Ginsburg 1995, p. 2122). In Australia, Parker (1998, p. 151) noted how 'given that the public's need is actually a need for *accurate* information, the function of these officers in preventing mistakes and correcting efforts is obviously an important one.' As the role of the CIO gained increased traction, this group of court professionals has been in a unique position to assist in the understanding of the courts and the processes of open justice, through facilitating and interpreting the law to the media and community sectors (Johnston 2011).

The courts also seek to serve the public interest while simultaneously giving voice to minority groups, although this can be a complex process, raising issues of the separation of powers between the courts and elected governments. O'Mohoney (2014b, p. 192) notes how the 'most controversial constitutional rights cases, on issues such as abortion, the death penalty, and same-sex marriage' are as much political issues as legal issues. Accordingly, constitutional scholars pay considerable attention to questions of whether courts or parliaments should be the final arbiter of the public interest (Keyzer 2010; O'Mohoney 2014b). O'Mohoney argues that courts:

> have long been the refuge of minority groups seeking to pursue a right that is denied to them. Since judges are charged with protecting individual rights without regard to popular opinion, oppressed or unpopular minorities can sometimes achieve legal change through constitutional litigation that might not have been possible through lobbying or electoral pressure.
>
> (O'Mohoney 2014a, n.p.)

Parliaments, on the other hand, are 'less suitable than courts for protecting minority rights' due to the imperative for parliamentarians to be elected by popular vote (O'Mohoney 2014a, n.p.). It should, however, also be acknowledged that in some judicial systems judges, like politicians, are also appointed by popular vote. O'Mohoney further argues that while constitutional courts might appear to be 'counter-majoritarian,' on closer and longer-term analysis, the alternative is often the case whereby:

> … viewing judicial review as a process of constructing the fundamental commitments of the people lends further weight to the argument that it is *not* actually counter-majoritarian: it may seem so in the short term, but over the long term, the court is actually giving expression to the will of the people.
>
> (O'Mohoney 2014b, p. 200 my emphasis)

His views find support from Australian constitutional law scholar Patrick Keyzer who argues how Australia's High Court, as the 'voice' of the Constitution, 'should have the capacity to gauge the views of the entire community in framing its judgments as to community values' (2010, p. 96). At the same time, Keyzer argues that the public interest can be served by constitutional courts in providing access to justice for those marginalized groups that do not have access to resources, also following the counter-majoritarian logic. The courts can provide opportunities for balancing minority and majority views in ways that may be inconceivable in parliaments. 'Interests might not otherwise be advanced because of prevailing power relationships within society that can be brought to a constitutional court and discussed and considered in an open and deliberative environment' (Keyzer 2010, p. 96). While minority claims should not displace the function of the legislature as the principle mechanism for the expression of the community, judicial review of the process, via constitutional adjudications, may be seen to 'involve value choices about the terms of our collective life' (Keyzer 2010, p. 96).

Lifeworld, Language and Indigenous Sentencing Courts

While Walsh and Hemmens (2011 p. 3) note the importance of looking to culture in their examination of law, identifying six elements of culture with which the law interacts—beliefs, values, norms, symbols, technology and language—courts can and do represent cultural conflict for many actors. At this point, we return to Habermas's understanding of lifeworld in exploring the cultural context of the courts. Rehg notes that a shared lifeworld facilitates acceptance of laws which stabilize 'a communicatively integrated group insofar as it removes a large body of assumptions from challenge' (1996, p. xvi). Thus, while Habermas suggests that within a systems theory approach legal systems are 'translated' by their own language to, for example, judges, lawyers and court staff (Rehg 1996, p. xxii), they can be likewise *not* translatable to outside actors who are brought into the legal environment, for example, defendants, witnesses, victims and onlookers. In such contexts, cultural disjunctures can occur. What happens when actors involved in the courts do not have access to the language, or indeed culture, of the lifeworld?

There is a solid body of literature that has examined the language of the courts and how legal discourse is both exclusionary and mystifying (Johnston & Breit 2010; McBarnet 1981; Vago 2009; Walsh & Hemmens 2011), generally accepting that 'there is a special rhetoric of law and it has its own vocabulary' (Vago 2009, p. 6). The law has even been referred to as a 'linguistically challenged profession' (Chambliss & Seidman 1982 cited in Vago 2009, p. 6).

This is not unique to the law. Foucault (1984) identifies language and discourse as part of all social structures, with professional discourses intended to exclude some and include others, thus bringing knowledge and power together. While one of the principle roles of the CIOs is to assist the media in interpreting the work of the courts, for members of the public who are required to engage with the process, culture, education, life experience, technology, context, circumstance, access and (mis)understanding, obstacles to understanding, empowerment and justice may occur. Weak and subaltern publics or individuals without means may be deeply disadvantaged. One response by the courts has been to adapt its language to be more responsive to all actors. Vago notes such a move has begun in the legal profession with 'law schools beginning to understand that good English makes sense' (2011, p. 6).

Extending this argument, legal scholar Mark Galanter in 1981 argued for a move away from 'legal centralism' toward 'indigenous law' (1981, p. 19). (It is important to note that Galanter used the term 'indigenous' to refer to the place of origin, rather than the First Nations' Peoples as applied later in this chapter.) Effectively, Galanter was arguing for more informal and less formal legal controls. He argued that 'just as health is not found primarily in hospitals, or knowledge in schools, so justice is not primarily to be found in official justice-dispensing institutions' (1981, p. 14). Galanter further proposed a move away from the 'institutional-intellectual complexes that we identify as national legal systems' which have displaced the previously diverse array of normative orderings of society (1981, p. 18).

Indigenous Courts

Since Galanter's treatise was written, alternative court practices have been developed in various common law systems, notably in Canada, New Zealand and Australia, to try to redress racial inequality in criminal justice systems and reduce the overrepresentation of Indigenous peoples in custody (Marchetti & Daly 2004; Tomaino 2009; Marchetti & Downie 2014). These reflect changed communication and cultural approaches from members of the judiciary in how they engage, enable and empower Indigenous people within the justice system. This includes the use of systems such as 'circles' whereby judicial officers sit face-to-face with offenders, elders, community members and victims, and the introduction of community sentencing panels. 'In changing how justice gets done, Indigenous sentencing courts can change judicial and legal actors, they can empower Indigenous elders and other community members, and they may change attitudes of Indigenous offenders' (Marchetti & Daly 2004, p. 4).

Marchetti and Daly (2004, p. 2) explain how Australia's first Indigenous court—the Nunga Court—was established in South Australia:

> Magistrate Chris Vass had worked for 15 years in Papua New Guinea (PNG). He returned to Australia in 1975 and was appointed magistrate in 1980. In the mid-1980s he started to do a circuit to the Pitjantjatjara Lands, travelling there six times a year for 17 years (with a two-year hiatus). His considerable time on the circuit, coupled with his years in PNG, shaped his thinking about British and Australian

colonial rule, race relations and law. A major element motivating Vass was to redress the deep distrust of Indigenous people toward the criminal justice system. In 1996 he began speaking with local Indigenous groups, the Aboriginal Legal Rights Movement and the Department of Aboriginal Affairs. From this, an Aboriginal Court Day was established and, soon after, it was named the Nunga Court.

This pioneering work became instrumental in courts in other Australian states which followed the lead and, while there is no uniform philosophy behind the operation of Indigenous courts in Australia, in some jurisdictions 'there is a commitment to tailoring court processes to create a culturally appropriate setting' (Tomaino 2009, p. 3). The public interest for those people involved in the system, and for the wider community, is illustrated in the aims of the Nunga Court:

- to provide a more culturally appropriate setting than mainstream courts;
- to reduce the number of Aboriginal deaths in custody;
- to improve court participation of Aboriginal people (rates in mainstream courts are less than 50% but up to 95% in Nunga courts. By reducing the number of arrest warrants, there is less time in custody, hence reducing the number of deaths in custody);
- to break the cycle of Aboriginal offending;
- to make justice proactive by seeking opportunities to address underlying crime-related problems with a view to making a difference;
- to recognize the importance of combining punishment with help so that courts are used as a gateway to treatment;
- to involve victims and the community as far as possible in the ownership of the court process; and
- to ensure that the court process is open and transparent to victims and the community at large (Tomaino 2009, pp. 3–4).

Soon after the development of the Nunga Courts, Australia's Federal Courts developed a practice of traveling to remote parts of Australia to engage with the First Nations' peoples of Australia and the Torres Strait, going 'on country,' as the following snapshot outlines.

Snapshot

Australian Federal Court Goes 'On Country'

Background

In 1994 the Australian *Native Title Act* was brought into operation, effectively changing the way the Commonwealth could handle claims for native title by the country's First Nations' peoples. Under the act, rules of the Federal

Court provide discretion as to where and how hearings should proceed, with section 82(2) stating that:

> In conducting its proceedings, the Court may take account of the cultural and customary concerns of Aboriginal peoples and Torres Straight Islanders, but not so to prejudice unduly any other party of the proceedings (Federal Court of Australia 2008, n.p.).

These provisions have enabled the Court to hear evidence 'on country,' often in remote locations, sitting under tents or trees, recognizing that for many native title claimants it is not possible to explain their relationship to land in an abstract setting. One of the Federal Court's earliest and longest on country hearings— *Ward v Western Australia* (1998)—included some 80 days of evidence taken in remote locations. Logistical and procedural issues for court staff included having to manage recording in windy (and noisy) conditions, ascertaining precise locations for GPS equipment, plus various other challenges involved in conducting public hearings hundreds of kilometers from the nearest substantial settlement. In one case the hearing covered 5,000 kilometers over 14 days; the longest day of traveling was 700 kilometers (Black 2007; Federal Court of Australia 2008).

The Federal Court thus established an entirely new field of jurisprudence in the 20-plus years since the *Native Title Act* was brought into operation. This has included the following:

- Developing 'men only' and 'women only' evidence in order to respect indigenous laws and customs.
- Developing specially adapted principles and procedures, such as taking of evidence in the form of song or dance, and in groups.
- Taking expert evidence from anthropologists and historians.
- Developing effective regional management of cases and mediation procedures as part of the overall framework.
- Developing a successful Indigenous research assistance project.
- Developing a series of resources, such as DVDs, to assist professional participants who are unfamiliar with the 'on country' framework (Black 2007; Federal Court of Australia 2008).

Adnyamathanha People and the Flinders Ranges

'On country' cases have been held all over Australia, from Fraser Island in Queensland, to Western Australia, and the Flinders Ranges of South Australia. In 1994, the Adnyamathanha people, which means 'ranges mob' or 'rock people,' of South Australia filed the first native title claim in that state, seeking a ruling relating to their customary rights and interests, including the right to hunt native fauna, collect and use native flora and conduct traditional practices such as funerals, on their country (Harbord & Withers 2008). In 2009 and 2014, respective claims were delivered in favor of the Adnyamathanha people.

In 2009 the Federal Court awarded the Adnyamathanha people non-exclusive rights over 41,000 square kilometers of land in the state's largest ever native title claim, subject to the applicable laws and valid rights of existing landholders (*Adelaide Advertiser* 2009). Then, in 2014, parts of the Adnyamathanha

Figure 7.1 Justice Tony North led into 'court' by Nyangumarta dancers for their consent determination in the Pilbara, Western Australia, June 2009.

Figure 7.2 Justice North with community member during Pilki hearing in the Central Desert, Western Australia, in 2013.

native title application not determined in 2009 were finalized (South Australian Native Title Services 2014). Following the finding, the solicitor for the Adnyamathanha group said one of the principle reasons for the success of the claims had been the way the Adnyamathanha people had maintained their spiritual and physical connection with their land, uninterrupted since the coming of the white-man (South Australian Native Title Services 2014, p. 1).

'Singing the Law'

In 2008, prior to the resolution of the cases, Adnyamathanha solicitors Graham Harbord and Johnston Withers wrote a discursive essay 'Singing the Law,' about an Indigenous elder who has since died (thus, for cultural reasons he should not be named) and his contribution to the Adnyamathanha native title claim. Harbord and Withers (2008, p. 22) explained how the system used was not 'a legal system as we know it, written in statutes or interpreted by courts, but rather a set of core beliefs and rules, asserted by the Adnyamathanha to have been handed down through the generations, including by way of stories, songs and rituals from the original ancestral beings.'

Following the initial 'preservation hearing' held in cases in which key witnesses are elderly or frail, the Court moved 'on country' to Hawker at Yourambulla Caves where the elder told of stories about that place and beyond (Harbord & Withers 2008). Harbord and Withers (2008, p. 23) describe the first instance in which the elder sang:

> It had not rained for a long time and the country was looking very parched. So [the elder] decided to sing a rain song. He said he wouldn't sing it for very long, just enough to bring a little rain. He told the judge that he didn't want to wash out the Federal Court hearing. On the second night of the hearing, it rained at Blinman in the Flinders Ranges. We are still considering how we might submit this as proof of the powerful connection that Adnyamathanha have with their country.

At several sites throughout the trip the elder sang songs associated with specific sites and occasionally performed a dance or told stories associated with the land, the history, the native fauna, flora, wild food, medications and poisons.

> He talked about the seeds on the Spinifex, for instance, which is called *wakati*. He told how the echidna one day was being cheeky with a yura [Adnyamathanha] boy. Having had enough of him, the boy seized the echidna and threw him in the Spinifex, and that's why the echidna got his spikes.
>
> (Harbord and Withers 2008, p. 23)

The court gathered valuable sound and video recordings about a part of Adnyamathanha culture in the Flinders Ranges. The elder told the Court at the conclusion of the trip: 'Sometimes there's time to cry for the place and sometimes to be sad for the place, but I'm glad to be back here and sing to all of you today. I'm glad to admit you all to this country' (Harbord & Withers 2008, p. 24).

Conclusion

Habermas contends that the law is both a symbolic and action system. This duality represents the natural and positive law and the functional and normative ways of understanding the law. This chapter has sought to expand this duality through philosophically and theoretically advancing our understanding of various public interest contexts, while also providing concrete action-based illustrations and arguments within the snapshots and illustrations. In examining two primary functions of the law—social change and social control—it presents both theoretical discussion and practical snapshots of the Irish referendum and the Australian Federal Court going 'on country,' which both richly illustrate the way the public interest is determined through legal and political systems. Clearly, as Habermas explained within the chapter, the law does not work in isolation. Laws are only part of the social systems that govern—ideology, technology, competition, conflict, communication, political and economic factors are among the other elements and mechanisms that impact on society (Habermas 1996; Vago 2009). This is affirmed by Foucault, who notes the law operates in a field of power relations within which it is only *one* directing force (Tadros 1998). At every turn we can find public relations both as a function of and process within these systems: in policy and communication roles in the bureaucracy, in government, in the courts, in commerce or within civil society. Sometimes individuals, organizations or social systems will seek to locate the public interest through the law, while at other times they will be guiding the public interest within courts or political processes.

By introducing the concept of the 'legitimation crisis' or the 'legitimation dilemma,' Habermas and Grodnick explain the issues that arise when law-making is estranged from the normative context or the citizenry is estranged from the state: the outcome is a democratic system that is not responsive to its citizenry. The normative and critical perspectives are aptly summed up in the following two illustrations.

On the one hand, John Rawls argues (1971, p. 60):

> ... each person is to have an equal right to the most extensive basic liberty compatible with a similar liberty for others.

On the other hand, Anatole France argues of the irony in the law's 'majestic equality' (France 1894 cited in McBarnet 1981, p. 167):

> ... the law forbids rich and poor alike to sleep under bridges, beg in the streets and steal loaves of bread.

In using France's quote to illustrate the inherent inequalities in society, which we can see starkly contrast with Rawls, McBarnet (1981) argues of the law's inherent contradictions. At the same time, the chapter provides examples of how inequality *can* be addressed. We conclude this chapter by anticipating a move to the next. Habermas points out how 'morality and law differ prime facie inasmuch as post traditional morality represents only a form of cultural knowledge, whereas law has, in addition to this, a binding character at the institutional level' (1996, p. 104). Following this, we now move forward to that field of higher abstraction—ethics and moral philosophy—in foregrounding the development of models for public relations and the public interest.

References

Adelaide Advertiser, 2009, 'Adnyamathanha people win Flinders Ranges native title claim', 30 March, viewed 25 May 2015, http://www.adelaidenow.com.au/news/historic-native-title-decision/story-e6freo8c-1225697821885.

Banks, S 1995, *Multicultural public relations: a social interpretive approach*, Routledge, London.

Bannister, J 2006, 'McKinnon v Secretary of Treasury—The Sir Humphrey Clause—review of conclusive certificates in freedom of information application', *Melbourne University Law Review*, vol. 30, no. 3, pp. 961–71, viewed 10 May 2015, https://www.law.unimelb.edu.au/files/dmfile/30_3_10.pdf.

Bentham, J 1843, 'On publicity', in J Bowring (ed.), *The works of Jeremy Bentham*, William Tait, Edinburgh.

Black, M 2007, 'The Federal Court of Australia: the first 30 years—a survey on the occasion of two anniversaries', *Melbourne University Law Review*, vol. 31, pp. 1017–52.

Bohman, J & Rehg, W 2011, 'Jürgen Habermas', in EN Zalta (ed.), *The Stanford encyclopedia of philosophy*, winter edn, viewed 1 May 2015, http://plato.stanford.edu/archives/win2011/entries/habermas/.

Carolan, E 2013a, 'Ireland's Constitutional Convention considers same-sex marriage: Part II', *International Journal of Constitution Law and Constitution Making* (weblog post), 25 April, viewed 18 May 2015, http://www.iconnectblog.com/2013/04/irelands-constitutional-convention-considers-same-sex-marriage-part-ii.

Carolan, E 2013b, 'Ireland's Constitutional Convention considers same-sex marriage', *International Journal of Constitution Law and Constitution Making* (weblog post), 9 April, viewed 18 May 2015, http://www.iconnectblog.com/2013/04/irelands-constitutional-convention-considers-same-sex-marriage-2.

Carter, M & Bouris, A 2006, *Freedom of information: balancing the public interest*, 2nd edn, The Constitution Unit-University College, London.

Clinard, M & Meier, R 2008, *Sociology of deviant behavior*, 13th edn, Wadsworth/Thomson Learning, Belmont, CA.

Cohn, M & Dow, D 1998, *Cameras in the courtroom: television and the pursuit of justice*, McFarland & Co., Jefferson, NC.

Demetrious, K 2013, *Public relations, activism and social change: speaking up*, Routledge, London.

Dozier, D & Lauzen, M 2000, 'Liberating the intellectual domain from the practice: public relations, activism, and the role of the scholar', *Journal of Public Relations*, vol. 12, pp. 3–22.

Ericson, R, Baranek, P & Chan, J 1987, *Visualizing deviance: a study of news organization*, University of Toronto Press, Toronto.

Ericson, R, Baranek, P & Chan, J 1989, *Negotiating control: a study of news sources*, University of Toronto Press, Toronto.

Farrell, D 2015, 'Constitutional Convention 'brand' is in jeopardy', *The Irish Times*, 17 May, viewed 25 May 2015, http://www.irishtimes.com/opinion/david-farrell-constitutional-convention-brand-is-in-jeopardy-1.2142826.

Federal Court of Australia 2008, 'A thumbnail outline of Federal Court achievements in the field of Native title', information sheet.

Foucault, M 1984, *The history of sexuality, vol 1: an introduction*, trans R Hurley, Penguin, Harmondsworth.

Galanter, M 1981, 'Justice in many rooms: courts private order and indigenous law,' *Journal of Legal Pluralism and Unofficial Law*, vol. 19, pp. 1–47.

Ginsburg, RB 1995, 'Communicating and commenting on the courts' work', *The Georgetown Law Journal*, vol. 83, pp. 2119–29.

Grodnick, S 2005 Rediscovering radical democracy in Habermas's Between Facts and Norms, *Constellations* vol 12 no 3: pp. 392–408.

Habermas, J 1974, 'The public sphere: an encyclopaedia article', *New German Critique*, no. 3, first published 1964, pp. 49–55.

Habermas, J 1984, *The theory of communication action, vol. 2*, Beacon Press, Boston.

Habermas, J 1989, *The structural transformation of the public sphere: an inquiry into a category of bourgeois society*, MIT Press, Cambridge, MA.

Habermas, J 1996, *Between facts and norms: contributions to a discourse theory of law and democracy*, MIT Press, Cambridge, MA.

Habermas, J 1998, *On the pragmatics of communication*, MIT Press, Cambridge, MA.

Harbord, G & Withers, J 2008, 'Singing the law', *Bulletin, Law Society of South Australia*, vol. 30, no. 4, pp. 22–24.

Hoebel, AE 1954, *The law of primitive man: a study of comparative legal dynamics*, Harvard University Press, Cambridge, MA.

Holtzhausen, DR & Voto, R 2002, 'Resistance from the margins: the postmodern public relations practitioner as organizational activist', *Journal of Public Relations Research*, vol. 14, no. 1, pp. 57–84.

Ihlen, Ø, van Ruler, B & Fredricksson, M (eds.) 2009, *Public relations and social theory*, Routledge, New York.

Johnston, J 2005, 'Communicating courts: A decade of practice in the third arm of government', *Australian Journal of Communication*, vol. 32, no. 3, pp. 77–93.

Johnston, J 2008, 'The court-media interface: bridging the divide', *Australian Journalism Review*, vol. 30, no. 2, pp. 27–39.

Johnston, J 2011, 'Courts' new visibility 2.0', in P Keyzer, J Johnston & M Pearson (eds.), *Courts and the media in the digital age*, Halstead, Sydney.

Johnston, J & Breit, R 2010 Towards a narratology of court reporting' *Media International Australia*, vol. 137, pp. 47–57

Johnston, J & McGovern, A 2013, 'Communicating justice: a comparison of courts and police use of contemporary media', *International Journal of Communication*, vol. 7, viewed 1 March 2015, http://ijoc.org/index.php/ijoc/article/view/2029.

Keyzer, P 2010, *Open constitutional courts*, Federation Press, Sydney.

Landau, P 2013, 'Whistleblowing: is new "public interest" test a good thing?', *The Guardian*, 25 June, viewed 30 June 2015, http://www.theguardian.com/money/work-blog/2013/jun/25/whistleblowing-public-interest-edward-snowden.

L'Etang, J 2008, *Public relations: concepts, practice and critique*, Sage, London.

Marchetti, E & Daly, K 2004, 'Indigenous courts and justice practices in Australia,' *Trends and Issues in Crime and Criminal Justice*, no. 277, Australian Institute of Criminology, viewed 25 April 2015 http://www98.griffith.edu.au/dspace/

bitstream/handle/10072/5041/25819.pdf;jsessionid=24DE4AA59936E2A
B0523C2C058199B46?sequence=1.

Marchetti, E & Downie, R 2014, 'Indigenous people and sentencing courts in Australia, New Zealand, and Canada', in S Bucerius & M Tonry (eds.), *The Oxford handbook of ethnicity, crime, and immigration*, Oxford Handbooks Online, Oxford.

McBarnet, D 1981, *Conviction: law, the state and the construction of justice*, Macmillan, London.

McDonald, H 2015, 'Ireland becomes first country to legalise gay marriage by popular vote', *The Guardian*, 24 May, viewed 23 May 2015 http://www.theguardian.com/world/2015/may/23/gay-marriage-ireland-yes-vote.

O'Mohoney, C 2014a, 'Is a referendum needed to introduce same-sex marriage?' *Irish Times*, 24 March, viewed 22 March 2015, http://www.irishtimes.com/news/crime-and-law/is-a-referendum-needed-to-introduce-same-sex-marriage-1.1733657.

O'Mohoney, C 2014b, 'If a constitution is easy to amend, can judges be less restrained? Rights, social change, and Proposition 8', *Harvard Human Rights Journal*, vol. 27, pp. 191–242.

Parker, S 1998, *Courts and the public*, AIJA, Melbourne.

Rawls, J 1971, *Theory of justice*, Harvard University Press, Cambridge, MA.

Rehg, W 1996 Translator's Introduction, *Between Facts and Norms: Contributions to a discourse Theory of Law and Democracy*, J Habermas, MIT, Cambridge.

Sedghi, A 2015, 'Irish same-sex marriage referendum: the laws around the world', *The Guardian*, 22 May, viewed 22 May 2015, http://www.theguardian.com/news/datablog/2015/may/22/irish-same-sex-marriage-referendum-world-laws.

Simon, J 1994, 'Between power and knowledge: Habermas, Foucault, and the future of legal studies', *Law & Society Review*, vol. 28, no. 4, 947–61.

Tadros, V 1998, 'Between governance and discipline: the law and Michel Foucault', *Oxford Journal of Legal Studies*, vol. 18, no. 1, pp. 75–103.

Tomaino, J 2009, 'Aboriginal (Nunga) Courts', *Information Bulletin*, Government of South Australia, viewed at 26 May 2015, http://www.ocsar.sa.gov.au/docs/information_bulletins/IB39.pdf.

Tuchman, G 1978, *Making news: a study in the construction of reality*, The Free Press, New York.

Vago, S 2009, *Law and society*, 9th edn, Pearson Education, London.

Walsh, A & Hemmens, C 2011, *Law, justice and society*, Oxford University Press, New York.

Legislation

Evidence Act 2006 (New Zealand) (Commonwealth) Section 68: Protection of Journalists' Sources, viewed 1 October 2015, http://www.legislation.govt.nz/act/public/2006/0069/latest/DLM393681.html.

Cases

McKinnon v Secretary, Department of Treasury NSD 70 of 2005, http://www.austlii.edu.au/cgi-bin/sinodisp/au/cases/cth/FCAFC/2005/142.html?stem=0&synonyms=0&query=%22The%20public%20interest%20is%20not%20one%20homogenous%20undivided%20concept%22.

8 The Public Interest, Ethics and Values
From Moral Philosophy to Professional Codes

> ... the very ubiquity of self-interest was the preservation of the public interest, as the aims of one individual or group would be checked and moderated by others.
>
> (Bentham 1816 in Gunn 1968, p. 411)

Introduction

This chapter takes us into the dense and murky field of moral philosophy and ethics, the epicentre of the public and self-interest. Atherton and colleagues (2008, p. 89) warn of the 'muddiness' of public and self-interest at the core of moral philosophy while virtue ethicist Michael Slote advises that the study of moral philosophy can provide only limited answers, that some moral questions simply '*outrun our human knowledge or reasoning powers*' (2013, p. 662 his italics). Hursthouse (2013) confirms none of the fields we examine in this chapter—virtue ethics, utilitarianism and deontology—can predict what ought to be done in particular situations. 'Just think of how incredible it would be were a moral theorist to present a slim volume containing a mathematical algorithm for moral decision making. If there were a simple recipe for invariably getting it right in ethics, we would have seen it a long time ago' (Hursthouse 2013, p. 612). And, in the translation of ethics into practice, Harrison and Galloway (2005, p. 1) observe how 'ethical nostrums designed to address professional practice issues' often rest on a need for clarity, but that formalized codes, models and guidance are not necessarily redemptive.

Yet, the Socratic question of how we ought to live seeks answers from ethics which provide deeper understanding, especially where complex issues such as the public interest and values are at stake (DesJardins 2008). Moral philosophy is premised on how we might live good lives. So, for example, Kantian rules of keeping promises, consequentialist rules to maximize good, and virtue rules to act charitably, kindly and honestly provide ways of interacting in the world; therefore:

> ... we must discern what is intrinsically valuable ... We must know how to balance options that generate different goods, on the assumption

that there is more than just one kind of intrinsic value. Again, there are no *precise rules* that offer guidance in resolving these sorts of puzzles.

(Shafer-Landau 2013, pp. 612–13, my italics)

Accepting these arguments, we now move into the slippery field of moral philosophy and ethics to examine the public interest, prescient that there are no clean and tidy lines around which to anchor the concept of the public interest, nor are there any simple answers to our questions. Thus, while some scholars (Martinson 2000; Harrison 2004; Harrison & Galloway 2005; Slote 2008; Fawkes 2009) advocate the need to look to the individual's character, motivations or wholeness rather than the code or the industry for guidance, others argue that codes and models have their place along with other guidelines in the articulation of an ethical position (Longstaff 1994; Beauchamp 2001; Tilley 2005; Messina 2007). Accordingly, this chapter takes a hermeneutic or interpretative approach to locating the public interest within ethical thinking, theories and codes; an exploration into the public interest which is not bound by positivist or empirical constraints, but neither does it discount them, noting how some scholars aim to combine various methodologies and develop new forms of 'situationism' or empirical ethics (Baker 2008, p. 2195).

This book has so far drawn on the work of many and varied ethical and philosophical perspectives in order to explicate the public interest and provide reflexive points of consideration and contestation (for example, Lippmann 1925, 1955; Dewey 1927; Rawls 1971; Friere 2005; Said 1978; Foucault 1978; Habermas 1989, 1996). This chapter now turns to developing further ethical underpinnings of the public interest, including the works and critiques of Aristotle, Bentham, Kant, Singer and others, first, through examining key fields of moral philosophy; second, by considering how public relations scholars have engaged with and assessed this space; and third, in presenting the findings of a preliminary study of public relations codes of ethics/practice/conduct in order to see how the public interest is presented to its practitioner base.

Public Interest and Moral Philosophy

On the face of it, utilitarian concepts of moral philosophy might seem to equate best with notions of the public interest because of the utilitarian principles that actions are right if they lead to the *greatest possible good* (or the least possible bad), and the subordination of 'duty, obligation and rights to *maximise good*' (Beauchamp 2001, p. 104 his italics). Criticisms of utilitarianism suggest that the theory therefore ignores a pluralist approach of the public interest *because* of its principle of utility through which the interests of the majority can overlook the interests of minorities. Such criticism continues that the cost-benefit analysis of utilitarianism, and the consequentialist outcomes that it seeks, can easily overlook individual human rights (Beauchamp 2001; Sandel 2009).

Defenders of this school of thought, though, say criticisms have pilloried the utilitarian idea of public good, 'reducing community to jarring bundles of appetites' (Gunn 1968, p. 398). Gunn's defence of Bentham's utilitarianism in *Jeremy Bentham and the Public Interest* clearly explains how, rather than trying to reduce all interests to a single homogeneity, Bentham's 'aim was that of giving all particular interests expression' (Gunn 1968, p. 410). At the same time he describes as 'unrealistic nonsense' any assumption that Bentham envisioned a public interest consisting in the satisfaction of *all* private interests. Rather, a more realistic summation is that government was useful insofar as it contributed to the 'common interests [of] subsistence, abundance, security and equality' which were unattainable by 'individual felicity' (1968, p. 405).

> He conceded that people were indeed self-seeking, wishing to give preference to their own interests. The whole problem was that some people had the opportunity to exercise this self-interest and others had not: "The wish is everywhere—the power not so." The answer was to change the political system, not human nature.
>
> (Gunn 1968, p. 407)

Indeed, for theorizing public relations' purposes, Bentham's approach to the public interest is doubtless worth further attention as 'far from hypostatizing the "People" as a single, irreducible interest, Bentham provided a most sophisticated analysis of society as a congeries of different interests' (Gunn 1968, p. 409).

A very useful development of public interest utilitarianism proposes an 'outsider,' 'objective' or 'third party' effect. Such thinking suggests a hypothetical third eye is introduced to judge the veracity of interest claims, thereby reinforcing the importance of greater accountability and openness to scrutiny (Campbell & Marshall 2002; Mickey 2003; Wheeler 2006). As such, moral reflection benefits from 'an interlocutor'—whether real or imagined (Sandel 2009, p. 29). This concept is described by Flathman (1966, p. 38) as a 'trans-subjective view of the public interest,' premised on three considerations:

- first, the existence of inequalities of various kinds (status, resources and other personal attributes) which requires someone (authority/government) to compensate for the differences;
- second, the notion that individuals may be mistaken in their interests or not have the wherewithal to know how to attain what they need;
- third, the acknowledgment that collective values and principles will transcend private interests and their summation (Flathman 1966, Campbell & Marshall 2002).

Flathman argues, 'It is true that self-interest has a legitimate place in the public interest, but deciding whose self-interest and to what extent requires the utilization of values and principles which transcend such interests' (1966, p 38).

Nevertheless, utilitarian's cost-benefit and consequentialist elements remain stumbling blocks to rights-based or deontological theory which, alternately, focuses not on substantive outcomes but on rights, fairness and justice. So while utilitarianism is therefore associated with the aggregate and consequentialist public interest typologies outlined elsewhere in the book, the individual rights-based or deontological approach is consistent with the process or proceduralist typology. In considering this view, Kant's concept of 'good will' and his categorical imperative are instructive. Kant argues, 'Nothing in the world ... can possibly be conceived which could be good without qualification except a *good will*' (in Beauchamp 2001, p. 150, his italics). Kant's use of universalizing—premised on duties that take the form of universal rules—in theory removes self-interest from consideration, thus rendering justifications 'impersonal, universal and rational' (Atherton, Cluett, McAdoo, Rawlinson & Sidoli 2008, p. 89). However, Beauchamp argues the deontological approach can also take account of consequences in what he calls 'a covert appeal to the utilitarian principle.' He explains (2001, p. 172):

> An action's consequences often cannot be separated from the nature of the action itself, so consequences too must be considered when an agent universalizes the action in order to determine whether it is permissible.

At the same time, the categorical imperative does not assist in 'how to handle conflicting obligations that give incompatible directives, both of which cannot be fulfilled' (Beauchamp 2001, p. 156). Such a question speaks to the issue of competing interests. Pluralist deontologists respond to this by arguing that the categorical imperative must therefore take account of *prima facie* obligations and duties of self-improvement, non-maleficence, beneficence and justice (Beauchamp 2001). At the extreme, however, rights-based ethics can spiral into moral absolutism which provides for the acceptance of fundamental ethical principles without any qualifications with regard to place or time. Accordingly, when absolutist beliefs, such as radical fundamentalist movements, are taken out of their religious context, they often do not stand up to rational criticism (Ceranic 2008).

Campbell and Marshall (2002) argue that postmodern and post-structural critiques have rendered the idea of universalizing concepts to be entirely problematic for the public interest. Indeed, 'class, gender, and race based critiques ... left this particular notion of "the public interest" in tatters, as have the lived realities of late twentieth century existence' (Sandercock 1998 in Campbell & Marshall 2002, p. 173). Accordingly, two key developments occurred with this turn away from universalizing: first, the shift toward greater understanding of plurality and heterogeneity that lie at the heart of postmodernism and other contemporary critiques; second, the acceptance of the agent as bringing subjective perspectives, with widespread agreement that 'ethical judgments are central to the day-to-day work of practitioners' (Campbell & Marshall 2002, p. 173; see also L'Etang & Pieczka 2006, p. 2). As such, these two developments—plurality and agent-based judgments—are each addressed in turn.

Many scenarios call for a plurality of moral judgment and moral argument. Beauchamp suggests the theory of 'moral disagreement [thus] allows one to criticize morally unacceptable conduct that violates universal standards while remaining sensitive to legitimate values, cultural and individual differences' (Beauchamp 2001, p. 34). He says a plurality of interests does not limit sound deliberation and decision making, indeed that while choices are not always easy 'we think through the alternatives, deliberate, and reach a conclusion' (2001, p. 38). Accordingly, while reason and judgment can be invoked to reflect on troublesome moral problems, moral pluralism will still render some moral disagreements systematically unresolvable because of the incompatibility of the rival premises of the disputing parties (MacIntyre 1978 in Beauchamp 2001). This idea is explicated by Bohman and Rehg (2014, n.p.) in their reading of Habermas, who argue that in pluralistic and multicultural settings, the categorical imperative of duties is not only problematic but also may be 'entirely untenable.' While they provide an escape-argument that 'one may plausibly claim to take an impartial moral point of view only by engaging in real discourse with all those affected by the issue in question' (Bohman & Rehg 2014, n.p.), there will inevitably be conflicts that cannot be resolved based on rights and resource distribution, power differentials and strategic communication practices that focus on achieving certain interests or outcomes. As such, there should be no naïve expectation that all interests will be achieved, rather that interests should be promised a hearing, 'not instant gratification' (Gunn 1968, p. 404, footnote 31).

The second issue—agent subjectivity—can be addressed through the prism of virtue ethics, a popular and recently revived school of philosophy that proponent Michael Slote argues has recently begun 'flexing its muscles' (Slote 2013, p. 663). Agent-based judgments are increasingly being tied to the concept of virtue ethics in modern ethical analysis though their genesis is with the ancient philosophers, notably Aristotle. Baker argues that ancient accounts proposed three components of virtue ethics: intellectual, dispositional and affective (Baker 2008, p. 2192). In other words, we know what is right and wrong (intellectual, e.g. stealing versus not stealing); we make doing the right thing a part of our lives (dispositional, e.g. we don't steal); and we take pleasure in doing the right thing and are not resentful of the benefits of those who do the wrong thing (affective, e.g. we don't want to steal). Such traditional accounts of virtue also saw it as being transformative, something one worked toward which required effort; however, this is deemed to be less a part of modern-day thinking (Baker 2008). Virtue ethics is explained as the agent's inward gaze effectively 'doubling back' on the world, allowing the agent to take facts about the world into account in determining what is morally acceptable or best to do (Slote 2013, p. 661).

Agent-based virtue ethics has received some attention within public relations scholarship. Harrison and Galloway (2005, p. 5) argue of the benefits of agent-based rather than action-based ethics:

> Action-based ethics asks whether a particular action is ethical, whereas agent-based ethics focuses on the individual agent's character and motivations, and asks whether they are virtuous.

Slote (2013), however, cautions about assuming that an agent who is usually virtuous is always virtuous. What happens if a virtuous person behaves out of character? Indeed, Aristotle points to inconsistencies:

> We ought to examine what has been said by applying it to what we do and how we live; and if it harmonizes with what we do, we should accept it, but if it conflicts we should count it [mere] words.
> (Aristotle 2013, p. 628)

Or, as Slote (2013, p. 655, his italics) puts it:

> If the evaluation of actions ultimately derives from that of (the inner states of) agents, then it would appear to follow that if one is the right sort of person or possesses the right sort of inner states, it doesn't morally matter what one actually *does*, so that the person, or at least her actions, are subject to no genuine moral requirements or constraints. In this light, agent-basing seems a highly autistic and antinomian approach to ethics, an approach that seems to undermine the familiar, intuitive notion that the moral or ethical life involves, among other things, *living up to* certain *standards* of behavior or action.

Codes and the Public Interest

Those scholars who sing the praises of agent-based ethics have advocated their benefits over codes of ethics and practice (Martinson 2000; Harrison 2004; Harrison & Galloway 2005). Harrison and Galloway (2005, p. 2) note that 'the virtue approach to ethics does more to illuminate the daily dilemmas of public relations practitioners than code and consequentialist approaches.' While there is great merit in this focus, the codes are not without their place, and indeed, though limited in scope, deserve close attention as they relate to self and public interests. Walle examined public relations codes of ethics from the Public Relations Society of America (PRSA), the Canadian Public Relations Society (CPRS), the Public Relations Institute of Australia (PRIA), the Public Relations Institute of New Zealand (PRINZ) and the Public Relations Institute of Southern Africa (PRISA), concluding there was 'a lack of society' in them all (Walle 2003, p. 1). She argued, 'The code that addresses the issue of public responsibility with the strongest wording is the PRISA code, which states that the members "shall respect the public interest and the dignity of the individual"' (Walle 2003, p. 3).

One view of codes holds that they serve a purpose as part of ethical thinking because, by their very nature, ethical theories and philosophies are insufficiently specific to provide concrete practical guidance. As such, they are part of ethical guidance frameworks, best used in conjunction with other elements (Longstaff 1994; Beauchamp 2001). For example, Beauchamp (2001) suggests a range of steps associated with resolving moral dilemmas or disagreements, which include the following:

- Obtain objective information.
- Provide definitional clarity.
- Adopt a code.
- Use examples and counterexamples.
- Analyze arguments.

Codes of ethics and practice provide fertile ground for investigating a concept such as the public interest because they incorporate specific discursive and linguistic choices, made by professional or industrial associations. As such, these documents present symbolic representations of that which is deemed to be important within these industry associations and professional bodies. As Simon Longstaff of the St James Ethics Centre (1994, n.p.) argues, codes 'should be understood as an authentic expression of what people hold to be right and proper.' Used for general guidance and to assist in circumstances of uncertainty or dispute, codes can also be considered within specific time contexts, reflecting temporal social and cultural moral frameworks (Beauchamp 2001).

Public Relations Codes

In public relations, codes of ethics/practice/conduct are established by peak national and international bodies intended to guide the practice of members. This chapter now presents the findings of a global study of 84 public codes of ethics/practice/conduct, undertaken with two primary aims: first, to gain a sense of how widely the expression 'the public interest' or 'interests of the public' is used within these codes; and second, to consider whether a reading of these codes could inform our understanding of how the public interest is viewed globally. The methodology followed a gathering of public relations codes of ethics, practice and conduct, using a range of online sites: the Global Alliance for Public Relations and Communication Management website; the International Public Relations Association website; the European Public Relations Association websites; and the African Public Relations Association website. Those which were not available in English were translated using

Google translator. It was proposed that the prevalence of the concept 'the public interest' and the context in which it was used were the two primary drivers of the study.

The study found that the phrases 'the public interest' or 'the interests of the public/society' were included in many codes from around the world (Table 8.1). Of the 84 codes under review, 34 incorporated the term 'the public interest,' or variations of it, on at least one occasion.[1]

Table 8.1 International Codes of Ethics/Practice/Conduct which include the public interest

Organization	Public interest references/mentions
Association of Public Relations Consultancies, Spain (ADECEC)	Code of Ethics: 1st of 11 points: 'Partner companies are required to provide and maintain just and impeccable treatment with … customers … colleagues … and the public in general, and they must respect the <u>interest of society</u> in their activities.'
Association of Public Relations Professionals of Puerto Rico (ARPPR)	Code of Ethics, Statement of Reasons: 'The duties of the professional public relations are the development of messages which directly impact on public opinion and responsibility of advising the organization or individual who provides services to the importance of their actions, not only respond to particular interests, but to the <u>public interest</u>'.
Canadian Public Relations Society Inc. (CPRS)	Code of Professional Standards, 1st of 9 points: 'Members shall conduct their professional lives in a manner that does not conflict with the <u>public interest</u> and the dignity of the individual, with respect for the rights of the public as contained in the Constitution of Canada and the Charter of Rights and Freedoms'.
Chartered Institute of Public Relations (CIPR)	Code of Conduct, under Principles of Good Practice: On integrity: 'Fundamental to good public relations practice are: Honest and responsible regard for the <u>public interest</u>'. On confidentiality: 'Not disclosing confidential information unless specific permission has been granted or the <u>public interest</u> is at stake or if required by law.'
China International Public Relations Association (CIPRA)	Code of Conduct, General provisions: 'For organizations to provide effective, responsible, public relations services, the education community and correctly guide public opinion, and to serve the <u>public interest</u>'. Under principles of honesty and credibility: 'Service organizations and the public in an honest manner, accurate and honest dissemination of information emphasizes business reputation, the <u>public interest</u> in the first place'.

(Continued)

Organization	Public interest references/mentions
	Code of Conduct introduction: 'The first piece of information dissemination is the basis of public relations services that only accurate and true information dissemination in order to better communication between the Organization's relationship with the news media, the Government, the public relations, and genuine service organizations and the <u>public interest</u>'
	2nd chapter: Membership should take into account '… the <u>public interest</u> and the interests of the Organisation'. Membership: 'Should do the subordination of organisation interests, institutional interests to the <u>public interest</u>'.
	Under the Standard of Public Relations Consultancy Services (55 articles): 51st point about honesty and credibility. 'PR consultancy services for honest, relying on reputation, should be honest about serving customers and the general public, to disseminate accurate and true information emphasizes business reputation and put the <u>public interest</u> first'. Conflicts of interest. 'Professional services will inevitably arise a conflict of interest, present and potential conflicts of interest should be avoided, personal interests to obey the interests of customers, subject to <u>the public interest</u> that a broad and lasting trust'.
European Association of Communication Directors (EACD)	Code of Conduct, under integrity: 'We believe that communications must be guided not solely by the interests of an organisation, but by a broader view of the <u>public good.</u>'
European Code of Professional Conduct in PR (Code of Lisbon)	Code of Ethics, clause 2: '… the pr practitioner undertakes … to act in accordance with the public interest and not to harm the dignity or integrity of the individual.'
Global Alliance for Public Relations and Communication Management (GA)	Code of Ethics, introduction, Mission: '… to be the global voice for public relations in the <u>public interest</u>'. Case study (PR counselling ethical principles): 'Protect and advance the flow of accurate and truthful information is essential to serving the <u>public interest</u>'.
Estonian Public Relations Association (EPRA)	Standards of the Code of Ethics (Loyalty): 'We are faithful to those whom we represent, and we are represented, while at the same time respecting the <u>interests of the society</u> …'
Hong Kong Public Relations Professionals' Association (HKPRPA)	Code of Professional Standards, 1st of 9 points: 'A member shall attempt to work in accord with the <u>public interest</u>'.
Hungarian Public Relations Association (MPRSZ)	Code of Ethics, part 4 of 7 parts (Interpretations section), point 3: 'The PR activity shall be in the <u>public interest</u>, in particular the core values of a democratic society'.

Organization	Public interest references/mentions
International Code of Ethics (Code of Athens)	Code of Ethics, clause 8: 'To act, in all circumstances, in such a manner as to take account of the respective interests of the parties involved; both the interests of the organisation which the practitioner serves and the interests of the publics concerned.'
Institute of Public Relations Malaysia (IPRM)	Code of Professional Conduct, based on International Code of Ethics (Code of Athens), 1st point: 'A member shall conduct his professional activities with respect for the public interest'.
Institute of Public Relations of Singapore (IPRS)	Code of Ethics, 1st of 15 points: 'A member shall conduct his professional activities with respect for the public interest and the interest of the profession'.
International Association of Business Communicators (IABC)	Code of Ethics (Articles), 1st of 12 points: 'Professional communicators uphold the credibility and dignity of their profession by practicing honest, candid and timely communication and by fostering the free flow of essential information in accord with the public interest'.
Israeli Association of Public Relations and Media Relations (ISPRA)	Professional Ethics, under appendix 2, rule 3: 'The member of the Association represented the client / employer in good faith. While there are expected to support a candidate or political issue, for which he works, to a member of the Union to act in accordance with the public interest, to seek the truth, ensure the accuracy and good taste.'
Italian Public Relations Federation (FERPI)	Code of Professional Conduct, Principles and rules relating to professional qualifications, article 15: 'Each member of FERPI in the exercise of their professional activity, must comply with public interests and the dignity of the individual.'
Komora Public Relations [Chamber of Public Relations Czech Republic] (KoPR)	Code of Ethics (Public interest – relation to the public), point 3 of 4: 'Members shall respect all opinions, support and promote the right to freedom of speech and expression, which is a clear public interest'.
Mexican Association of Public Relations Professionals (PRORP)	Code of Ethics (Loyalty): 'Insist that members are loyal to their clients, at the same time that they fully comply with their obligations to the interests of society ...'
Nigerian Institute of Public Relations (NIPR)	Code of Professional Conduct, Conduct towards the public, the media and other professionals (points 2.1 and 2.6). A member shall: 'Conduct his or her professional activities with proper regard to the public interest'. 'Neither offer nor give, or cause an employer or client to give any Inducement in holders of Public office or members of any statutory body or organization who are not directors, executives or retained consultants, with intent to further the interests of the employer or client if such action is inconsistent with the public interest'
Norwegian Communication Association (NCA)	Professional Ethical Principles (Integrity, point 1): Members shall have a: 'Responsible attitude to the public interests'.

(Continued)

Organization	*Public interest references/mentions*
Public Relations Association of Indonesia (PERHUMAS)	Code of Conduct (Article 3 regarding behaviour towards society and mass media), 1st point: 'Run the PR profession activities with attention to the <u>interests of the community</u> ...'
Public Relations Association of Uganda (PRAU)	Code of Ethics, 1st point: 'Endeavour to work for mutual understanding, peaceful coexistence and <u>public interest</u>'.
Public Relations Consultants Association – UK (PRCA)	Professional Charter, Conduct towards the public, media and other professionals, section 2 (1st and 8th points): A member shall: 'Conduct their professional activities with proper regard to the <u>public interest</u>.' 'Neither offer nor give any inducement to persons holding public office or members of any statutory body or organisation who are not directors, executives or retained consultants, with intent to further the interests of the organisation if such action is inconsistent with the <u>public interest</u>.'
Public Relations Institute of Ireland (PRII)	PRII Code of Professional Practice for Public Affairs & Lobbying, conduct towards the public (1st point): All members 'Shall at all times be familiar with and observe all relevant EU, local, national and international law in force, shall have due regard for the <u>public interest</u> ...'
Public Relations Institute of New Zealand (PRINZ)	Code of Ethics, overview: 'We balance our role as advocates for individuals or groups with the <u>public interest</u>. Under values, Advocacy 'We serve the <u>public interest</u> by acting as responsible advocates for those we represent'. Under Loyalty: 'We are faithful to those we represent, while honouring our obligations to serve the <u>public interest</u>.' Under principles (Balancing openness and privacy), 1st point 'A member shall: Promote open communication in the <u>public interest</u> wherever possible'
Public Relations Institute of Southern Africa (PRISA)	Code of Ethics and Professional Standards, point 2.5: 'We shall accurately define what public relations activities can and cannot accomplish. In the conduct of our professional activities, we shall respect the <u>public interest</u> and the dignity of the individual.' Point 2.6: 'We shall conduct our professional lives in accordance with the <u>public interest</u>'.
Public Relations Society of Kenya (PRSK)	Code of conduct, (1st point): 'Member shall conduct his professional activities with respect for the <u>public interest</u>'.
Public Relations Society of America (PRSA)	Code of Ethics professional values: Advocacy: 'We serve the <u>public interest</u> by acting as responsible advocates for those we represent'.

Organization	Public interest references/mentions
	Loyalty: 'We are faithful to those we represent, while honoring our obligation to serve the <u>public interest</u>'.
	Code Provisions Free Flow of Information: 'Core Principle Protecting and advancing the free flow of accurate and truthful information is essential to serving the <u>public interest</u>'. Competition: 'To serve the <u>public interest</u> by providing the widest choice of practitioner options'.
Public Relations Society of Slovenia (PRSS)	Code of Professional Conduct, general professional obligations: 'Professional consultant for public relations is also obliged to act in accordance with the <u>public</u> <u>interest</u> ...'
Russian Public Relations Association RPRA	Code of professional and ethical principles in the field of public relations, General Principles of Professional (1st point)' '... the work of the consultant or agency providing services in the field of public relations, should make public good and cannot prejudice the legitimate interests of the person, honour, dignity. Participation in any activities that jeopardize the <u>public interest</u> or pursuing covert, unannounced public purpose, firmly denied'.
SYNTEC Public Relations Council, France	Code of Ethics, under professional and moral qualifications: It is thus required to comply with both the interests of its customers and the <u>public interest</u> in the conduct of its business.
Turkish Public Relations Association (TUHID)	The Profession's Principles, about members (point 2 of 14 points): 'Public relations profession [be] exercised in a manner that will not damage the <u>interest of the public</u>'.
Ukrainian Association of Public Relations (UAPR)	Code of professional ethics. Members obligations (3 of 11 points). Members are obliged to: 'Carry out their professional activity with proper consideration of <u>public interest</u>. 'Clearly observe the fundamental principles of the Association regarding transparency towards the gifts do not offer and do not give, do not force the client to offer or give any gift or other remuneration to the media, officials of government agencies, employees of any institutions or organizations in order to promote the interests of the client through the unauthorized disclosure of information, or if such action is contrary to the <u>public interest</u>. 'To not use personally and do not allow their clients to use the official position of officials of government agencies or the media, to promote the interests of the customer, if such actions are contrary to the <u>public interest</u>'.

Public relations codes of ethics/conduct/practice or professional standards which incorporate the term 'the public interest'. Some variation in expression may apply to translated codes and in some instances codes may consist of multiple documents. This table is indicative only: additional codes may have been inadvertently missed.

One notable observation of the sample of 34 codes was that many public relations associations and institutes have adopted the Code of Athens (1965) (otherwise known as the International Code of Ethics) and/or the Code of Lisbon (1978) (otherwise known as the European Code of Professional Practice) which both cite the public interest. These codes have been adopted by 18 national associations (from 15 European countries) which are institutional members of European Public Relations Confederation (CERP).

The Code of Lisbon distinguishes between public and individual interests:

> *He/she likewise undertakes to act in accordance with **the public interest** and not to harm the dignity or integrity of the individual.*

While the Code of Athens requires a balance between interest of the public and organization:

> *To act, in all circumstances, in such a manner as to take account of the respective interests of the parties involved: both the interests of the organization which he serves and the **interests of the publics** concerned.*

In some instances, additional codes have also been adopted. The Public Relations Institute of Ireland (PRII), for instance, subscribes to Codes of Lisbon and Athens, plus the PRII Code of Practice for Public Affairs and Lobbying.

Findings further showed that different codes draw a range of interpretations of the public interest and how it aligns with sectional interests or advocacy. For example, the PRSA associates advocacy and the public interest with a aggregate approach:

> *We serve the public interest by acting as responsible advocates for those we represent.*

The Public Relations Institute of New Zealand (PRINZ), on the other hand, aims to find the balance between client and the public:

> *We are faithful to those we represent, while honouring our obligations to serve the public interest.*

In its reference to the public and the individual, the Canadian Public Relations Society (CPRS) has possibly the only code that includes its country's constitution in its terms of reference:

> *Members shall conduct their professional lives in a manner that does not conflict with the public interest and the dignity of the individual, with respect for the rights as contained in the Constitution of Canada and the Charter of Rights and Freedoms.*

A significant strength of the link to the Canadian constitution lies not only with the endorsement it brings but also that it incorporates a higher national and legal imperative, thus extending its impact beyond the CPRS's own industry parameters. Canada's embrace of the public interest within its professional code was also addressed when the CPRS revised its definition of public relations in order to include the public interest (Begin 2012).

At the same time, all codes of ethics/practice/conduct—across all industries, not just public relations—include inherent limitations. This analysis does not attempt a full critique of codes *per se*—this is well covered in the literature (see, for example, L'Etang 2003; Walle 2003; Harrison & Galloway 2005). Rather, it is worth outlining some of the limitations that relate to interests. The very nature of codes means that they are summary documents which cannot anticipate the complexity that comes with all ethical challenges and contexts; this includes understanding how to deal with competing interests, conflicts of interest and how to determine or define the public interest within all potential contexts. Indeed, some guidance clauses call for the practitioner to serve clients and/or the profession while *also* serving the public interest, so codes may include potential degrees of confusion. Moreover, since practitioners rarely work in isolation, codes are also limited in providing guidance about how to deal with others who hold different ethical positions.

Additionally, codes' limited enforceability rests with the voluntary nature of membership. At best, codes can only enforce behavior from members, and though the lack of enforceability is a limitation of any code of ethics/practice/conduct, in an industry which is unregulated, like public relations, breaches of the code provide for limited sanctions. This sits in contrast to professions such as medicine, teaching or accounting, which are far more likely to require registration and thus adherence to codes in order to practice.

Finally, while mindful of the limitations in any code, the preamble of the Global Alliance for Public Relations and Communication Management's Code of Ethics provides one of the most comprehensive navigations through potential conflicts (n.d., p. 2):

> A code of ethics and professional conduct is an individual matter that should be viewed as a guide to make sound values-based decisions. Ethical performance, not principles, is ultimately what counts. No one can dictate precise outcomes for every situation. However, we can apply common values and decision-making processes to arrive at a decision and justify it to others. In making decisions, we should be guided by a higher sense of serving the public as a whole as opposed to specific constituencies on an exclusive basis. Consideration should be given to the protection of privacy of individuals and respect for the spirit as well as the letter of applicable laws.

This passage places virtue ethics, agency and codes into the same space, with codes therefore juxtaposed against individual ethical choice. Moreover, it also addresses societal values as underpinning ethical practice, an issue to which we now turn.

Public Values

Bozeman argues one way of working through the vague, ambiguous nature of the public interest is to determine public values in support of it. Arguably then, public values can help bring the public interest into focus and assist in providing a degree of tangibility where one is sought (Bozeman 2007; Sandel 2009; Institute of Chartered Accountants in England and Wales [ICAEW] 2012, 2014). Value systems are not universal; however, we can apply a normative consensus about the following:

- basic rights, benefits and prerogatives to which citizens should and should not be entitled to;
- basic obligations of citizens to society, the state and each other; and
- basic principles on which governments and policies are made (Bozeman 2007).

Bozeman suggests it can be useful to alter the discussion beyond 'the public interest' to that of 'publicness or public values' in helping to progress our understanding of the public interest (2007, p. 139). In reality, the idea of values is often used interchangeably with interests, with values held by society at the top of an interest hierarchy (Wheeler 2006). Alternately, as Campbell and Marshall (2002) note, collective values transcend self-interests. While such distinctions might appear as fraught as locating a collective public interest, Bozeman suggests that they can be determined through the voice of the people via polling, plebiscites, referenda and research, though he adds 'intuition' should not be ignored as a way of understanding what values may apply (Bozeman 2007, p. 133). We might add to this the use of common sense and values that are consistent with long-argued ethical foundations such as do no intentional harm; enhance public welfare; and practice truthfully, openly and transparently.

As such, moral accountability is a direct result of understanding and applying public values. Agents need to have a clear understanding of the values held within a specific society and the expectations around decisions and actions that these values create. 'This notion of accountability relies heavily on the belief that decision makers are capable of developing a clear, "objective" view of what is "right" and "wrong" in any given situation' (Painter-Morland 2008, p. 6) and that public values provide 'guideposts rather than just a consideration or a check and balance' for citizens (Bozeman 2007, p. 177).

Elsewhere in the book we have examined the importance of considering and being open to the cultural values of others and the role this plays in understanding a diversity of public interests. In a business sense, a new approach to working within communities while acknowledging their values is seen in the practice of the 'social license to operate.' Occurring when a project requires the ongoing approval of the local community (or other relevant stakeholders), this requires an understanding and acceptance of the values of the community. Such a process calls for learning about local stakeholder values relating to their existing lifestyle, what they wish to maintain, where there may be flexibility for change, and so on (Business for Social Responsibility 2003, p. 15). The field of social license to operate has emerged as significant within the industries of mining and food integrity. The literature is littered with examples of crises which have emerged because, for example, mining companies have 'muscled into' environments without consideration of the values and interests they were affecting (see, for example, Business for Social Responsibility 2003; Pike 2012).

At the same time, the reader will recall the identification of natural capital as one of six to be reconciled in the public interest. As such, the environment provides a classic example of a public value which has emerged and shifted over time. Environmental or green values bring together ethics and ecology to involve giving greater normative consideration to nonhuman interests, including the status of animals and other natural objects, the preservation of biological diversity, the protection of ecosystems and the aesthetic impacts of human operations on the environment (DesJardins 2008, p. 1043). International laws are changing to accommodate this shift, for example, in climate change action by some countries (though not all); in identifying cultural connections between the environment and Indigenous people, such as the Australian Indigenous land rites; and in the landmark legal recognition of the personhood status achieved by the Whanganui River in New Zealand. This agreement between the New Zealand government and the Whanganui River Iwi people recognizes the river and all its tributaries as a single entity, giving it the status of a legal entity, complete with rights and interests (Shuttleworth 2012; Archer 2014).

> By granting legal status to the river, the parties found an innovative way to use the Crown's existing legal framework regarding legal standing, guardianship and property ownership in a manner that serves and defends *the best interests* of the river, while also respecting and preserving the iwi's traditional worldview and laws regarding their sacred duties to protect the river.
>
> (Archer 2014, p. 8, her italics)

The historic move which required 'renewed dialogue and cooperation with respect to waterways' between the Crown and Indigenous peoples is said to have provided impetus for similar claims in Canada's British Columbia over rivers, lakes and coastal waters (Archer 2014, p. 1). Archer (2014) notes how Indigenous peoples have identified key shared values within their laws and traditions which recognize the primacy of the environment and duties to protect the natural environment and future generations.

Bozeman argues that 'public values failure occurs when core public values are not reflected in social relations, either in the market or public policy' (2007, p. 145). In such instances, flaws in regulatory or policy-making processes may be found, such as those identified in the following list:

- poor public information, as seen in government non-disclosure;
- unequal/uneven distribution of benefits, as seen in public education;
- 'capture' of a regulatory system that does not consider external opinions;
- inadequate provider availability for a core public value, such as nuclear waste disposal;
- inadequate attention to 'the time-horizon,' which prioritizes the now over the future. (See the discussion in Bozeman 2007, pp. 148–53; Mitnick, and Mitnick and Getz chapter 2 in this book; Habermas chapter 7 in this book).

Conclusion

Thomas Bivins's groundbreaking article on the public interest begins by posing the following statement and questions (1993, p. 117):

> As the practice of public relations attempts to become the profession of public relations, clarification of its ethical obligation to serve the public interest is vital if it is to accomplish its goal ... The primary question discussed here is: Can public relations as mediator, respondent, and advocate, serve the public interest? And, if so, how?

The answer, in part, can be found from within public relations scholarship. A major development since Bivins wrote his paper in 1993 has been the move within public relations scholarship to engage in significant self-critique, with a growing critical literature, including debates on ethical practice (see, for example, L'Etang & Pieczka 1996; Moloney 2006; Weaver, Motion & Roper 2006; L'Etang 2006; Messina 2007; Bardham & Weaver 2011; Curtin & Gaither 2007, 2012; Holtzhausen 2012; Demetrious 2013; L'Etang, McKie, Snow & Xifra 2016). As public relations continues on the path to questioning and challenging what the industry does, how it goes about it, and how it might do it better, the increased self-critique and the public debate and transparency that follow have great potential for claims to the public interest.

Answers are not found simply in ethical investigations. As Slote (2013, p. 663) argues, 'Any ethical theory that makes it too easy always to know what to do or to feel will seem to that extent flawed or even useless because [it is] untrue to our soberer sense of the wrenching complexity of moral phenomena' (Slote 2013, p. 663). It would seem that the public interest represents such a complex moral phenomena—making it near impossible to answer Bivins's questions with any absolute certainty. On the other hand, ethics and moral philosophy—as theory or code—can assist in raising critical awareness and consciousness, placing public values such as environmental sustainability and Indigenous rights unavoidably in the path of big business and government. Public relations codes, as we have seen, do include some attention to the public interest and some attempt to reconcile conflicts or competing interests. Thus, as a starting point, educational spaces can be used as sites for interrogating a range of codes—perhaps not only the local one—to locate strengths, weaknesses, challenges and opportunities in navigating potential conflicts and competing interests. Codes provide a starting point for addressing the questions: 'Whose interest?' and 'How do we define the public interest in this particular circumstance?'

The book now continues examining some of these themes in its closing chapter, in a final consideration of the contested nature of the public interest in the theory and practice of public relations.

Note

1. This table is drawn from 84 codes which were freely accessed from the internet. Although every attempt was made to translate the 84 codes, it may be that some which included the public interest, or a variation of it, may be excluded from this list. Translations may vary using means other than used here (Google translator).

References

Archer, JL 2014, 'Rivers, rights and reconciliation in British Columbia: lessons learned from New Zealand's Whanganui River agreement', *Social Science Research Network,* pp. 1–21, viewed 12 June 2015, http://papers.ssrn.com/sol3/papers.cfm?abstract_id=2374454.

Aristotle, 2013, 'The nature of virtue', in R Shafer-Landau (ed.), *Ethical theory: an anthology,* 2nd edn, John Wiley & Sons, New York, pp. 615–30, from *Nichomachean ethics,* trans. T Irwin, Hackett Publishing, Indianapolis, IN, 1999.

Atherton, M, Cluett, C, McAdoo, O, Rawlinson, D & Sidoli, J 2008, *AQA philosophy,* Thomas Nelson, Cheltenham.

Baker, J 2008, 'Virtue ethics', in RW Kolb (ed.), *Encyclopaedia of business ethics and society, vol. 5,* Sage, Los Angeles, pp. 2190–96.

Bardham, N & Weaver, K (eds.) 2011, *Public relations in a global cultural context,* Routledge, New York.

Beauchamp, TL 2002, *Philosophical ethics: an introduction to moral philosophy,* McGraw Hill, Boston.

Begin, D 2012, 'Can public relations be in the public interest?' *Where to begin: life as my muse* [weblog], viewed 20 November 2013, http://www.wheretobegin.ca/can-public-relations-be-in-the-public-interest/.

Bivins, TH 1993, 'Public relations, professionalism, and the public interest', *Journal of Business Ethics,* February, vol. 12, no. 2, pp. 117–26.

Bohman, J & Rehg, W 2011, 'Jürgen Habermas', in EN Zalta (ed.), *The Stanford encyclopedia of philosophy*, winter edn, viewed 1 May 2015, http://plato.stanford. edu/archives/win2011/entries/habermas/.

Bozeman, B 2007, *Public values and public interest: counterbalancing economic individualism*, Georgetown University Press, Washington, DC.

Business of Social Responsibility 2003, *Social license to operate*, viewed 12 August 2015, http://commdev.org/files/858_file_BSR_Social_License_to_Operate.pdf

Campbell, H & Marshall, R 2002, 'Utilitarianism's bad breath? A re-evaluation of the public interest justification for planning', *Planning Theory*, vol. 1, no. 2, pp. 163–87.

Canada Public Relations Society CPRS 2013, *Mission, definition and values*, viewed 15 December 2013, http://www.cprs.ca/aboutus/mission.aspx

Ceranic, T 2008, 'Ethical absolutism', in RW Kolb (ed.), *Encyclopaedia of business ethics and society*, vol. 5, Sage, Los Angeles, pp. 2–3.

Curtin, PA & Gaither, TK 2007, *International public relations: negotiating culture, identity and power*, Sage, Thousand Oaks, CA.

Demetrious, K 2013, *Public relations, activism and social change: speaking up*, Routledge, London.

DesJardins, JR 2008, 'Environmental ethics,' in RW Kolb (ed.), *Encyclopaedia of business ethics and society*, vol. 5, Sage, Los Angeles, pp. 733–40.

Dewey, J 1927, *The public and its problems*, H. Holt & Co, New York.

Fawkes, J 2009, 'Integrating the shadow: a Jungian approach to professional ethics in public relations,' *Ethical Space: The International Journal of Communication Ethics*, vol. 6, no. 2, pp. 30–38.

Flathman, RE 1966, *The public interest: an essay concerning the normative discourse of politics*, John Wiley & Son, New York.

Foucault, M 1978, *The history of sexuality*, vol. 1: *an introduction*, trans. R Hurley, Penguin, Harmondsworth.

Freire, P 2005, *The pedagogy of the oppressed*, trans. MB Ramos, Continuum, New York, original work published 1970.

Gunn, JAW, 1968, Jeremy Bentham and the public interest, *Canadian Journal of Political Science*, vol. 1, no. 4, pp. 398–413.

Gunn, JAW, 1968a, 'Interest never lies: a 17th century political maxim', *Journal of the History of Ideas*, vol. 29, no. 8, pp. 551–64.

Harrison, J 2004, 'Conflicts of duty and the virtues of Aristotle in public relations ethics: continuing the conversation commenced by Monica Walle', *Prism*, 2, viewed 27 June 2015, http://www.prismjournal.org/fileadmin/Praxis/Files/ Journal_Files/Issue2/Harrison.pdf.

Harrison, K & Galloway, C 2005, 'Public relations ethics: a simpler (but not simplistic) approach to the complexities', *Prism*, 3, pp. 1–17, viewed 26 June 2015, http://www.prismjournal.org/fileadmin/Praxis/Files/Journal_Files/Issue3/ Harrison_Galloway.pdf.

Habermas, J 1989, *The structural transformation of the public sphere: an inquiry into a category of bourgeois society*, MIT Press, Cambridge, MA.

Habermas, J 1996, *Between facts and norms: contributions to a discourse theory of law and democracy*, MIT Press, Cambridge, MA.

Holtzhausen, D 2012, *Public relations as activism: postmodern approaches to theory and practice*, Routledge, New York.

Hursthouse, R 2013, 'Normative virtue values', in R Shafer-Landau (ed.), *Ethical theory: an anthology,* 2nd edn, John Wiley & Sons, New York, pp. 645–53.

Institute of Chartered Accountants in England and Wales (ICAEW) 2012, *Acting in the public interest: a framework for analysis,* Market Foundations Initiative, viewed 1 March 2015, http://www.icaew.com/s/media/corporate/files/technical/ethics/professional_ethics/acting%20in%20the%20public%20interest%20framework%20template%2004%2014.ashx.

Institute of Chartered Accountants in England and Wales (ICAEW) 2014, *Acting in the public interest: framework template,* viewed 1 March 2015, http://www.icaew.*com*/en/technical/ethics/the-public-interest.

L'Etang, J 2003, 'The myth of the "ethical guardian": an examination of its origins, potency and illusions', *Journal of Communication Management,* vol. 8, no. 1, pp. 53–67.

L'Etang, J & Pieczka, M (eds.) 1996, *Critical perspectives in public relations,* Thomson Business Press, London.

L'Etang, J & Pieczka M (eds.) 2006, *Critical debates and contemporary practice,* Lawrence Erlbaum, Mahwah, NJ.

L'Etang, J, McKie, D, Snow, N & Xifra, J (eds.) 2016, *The Routledge handbook of critical public relations,* Routledge, London.

Lippmann, W 1927, *The phantom public,* Harcourt, Brace and Co., New York.

Lippmann, W 1955, *Essays in the public philosophy,* Little Brown, Boston.

Longstaff, S 1994, *A statement about codes of ethics and conduct,* St James Ethics Centre, 5 November, viewed 2 January 2015, http://www.ethics.org.au/on-ethics/our-articles/november-1994/a-statement-about-codes-of-ethics-and-conduct.

Martinson, DL 2000, 'Ethical decision making in public relations: what would Aristotle say?', *Public Relations Quarterly,* vol. 47, no. 3, pp. 18–39.

Messina, A 2007, 'Public relations, the public interest and persuasion: an ethical approach,' *Journal of Communication Management,* vol. 11, no. 1, pp. 29–52.

Mickey, RJ 2003, *Deconstructing public relations: public relations criticism,* Lawrence Erlbaum, Mahwah, NJ.

Mitnick, B 1980, *The political economy of regulation,* Columbia University Press, New York.

Mitnick, B & Getz, KA 2008, 'Regulation and regulatory practices', in RW Kolb (ed.), *Encyclopedia of business ethics and society, vol. 5,* Sage, Los Angeles, pp. 1787–1802.

Moloney, K 2006, *Rethinking public relations,* Routledge, London.

Painter-Morland, M 2008, 'Accountability', in RW Kolb (ed.), *Encyclopedia of business ethics and society, vol. 5,* Sage, Los Angeles, pp. 4–8.

Pike, R 2012, *Social license to operate,* Schroders, New York.

Rawls, J 1971, *Theory of justice,* Harvard University Press, Cambridge, MA.

Said, E 1978, *Orientalism,* Pantheon, New York.

Sandel, MJ 2009, *Justice: what's the right thing to do,* Penguin, London.

Shafer-Landau, R 2013, 'Introduction to part XI: virtue ethics,' in R Shafer-Landau (ed.), *Ethical theory: an anthology,* 2nd edn, John Wiley & Sons, New York, pp. 611–15.

Shuttleworth, K 2012, 'Agreement entitles Whanganui River to legal identity', *New Zealand Herald,* 30 August, viewed 12 June 2015 http://www.nzherald.co.nz/nz/news/article.cfm?c_id=1&objectid=10830586.

Slote, M 2013, 'Agent-based virtue ethics', in R Shafer-Landau (ed.), *Ethical theory: an anthology*, 2nd edn, John Wiley & Sons, New York, pp. 653–64.

Tilley, E 2005, 'The ethics pyramid: making ethics unavoidable in the public relations process', *Journal of Mass Media Ethics*, vol. 20, no. 4, pp. 305–20.

Walle, M 2003, 'Commentary: What happened to public responsibility? The lack of society in public relations codes of ethics', *Prism*, no. 1, pp. 1–5.

Weaver, CK, Motion, J & Roper, J 2006, 'From propaganda to discourse (and back again): truth, power, the public interest, and public relations', in J L'Etang, & M Pieczka (eds.), *Public relations: critical debates and contemporary practice*, Lawrence Erlbaum, Mahwah NJ, pp. 7–23.

Wheeler, C 2006, 'The public interest: we know it's important, but do we know what it means', in R Creyke & A Mantel (eds.), *AIAL Forum no. 48*, Australian Institute of Administrative Law, pp. 12–26.

Codes of Ethics

Association of Consulting in Public Relations and Communication, Spain, ADECEC, http://www.adecec.com/quienes_somos/codigo_etico.php; http://www.microsofttranslator.com/bv.aspx?from=&to=en&a=http%3A%2F%2Fwww.adecec.com%2Fquienes_somos%2Fcodigo_etico.php.

Association of Public Relations Agencies Czech Republic, APRA, PR Code of Ethics for ordering parties, http://www.apra.cz/en/about_apra/professional_standards.html.

Association of Swedish Communication Professionals, SACP, http://www.sverigeskommunikatorer.se/om-oss/in-english/statutes-and-ethics/.

Bahrain Public Relations Association, BPRA, http://www.prbahrain.org/en/; http://www.prbahrain.org/en/details.php?artid=26.

Chamber of Commerce Public Relations Czech Republic, KoPR, http://www.komorapr.cz/; http://www.microsofttranslator.com/bv.aspx?from=&to=en&a=http%3A%2F%2Fwww.komorapr.cz%2Fkodex.

Code of Athens, http://www.ipra.org/pdf/Code_of_Athens.pdf.

Code of Lisbon, http://www.polisphere.eu/database/verhaltenskodizes/european-code-of-professional-conduct-in-pr-code-of-lisbon/.

Danish Association of Public Relation Consultancies, BPRV, Ethical Norms, http://www.corresponsables.com/servicios/directorio/danish-association-public-relations-consultancies-bprv.

Danish Communication Association, DKF, http://www.kommunikationsforening.dk/.

Estonian Public Relations Association, EPRA, http://www.microsofttranslator.com/bv.aspx?from=&to=en&a=http%3A%2F%2Fwww.epra.ee%2F%3Fpage_id%3D71.

Finnish Association of Communications Professionals, ProCom, Ethical Guidelines, http://www.microsofttranslator.com/bv.aspx?from=&to=en&a=http%3A%2F%2Fprocom.fi%2Fviestintaala%2Fohjeet-ja-periaatteet%2Fprocomin-eettiset-ohjeet%2F.

German Public Relations Consultancies Association, GPRG, http://www.dprg.de/_Verband.aspx; http://www.microsofttranslator.com/bv.aspx?from=&to=en&a=http%3A%2F%2Fwww.gpra.de%2F.

Global Alliance for Public Relations and Communication Management, GA, http://www.globalalliancepr.org/website/sites/default/files/nolie/Governance/Code%20of%20ethics/GA-Code%20of%20Ethics.pdf.

Hungarian Public Relations Association, MPRSZ, http://www.mprsz.hu/; http://www.microsofttranslator.com/bv.aspx?from=&to=en&a=http%3A%2F%2Fwww.mprsz.hu%2Fetikai-kodex%2F.

Information Press & Communication, France, IPC, http://www.infopressecom.org/; http://www.microsofttranslator.com/bv.aspx?from=&to=en&a=http%3A%2F%2Fwww.infopressecom.org%2Fcms%2Fpages%2Fcode-de-deontologie.

Information Presse & Communication IPC, http://www.infopressecom.org/.

Institute of Public Relations Malaysia, IPRM, http://iprm.org.my/download/accreditation-programme-2011.pdf.

Institute of Public Relations of Singapore, IPRS, http://iprs.org.sg/iprs-code-of-ethics.

International Association of Business Communicators, IABC, http://www.iabc.com/about/code.htm; http://www.iabc.com/about-us/leaders-and-staff/code-of-ethics/.

Israel Public Relations Association, ISPRA, http://www.microsofttranslator.com/bv.aspx?from=&to=en&a=http%3A%2F%2Fwww.allmarketing.co.il%2Fminisites%2FIndex.asp%3FArticleID%3D778%26CategoryID%3D507%26Page%3D1.

Israeli Association of Public Relations and Media Relations, ISPRA, Professional ethics, http://www.ispra.org.il/ http://www.ispra.org.il/196019/%D7%9B%D7%9C%D7%9C%D7%99-%D7%90%D7%AA%D7%99%D7%A7%D7%94-%D7%9E%D7%A7%D7%A6%D7%95%D7%A2%D7%99%D7%AA.

Italian Public Relations Federation, FERPi, http://www.ferpi.it/ferpi/associazione; http://www.microsofttranslator.com/bv.aspx?from=&to=en&a=http%3A%2F%2Fwww.ferpi.it%2Fferpi%2Fassociazione%2Fstatuto_e_codici%2Fcodici-ferpi.

Komora Public Relations (Chamber of Public Relations Czech Republic), Komora, komoraPRhttp://www.komorapr.cz/kodex; http://www.microsofttranslator.com/BV.aspx?ref=IE8Activity&a=http%3A%2F%2Fwww.komorapr.cz%2Fkodex.

Mexican Association of Public Relations Professionals, PRORP, http://www.prorp.org.mx/; http://www.microsofttranslator.com/bv.aspx?from=&to=en&a=http%3A%2F%2Fwww.prorp.org.mx%2Findex.php%3Foption%3Dcom_content%26view%3Darticle%26id%3D95%26Itemid%3D223.

National Association of Public Relations of Luxembourg, CENARP, http://www.cenarp.lu/index.php/qui-sommes-nous; http://www.microsofttranslator.com/bv.aspx?from=&to=en&a=http%3A%2F%2Fwww.cenarp.lu%2Findex.php%2Fqui-sommes-nous.

National Committee of Public Relations from the Cuban Association of Social Communicators, ACCS, http://www.accs.co.cu/ http://www.accs.co.cu/images/docs/CODIGO DE ETICA PROFESIONAL ACCS.

Netherlands Association of Public Relations Consultants, VPRA, http://www.vpra.nl/nl/Nieuws/; http://www.microsofttranslator.com/bv.aspx?from=&to=en&a=http%3A%2F%2Fwww.vpra.nl%2Fnl%2FNieuws%2F.

Nigerian Institute of Public Relations, NIPR, http://nipr.com.ng/about-us/ethics-code/.

Polish Public Relations Association, PSPR, http://www.polskipr.pl/english/ http://www.microsofttranslator.com/bv.aspx?from=&to=en&a=http%3A%2F%2Fwww.polskipr.pl%2Fo-stowarzyszeniu%2Fkodeks-etyki%2F.

PR Suisse, PR. http://www.prsuisse.ch/.

Public Relations Association of Indonesia, PERHUMAS, http://www.perhumas. or.id/; http://www.microsofttranslator.com/bv.aspx?from=&to=en&a=http%3A% 2F%2Fwww.perhumas.or.id%2F%3Fpage_id%3D24;   http://www.perhumas. or.id/?page_id=24.

Public Relations Association of Uganda, PRAU, http://www.prauganda.com/ component/k2/130-code-of-ethics.html.

Public Relations Industry Denmark, PRB, Ethical Rules, http://www.microsofttrans- lator.com/bv.aspx?from=&to=en&a=http%3A%2F%2Fwww.publicrelations- branchen.dk%2Fetiske-regler.

Public Relations Institute of Australia, PRIA, http://www.pria.com.au/documents/ item/6317.

Public Relations Institute of New Zealand, PRINZ, https://12248-console.member- connex.com/Folder?Action=View%20File&Folder_id=73&File=PRINZ%20 Code%20of%20Ethics_WEB.pdf.

Public Relations Institute of Southern Africa, PRISA, Code of Ethics and Professional Standards, http://www.prisa.co.za/images/downloads/Code_of_Ethics/Prisa%20 code%20of%20ethics%20%20professional%20standards.pdf.

Public Relations Society of America, PRSA, http://www.prsa.org/AboutPRSA/Ethics/ documents/Code%20of%20Ethics.pdf.

Regional Council of Public Relations Practitioners Brazil, CONRERP, http://www. conrerp4.org.br/home/show_page.php?id=2021; http://www.microsofttranslator. com/BV.aspx?ref=IE8Activity&a=http%3A%2F%2F65.55.108.4%2F- proxy.ashx%3Fh%3DV0XNM40r2j1gUTXI7ytc7UAWdfjJPNpB%26a% 3Dhttp%253A%252F%252Fwww.conrerp4.org.br%252Fhome%252Fshow_ page.php%253Fid%253D5271%2526.

Russian Public Relations Association, RPRA, Code of Professional and Ethical Prin- ciples in the Field of Public Relations 2001, http://www.raso.ru/; http://www. microsofttranslator.com/bv.aspx?from=&to=en&a=http%3A%2F%2Fwww. raso.ru%2Fpro%2Fpr_ethics%2Frussian_codex.

Spanish Association of Communicators, DIRCOM, http://www.dircom.org/; http://www.microsofttranslator.com/bv.aspx?from=&to=en&a=http%3A% 2F%2Fwww.dircom.org%2Fsobre-dircom%2Fcodigo-etico.

Swiss Public Relations Association, SPRV, Professional Ethics, http://www. prsuisse.ch/de; http://www.microsofttranslator.com/bv.aspx?from=&to=en&a= http%3A%2F%2Fwww.prsuisse.ch%2Fde%2Fpr-der-schweiz%2Fpr- wissen%2Fberufsethik.

Syndicat national des attachees de presse et des conseillers en relations public, SYNAP, http://www.synap.org/index.php; http://www.microsofttranslator.com/ bv.aspx?from=&to=en&a=http%3A%2F%2Fwww.synap.org%2Findex. php%3Faction%3Drubrique%26id%3D20.

SYNTEC Public Relations Consultants Organization France, http://www.microsoft- translator.com/bv.aspx?from=&to=en&a=http%3A%2F%2Fwww.syntec-rp. com%2F8-syntec-conseil-en-relations-publics%2F211-qui-sommes-nous%2F56 3-deontologie.aspx.

The Federal Association of German Press Officer, BdP, http://www.bdp-net.de/.

The Norwegian Communication Association, NCA, Professional Ethical Principles, http://www.kommunikasjon.no/Foreningen/om-oss/etisk-r%C3%A5d; http://www. microsofttranslator.com/bv.aspx?from=&to=en&a=http%3A%2F%2Fwww. kommunikasjon.no%2FForeningen%2Fom-oss%2Fetisk-r%25C3%25A5d.

Turkish Public Relations Association, The Profession's Principles, TUHID, http://www. tuhid.org/; http://www.microsofttranslator.com/bv.aspx?from=&to=en&a= http%3A%2F%2Fwww.tuhid.org%2Ftuhid-meslek-ilkeleri.html.

Ukrainian Association of Public Relations, VRPL, Code of Professional Ethics, http://www.uapr.com.ua/en; http://www.microsofttranslator.com/BV.aspx?ref= IE8Activity&a=http%3A%2F%2Fwww.uapr.com.ua%2Fua%2Fethics.

Codes of Conduct

Belgian Public Relations Consultants Association, BPCA, http://bprca.be/site/images/ stories/pdfs/stockholm.pdf.

Chartered Institute of Public Relations, CIPR, http://www.cipr.co.uk/sites/default/ files/CIPR%20Code%20of%20Conduct%2008-03-2012_0.pdf.

China International Public Relations Association, CIPRA, http://www.cipra.org.cn/; http://www.microsofttranslator.com/bv.aspx?from=&to=en&a= http%3A%2F%2Fwww.cipra.org.cn%2Ftemplates%2FT_List%2Findex. aspx%3Fnodeid%3D2%26page%3DContentPage%26contentid%3D102.

European Association of Communication Directors, EACD, http://www.eacd-online. eu/membership/code-conduct.

International Public Relations Association, IPRA, http://ipra.org/about/ipra-codes.

Italian Public Relations Federation, FERPi, http://www.ferpi.it/ferpi/associazione; http://www.microsofttranslator.com/bv.aspx?from=&to=en&a= http%3A%2F%2Fwww.ferpi.it%2Fferpi%2Fassociazione%2Fstatuto_e_ codici%2Fcodici-ferpi%2Fcodice-di-comportamento-professionale-della- ferpi%2Fshow_codici_recepiti%2F26409.

Middle East Public Relations Association, MEPRA, http://www.mepra.org/about-us/ standards-and-governance/.

Public Relations Association of Austria/ Public Relations Verband Austria, PRVA, http://prva.at/about-us/our-concept; http://www.microsofttranslator.com/bv. aspx?from=&to=en&a=http%3A%2F%2Fwww.prva.at%2Fueber-uns%2F- grundlagen%2Fethische-grundsatze%2Fethik-ehrenkodex%2F.

Public Relations Consultants Association of Ireland, PRCA, http://www.prca.ie/; http://www.prca.ie/article.aspx?cat=3&sub=5.

Public Relations Institute of Australia, PRIA, Code of Conduct for Registered Con- sultancies, http://www.pria.com.au/documents/item/6494.

Public Relations Society of Kenya, PRSK, http://www.prsk.co.ke/index.php/ membership/code-of-conduct.

Public Relations Society of Slovenia, PRSS, http://www.piar.si/o-drustvu/temeljni- dokumenti; http://www.microsofttranslator.com/bv.aspx?from=&to=en&a=http% 3A%2F%2Fwww.piar.si%2Fo-drustvu%2Ftemeljni-dokumenti%2Fkodeks- etike-prss%2F.

Codes/Charters by other names

Association of Public Relations Consultancies in Sweden, PRECIS, Standards, http://www.precis.se/.

Canadian Public Relations Society Inc, CPRS, Code of Professional Standards, http://www.cprs.ca/aboutus/code_ethic.aspx.

German Public Relations Society, DPRG, Communication Code, http://www.micro-softtranslator.com/bv.aspx?from=&to=en&a=http%3A%2F%2Fwww.dprg.de%2F_Verband.aspx.

Hong Kong Public Relations Professionals' Association, HKPRPA, Code of Standards, http://prpa.com.hk/?p=84.

Public Relations Consultants Association—UK, PRCA, Professional Charter, http://www.prca.org.uk/assets/files/PRCA%20Professional%20Charter%20and%20Codes%20(October%202013).pdf.

Public Relations Consultants Association of India, PRCAI, Consultancy Management Standard, http://prcai.org/; http://prcai.org/about-us/consultancy-management-standard-cms/.

Public Relations Institute of Ireland, PRII, PRII Code of Professional Practice for Public Affairs & Lobbying, http://www.prii.ie/show_content.aspx?idcategory=1&idsubcategory=1#PRRIICode.

Sweden Communicators, SACP, Professional Standards, http://www.sverigeskommu-nikatorer.se/fakta-och-verktyg/om-yrket-kommunikator/yrkesetik/.

Syrian Public Relations Association, SPRA, Code of Professional Standards, http://www.spra-sy.com/english/?more=1311&category_id=117.

9 The Public Interest and Public Relations

Key Intersections and Considered Directions

... the agent himself must consider on each occasion what the situation
requires.
(Aristotle, *The Nicomachean Ethics* in Flathman 1966, epigraph).

Introduction

Although the public interest is by no means an unknown concept for public relations, it has not gained the attention it might have. Though it has been examined on and off since the 1950s, it has not taken root as a theory or paradigm. Contemporary public relations books and monographs, rarely, if ever, include the public interest in their indexes, nor is it generally linked by keyword searches to online public relations research. As we examined in chapter 1, a crowd-sourced effort to define public relations in the United States earlier this decade found *no one* prioritized the public interest, a point which caused leading practitioner Harold Burson to speak out in concern: 'Yes, communications and establishing relationships are part of the mix, but the process must start with appropriate behaviour that serves the public interest,' (Burson 2012, n.p.). Burson was not alone in identifying this lacuna in current public relations thinking. At the same time, Canadian practitioners also called for a re-engagement with the public interest, embedding it in their definition and within their code of practice (CPRS 2013; Begin 2012).

At a history of public relations conference in 2015, a paper based on the origins of the public interest, as outlined in this book, was described by conference delegates as 'provocative' and 'controversial.' The idea of applying the concept to public relations was received with both overwhelming enthusiasm and total rejection, the latter summed up in the argument that 'it is not consistent with capitalism' ... how can the public interest exist when there are campaigns that have a deleterious effect on society? Yet, for every argument against, a counter can be made; public relations can and does develop campaigns that have harmful effects. It also develops alternative campaigns through which society can make informed choices, debate truths, help others and sometimes even raise the bar so that, through debate and discussion, more information is known and social progress is made. This is where the public interest, as outlined in this book, makes its mark. Fundamentally, the public interest is as much a way of thinking and doing as a way of achieving outcomes, essentially a theoretical approach that does not easily translate to 'this' campaign or 'that' tactic. Wheeler explains it is 'the objective of, or the approach to be adopted, in decision making rather than a specific or immutable outcome to be achieved' (2006, p. 24).

In its early analysis, the public interest was used as a political concept to express approval or commendation of public policy which benefitted a particular section of society (Flathman 1966). This has been embraced and further developed, ubiquitously incorporated across society, as incorporated in this book for the following reasons:

- in media, 'it will often be a matter of balancing a number of outcomes which would be for the common good, but which cannot all be achieved simultaneously' (Leveson 2012, p. 69);
- in law and policy, 'Legislators and policy makers recognise that the public interest will change over time and according to the circumstances of each situation' (Carter & Bouris 2006, p. 4);
- in politics and regulation, when regulatory systems work in the public interest, they efficiently and openly balance external interests (Mitnick & Getz 2008);
- in anthropology, it operates on 'macrosocial issues related to equality of educational opportunity, social justice, health and nutrition, human rights, and social wellbeing' (Sanday & Jannowitz 2004, p. 65);
- in accounting, it seeks 'to allow for variation in circumstances and public interest meaning' (ICAEW 2012, p. 4);
- in planning, it is used as 'the pivot around which debates about the nature of planning and its purposes turn' (Campbell & Marshall 2002, p. 181); and
- in public health, through proposing the 'representative individual,' that is, a hypothetical individual who equates with the public interest because it could be anyone (Ho 2013, p. 13; see later in this chapter).

Scholars and practitioners have thus considered the public interest and constructed their own interpretations for how it can apply to their respective, sometimes overlapping, fields. It would seem that, despite its problems and limitations, the public interest remains a constant and ubiquitous force across a very wide range of disciplines and fields.

This final chapter pieces together the many and diverse theories, paradigms and practices we have moved through in this book: it responds to criticisms, proposes frameworks and models, and brings the journey to a point at which we can move forward in debate and discussion about the public interest in public relations; not an end, rather a beginning.

Responding to the Criticisms

Several key reasons have been asserted over the years by public interest nay-sayers, those who see it as unworkable and largely unachievable. The first two are closely aligned, fundamentally found in its ambiguous and nebulous nature and the interest-based conflict it represents. Concerns are also raised for the absence of a mechanism through which to advocate, defend and manage the formal decision-making process of what is in the public interest. These issues have been variously addressed, both implicitly and explicitly, in the preceding chapters, and we will briefly summarize each one as we also draw together some of the book's key themes.

On Conflicting Interests and Ambiguity

Dewey noted in *Liberalism and Social Action* (1935 cited in Bozeman 2007, p. 105): 'Of course there are conflicting interests: otherwise there would be no social problems.' Debates will be forever ongoing over conflicting interests, those which are resolved will make space for new ones, be they same-sex marriage, asylum seekers, childhood immunization, animal rights, women's rights, Indigenous rights, greenhouse gas emissions and renewable energy, spending cuts, genetically modified foods, gun laws, and so the list goes on. As a starting point, to paraphrase Mansbridge (1998), any question of the public interest needs to ask: 'Whose interest?'

The contest of competing interests can, and should, lead to discussion and debate where ideas are 'thrashed out,' where decision makers and members of the public are placed in positions where they have to justify their reasoning. As we have examined within the book, resources that embed power are unevenly applied within political systems and, as such, there are 'myriad forms inequality can take' (Mansbridge 1998, p. 12). However, at the same time, weak publics can hold governments accountable through the systems that exist within civil society (Habermas 1996). So, the fact that the public interest is open to contest and scrutiny can provide the context for social change, exposing 'capture' or corruption and enabling social justice imperatives to come under review.

A positive outcome of the postmodern turn has been an awareness of difference, otherness and the dynamic nature of situations, plus the rejection of universalism and the supremacy of scientific reasoning. Through postmodernism, feminism, postcolonialism and other critical critiques has come the recognition of the fragmented, pluralistic and heterogeneous nature of many contemporary societies and the variety of lived experiences of people within them (Campbell & Marshall 2002). As such, the politics of difference brings with it multiple publics and multiple perspectives, enabling 'struggle for the right to difference, as well as the right to a voice in decisions affecting a wide range of groups, including indigenous peoples, migrants and refugees, women, and gays and lesbians' (Sandercock 2000 in Campbell & Marshall

2002, p. 173). Accordingly the public interest should reflect the diversity of society's interests, discovered discursively through participant involvement (Healey 1992). The result then is that pluralist, process-driven, rights-based, participant-oriented and dialogic directions have emerged as critical elements within contemporary public interest thinking.

With such diversity comes an inherent need for adaptability, which finds the public interest's lack of specificity can also be a strength. Because the public interest is not fixed in time, policies, regulations and laws can be responsive to norms, mores and value systems that reflect change and, over time, change themselves. This level of adaptability, even ambiguity, must therefore remain open to scrutiny and criticism which, when placed within time and context, can translate from conceptual to functional, such as the freedom of information laws, the Indigenous courts, the referendum on gay marriage, social capital fueled regeneration, and so on, as examined throughout this book. Indeed, the public interest is generally employed in such a fashion that the meaning will be inferred from its usage at the time (Bozeman 2007) as courts, legislators and policy makers find the 'rich and variable' nature of the public interest to be useful as a guide for decision makers (Wheeler 2006, p. 18).

On the Role of the Agent

Mitnick (1980, 2008) identifies how the public interest can be managed through the mechanism of agency. Those in agency roles may be legal counsel, accountants, public relations practitioners or others who 'negotiate' the public interest. In formal contexts, contracts will thus require the agent to act with a fiduciary interest, that is, in the interests of another. So, where does this leave the public interest if the agent is acting for a special interest? Mitnick argues that 'the genuinely held, terminal preferences of public interest agents for the concept of the public interest for which they act may even reinforce their fiduciary preferences' (1980, p. 92). In other words, agents may (perhaps should?) bring an advisory role to their agency where they believe a public interest may outweigh the special or private interest of their employer or to whomever they hold the fiduciary duty.

Agency is examined and used in two principal ways. Moral agency is a philosophical concept which centers on living within society and making moral judgments, as well as balancing intentions with consequences (Crozier Garcia 2007, p. 1411). Alternately, as agency theory, it is a concept derived initially from economic theory but now part of sociology and political theory, based within an agent-principal relationship, incorporating service, control and power differentials (Mitnick 2008). In critical communication terms these two approaches are brought together, explained as 'the capacity of human beings to engage with structures that encompass their lives, to make meanings through this engagement, and at the same time, creating discursive openings to transform these structures' (Dutta, Ban & Pal 2012, p. 7), as previously outlined in chapter 3. Through the role of agency, public interest information will 'inform governments about policy making which, in turn, deliver benefits to society, build social capital, and place the information in the public domain, open to scrutiny, to ensure government accountability and transparency' (Henninger 2013, p. 81). It is precisely because of these functions of informing, interpreting and advising that public relations may be one of *the* best jobs for the task, providing information and clarifying the contemporary social and political currents of thought on issues such as:

- Is it acceptable to keep children seeking asylum in off-shore detention centers?
- Is it time to consider introducing gay marriage legislation?
- Is it time to educate women and men about the health and personal risks associated with genital mutilation?
- Is it appropriate to use an online information facility such as Wikipedia to mask a personal and commercial agenda?
- Is it appropriate to develop a cultural facility without sufficient consultation with the affected community?
- Can Indigenous deaths in custody and Indigenous incarceration numbers be reduced by using a more culturally appropriate legal model?
- Can regional communities re-invent themselves when they pool their talents and gain government support?
- How do we best connect with diverse stakeholders and communities on important matters of literacy?

Each one of these questions has been asked within the snapshots of this book. Each presents a complex situation—some more so than others—which requires research, reflection and consultation with multiple stakeholders. And, finally, each requires sensitivity to pluralist thinking, diversity and cultural difference because each represents a problem or challenge which calls for social change or development.

Ex Ante *and* Ex Post *Frameworks*

Throughout the book we have explicitly and implicitly considered the public interest from *ex ante* (before) and *ex post* (after) perspectives in determining its usefulness. It is to these concepts that we now turn. Economist and health policy scholar Lok-Sang Ho (2011, 2013) argues for an *ex ante* approach to the public interest; that is, it should be applied *before* decisions are made or actions are taken. His analysis departs from many others who view it as best applied *ex post*, or determined after decisions are made, with actions considered on a case-by-case basis. Ho's theoretical direction places the question of how to manage the public interest firmly at the start of any process. He bases his findings on an examination of health policies from 12 countries, premising his observations on the idea of policy makers taking an impartial position, using *ex ante* policy development in order to maximize the benefits for what he calls the 'representative individual,' that is, a hypothetical individual who has no fixed identity (2013, p. 13). In effect, he argues, this 'representative individual' equates with the public interest because it could be anyone. '[W]e simply imagine ourselves to be blind to our identities but ... we could be anyone in the community, including the unfortunate ones' (Ho 2013, p. 13). Based on this, he argues that the public interest is maximized through the *ex ante* welfare of this individual, which provides clearer choices for policy development. He presents a hypothetical example:

> Consider a city with a population of seven million, such as Hong Kong in 2011. Should we spend $7 million on one patient to cure a rare and crippling disease that is expected to hit one out of the seven million population each year? If we imagine that the disease randomly strikes anyone in the city, then since spending only $1 per capita a year can eliminate a real and serious threat, the city should certainly spend the money. The cost of $1 per person per year should be far smaller than the *ex ante* loss of welfare due to the threat of an untreated crippling disease.
> (Ho 2013, p. 13)

As a summary, we could apply it in the following formula: *Ex ante welfare + representative individual = public interest*. According to Ho, the hallmark of the public interest is the impartiality or lack of personal interest in health decisions. He argues that what makes a 'good health care system ... should be funded in part by taxes, and in part by user charges, in part by insurance funds. It should avail citizens of choice, but it should provide basic protection to all' (2013, p. 147). In addressing how health care can line up with the public interest, Ho notes how such policies are not only about health; how they should take a holistic approach in order to best promote the public interest; and how they include everything from food safety and driving habits to workplace safety and crime prevention. Thus, Ho presents a major challenge to the public interest, that is, the interconnectedness of policies, each to be considered in its own right, by unconnected policy makers, while ultimately incorporating those in every part of the process, including communication and information exchange functions. Though he couches his public interest imperative within an *economic framework*, social benefits are also apparent.

In contrast to the *ex ante* approach, the Institute of Chartered Accountants in England and Wales (ICAEW) argues for an *ex post* approach to develop what may be the first 'industry framework' for working in the public interest (ICAEW 2012). It includes a set of criteria for evaluating how to judge the public interest, using transparency and balance as fundamental tools, and taking the view that the validity of the public interest rests with both 'a pattern of behaviour that builds up reputation over time, as well as information directly relevant to the proposal' (ICAEW 2012, p. 4). As with other reports which have been examined in the book—for example, Wheeler (2006), Carter and Bouris (2006) and Leveson (2012), and a general theme that has emerged throughout the literature—the ICAEW chose not to define the public interest but instead developed a framework to assist policy makers and others involved in implementing measures acting in the public interest. It noted:

> … the framework should be useful to anyone as a tool for challenge and relevant to any of the wide range of actions that are asserted to be in the public interest … the framework also has a role for individuals considering an action such as disclosure of a matter that would otherwise be confidential, in the public interest (2012, p. 5).

The framework is particularly relevant for an analysis of the public interest in public relations because it emerged from an industry that, like public relations, is tasked with agency. It also acts as a reflexive point on ethical standards and professionalization. Thus, for those in public relations seeking to advance the field's professionalism, the framework represents useful scaffolding for better understanding and applying the public interest as part of professional status. This link between the public interest and professionalism runs through much of the literature across various disciplines (see, for example, Campbell & Marshall 2002, p. 169; Bivins 1993; Harrison 2004; Messina 2007).

The ICAEW use seven key elements to determine whether a party may be acting in the public interest. These have been used to develop a process framework, as represented in Table 9.1.

Table 9.1 A 7-step public interest process framework

Key Issues	Key Questions
Credentials for invoking the public interest:	Should credentials be questioned? What safeguards can be/have been put in place to check these?
A public interest matter:	What advantage is being sought in arguing that the issue is a public interest matter (improved implementation, persuasion, justification, serving remit)? Should it be a public interest matter?
The relevant publics:	Is it clear who the public/s is/are?
The relevant public's wants:	What do the relevant public/s really want (freedom to go about business, defence of interests, defence of basic living standards, preservation of core values)?
Constraints to wants:	Are there reasons why the wants might have been 'wrong' (under or misinformation, emotional or charismatic sway, inadvertent collective harm)? Are there externalities that have not been factored in? Has the future been taken into account properly? Are there over-riding values (virtue, consequence, duty, justice)? If over-riding values are being applied, are they transparent, including how conflicts between values have been considered and/or resolved?

(Continued)

Key Issues	Key Questions
Aggregation & Decision:	Have the problem, objectives and potential alternative actions been established? Has a rational assessment of the outcome of each potential action been made (e.g. on an expected value, or utility basis)? Are there measurement issues? Can they be overcome? (Consider incommensurability, subjectivity, interaction, weighting, trade-offs. Is it clear whether the outcome is supportable in terms of ends and means? Does the solution stack up on an 'informed intuition' basis)?
Implementation:	Is the right approach carrot, stick or sermon (or combination)? What infrastructure and support tools are available? What do we need for implementation?

While this table provides a seven-step approach for working through issues related to the public interest, others have also suggested simple approaches to balancing interest determinations. For example, Ombudsman Chris Wheeler (2006) advocates a three-step process of, first, identifying the relevant public/s; second, identifying the 'public interest' based on primary, secondary and tertiary research; and, finally, assessing and weighing the competing or conflicting interests including the revealed majority views, the views of the elected members of the public and an objective assessment from a third party. Another model is provided by ethicist Thomas Beauchamp (2001) who suggests a five-step approach to resolving moral dilemmas or disagreements:

- Obtain objective information.
- Provide definitional clarity.
- Adopt a code.
- Use examples and counterexamples.
- Analyze arguments.

Despite the absence of definitional clarity—an issue dealt with elsewhere in the book—Beauchamp's approach is nevertheless useful. These approaches are consistent with introducing a *Public Interest Standards Test* to ensure transparency, participation, consultation, reasoned argument, and analysis of issues such as monopolies. Though formalizing any set of standards comes with its own challenges and hurdles, it could provide a useful adjunct to the existing public relations codes in assisting with the abstract nature of the public interest.

But how then do we reconcile the *ex ante* and the *ex post*? The *ex post* approach has provided the rationale for determining the public interest, specific to *each* context and time, on a case-by-case basis. So, are the *ex ante* and *ex post* necessarily at odds with each other, as they have been previously presented (Ho 2011, 2013; Messina 2007) or can the two co-exist, conceived at the start of a problem/issue/dilemma/project in *planning* and reviewed throughout *evaluation* when information is made available, in a manner quite consistent with public relations research and evaluation practices that work as a cycle? Wheeler (2006) proposes the public interest is best understood as having two separate components: objectives and outcomes, and process and procedure. This provides an alternative, flexible way of considering the two approaches and one which is more consistent with public relations methodologies and discourse. Accordingly, it is suggested that *ex ante* and *ex post* approaches can both be useful.

Public Interest Models for Public Relations

Seib and Fitzpatrick (1995) identify an ethical model for public relations practice based on five duties: duty to oneself, the client, the employer, the profession and society. Various sections of this book, and common sense, indicate we must include 'the future' and 'the environment' in our understanding of society. Accepting that duties may be contested, (see, for example, Messina 2007) a fundamental question: 'Will my decision hurt society, even if I benefit myself, my client, my employer or my profession?' thus gives rise to *a public interest service model* for public relations. The idea of applying a service orientation to public relations is not new to the discipline, as previously advocated by Bivins (1993) who saw it as a way to professionalize public relations, and later developed by Sallot, Cameron and Lariscy (1997) and others (Harrison 2004). Harrison argues how it is 'this very notion of service to the community, and the upholding of the public interest against private interests—or the singular interest of publics—which is at the core of any definition of what it means to be a profession' (2004, p. 1). At the same time, the role played by civil society, seen in the rise of advocacy and interest groups and individuals, presents an alternate approach where service may be less a motivation than advocacy in a *public interest action model*, driven by social cause and a desire for change. The models are not a binary; they simply provide two ways of conceptualizing the relationship between public relations and the public interest. Because public relations is not 'one way' of doing things, flexible modeling is necessary. At the same time, in acknowledging the existence of self-interest we can be more open to the interests of others through open discourse and effective rhetorical engagement (Habermas 1998; Edwards 2011; Bohman & Rehg 2014) whether through advocate or service orientation.

Public Interest as a Way of Thinking and Doing

Public relations scholars have engaged with and embraced a diverse range of theoretical and paradigmatic streams in recent years. This book proposes that the public interest can now be added to this growing and dynamic field of knowledge in advancing and extending how we might think about public relations. While the public interest can be a complex, mutable and abstract concept, it is also thought-provoking, critical and provocative, consistent with the diversity and plurality of modern societies, to be discovered discursively through participatory engagement and practice.

Within the book we have located strong synergies and intersections with concepts which are fundamental to public relations: social capital and other capital, the public sphere, participatory and communicative action, social change, legal and social order, cultural theory, agency, postmodernism and postcoloniality and many others. In drawing on these theories and concepts, we have expanded and developed the already well-established public interest literature and the dedicated public interest typologies, such as normative, abolitionist, proceduralist/process and consensualist, which have provided a starting point for understanding how others have learned to understand, explain or reject the public interest. Having ventured into the public interest from alternate entry points, many scholars advocated for a process-driven approach that accommodated diversity and plurality. Those professing this view found that many publics, rather than a single public, and many interests, rather than any universal interest, were more consistent with modern-day thinking of the public interest. At the same time, this does not preclude the typology of consensualism or consensus being achieved in some form, where deliberation and balance are actively and honestly sought, returning us to the 'pragmatic idealism' that was proposed by Dewey and Bozeman, consistent with Habermas's concept of communicative action. Public interest theories, however, have not included a critical public interest paradigm. As this book shows, critical theory can provide an extended or alternate dimension for viewing the public interest, especially when considering resource and access inequalities and the dialectic that is so often inherent in interest conflicts. For public relations, these fundamental elements of the public interest provide wide scope for further and deeper examination.

To paraphrase Bozeman, the public interest begins with a problem and then addresses the public values failure by suggesting public policies and other putative solutions such as market approaches and public-private partnerships (Bozeman 2007). This book has used such approaches, together with government and public relations initiatives, in providing various access points through which to engage and better understand how public problems and issues can be addressed, using a range of solutions and, equally, how 'capture' in systems and maleficence can override claims to the public interest. The public interest, then, can also be viewed through the normative typology, based on deliberative processes 'shedding light on an ideal ... that is either intersubjective or consensual' (Bozeman 2007, p. 177).

For public relations, through either service, advocacy or a combination of the two, the public interest is affected via interference or enabling mechanisms which can be provided through agency, often moved forward through a dialectical tension. Because society is dynamic, the answer to whether the public interest best falls into the *ex ante* or *ex post* time frame is simply that it can be both; problems and issues present differently, society is not static, cycles and continuums exist everywhere, as our snapshots and illustrations have shown. As with any theory, the public interest is a reflexive process which can assist with understanding practice but will not necessarily give the agent a simple application or solution. However, 'what is important is that a conscientious attempt is made to find appropriate answers, and that the decision-maker is able to demonstrate that the appropriate approach was followed and all relevant matters were considered' (Wheeler 2006, p. 24). At the same time, far from being just a box to tick, the public interest is better seen in the analogy of the 'hair shirt' (Sorauf 1957), the uncomfortable irritation that reminds the agent that alternatives and inequalities exist. As L'Etang and Pieczka (2006) point out, 'there is no simple way of providing moral and intellectual comfort to practitioners ... fundamental ethical questions have to be confronted daily in routine practice' (2006, p. 2). At the same time, the public interest, which exists across society and is used as a guidepost for good and fair practice, will remain a constant force, whether or not public relations chooses to acknowledge or engage with it.

In arguing in favor of the adaptability and breadth of the public interest, Lord Hailsham of Marylebone reported, 'The categories of the public interest are not closed and must alter from time to time ... as social conditions and social legislation develop' (in Wheeler 2006, p. 14). As such, the public interest has also emerged as a methodology as well as a theory and paradigm. Rejected in the past as too vague, too ambiguous and too utopian by positivist schools of thought, it has rebounded across a diverse range of fields—from anthropology to media, law and accountancy—following what Denzin and Lincoln (2011, p. 1) refer to as the 'decolonization' of methodologies arising out of postmodernism, postbehavioralism, postcolonialism, reflexive ethnographies, participant action, naturalistic approaches and other interpretive *bricolage*. They point out how qualitative research is a situated activity that is based on a set of interpretive practices intended to gain a clearer understanding of the subject matter at hand. The public interest may be viewed in this light with public benefit as the societal outcome, and the public interest as what activates it, in a process of advancing social change and redressing social injustice, 'imagining radical democracy that is not yet a reality' (Weems 2002 cited in Denzin & Lincoln 2011, p. xiii).

References

Beauchamp, TL 2002, *Philosophical ethics: an introduction to moral philosophy*, McGraw Hill, Boston.

Begin, D 2012, 'Can public relations be in the public interest?' *Where to begin: life as my muse* [weblog], viewed 20 November 2013, http://www.wheretobegin.ca/can-public-relations-be-in-the-public-interest/.

Bivins, TH 1993, 'Public relations, professionalism, and the public interest', *Journal of Business Ethics*, February, vol. 12, no. 2, pp. 117–26.

Bohman, J & Rehg, W 2014, 'Jürgen Habermas', in EN Zalta (ed.), *The Stanford encyclopedia of philosophy,* winter edn, viewed 1 May 2015, http://plato.stanford.edu/archives/win2011/entries/habermas/.

Bozeman, B 2007, *Public values and public interest: counterbalancing economic individualism,* Georgetown University Press, Washington, DC.

Burson, H 2012, 'A "modern" definition of public relations? Why?', 5 March 2012 [weblog], viewed 2 January 2015, www.burson-marsteller.com/harold-blog/a-modern-definition-of-public-relations-why/.

Campbell, H & Marshall, R 2002, 'Utilitarianism's bad breath? A re-evaluation of the public interest justification for planning', *Planning Theory,* vol. 1, no. 2, pp. 163–87.

Canada Public Relations Society CPRS 2013, *Mission, definition and values,* viewed 15 December 2013, http://www.cprs.ca/aboutus/mission.aspx.

Carter, M & Bouris, A 2006, *Freedom of information: balancing the public interest,* 2nd edn, The Constitution Unit-University College, London.

Cochran, CE 1974, 'Political science and the public interest', *The Journal of Politics,* vol. 36 no. 2, pp. 327–55.

Crozier Garcia, C 2007, 'Moral agency', in RW Kolb (ed.), *Encyclopedia of business ethics and society, vol. 5,* Sage, Thousand Oaks, CA, pp. 1409–12.

Denzin, NK & Lincoln, YS 2011, 'Introduction: the discipline and practice of qualitative research', in NK Denzin & YS Lincoln (eds.), *The Sage qualitative handbook of research,* 4th edn, Sage, Thousand Oaks, CA, pp. 1–21.

Dutta, M, Ban, Z & Pal, M 2012, 'Engaging worldviews, cultures, and structures through dialogue: the culture-centred approach to public relations', *Prism,* vol. 9, no. 2, pp. 1–10.

Edwards, L 2011, 'Questions of self-interest, agency and the rhetor,' *Management Communication Quarterly,* vol. 25, no. 3, pp: 531–540.

Flathman, R 1966, *The public interest,* John Wiley & Sons, New York.

Habermas, J 1996, *Between facts and norms: contributions to a discourse theory of law and democracy,* MIT Press, Cambridge, MA.

Habermas, J 1998, *On the pragmatics of communication,* MIT Press, Cambridge, MA.

Harrison, J 2004, 'Conflicts of duty and the virtues of Aristotle in public relations ethics: continuing the conversation commenced by Monica Walle', *Prism,* 2, viewed 27 June 2015, http://www.prismjournal.org/fileadmin/Praxis/Files/Journal_Files/Issue2/Harrison.pdf.

Healey, P 1992, 'Planning through debate: the communicative turn in planning theory', *Town Planning Review,* vol. 63, no. 2, pp. 143–62.

Henninger, M 2013, 'The value and challenges of public sector information', *Cosmopolitan Civil Societies Journal,* vol. 5, no. 3, pp. 75–95, ISSN: 1837–5391.

Ho, Lok-Sang 2011, *Public policy and the public interest,* Routledge, London.

Ho, Lok-Sang 2013, *Health policy and the public interest,* Routledge, London.

Institute of Chartered Accountants in England and Wales (ICAEW) 2012, *Acting in the public interest: a framework for analysis,* Market Foundations Initiative, viewed 1 March 2015, http://www.icaew.com/~/media/corporate/files/technical/ethics/professional_ethics/acting%20in%20the%20public%20interest%20framework%20template%2004%2014.ashx.

Institute of Chartered Accountants in England and Wales (ICAEW) 2014, *Acting in the public interest: framework template,* viewed 1 March 2015 http://www.icaew.com/en/technical/ethics/the-public-interest.

L'Etang, J & Pieczka, M 2006, 'Introduction', in J L'Etang & M Pieczka (eds.), *Public relations: critical debates and contemporary practice,* Lawrence Erlbaum, Mahwah, NJ, pp. 1–3.

Leveson, Lord Justice 2012, *An inquiry into the culture, practice and ethics of the press,* 29 November, viewed 29 May 2013, http://www.levesoninquiry.org.uk.

Mansbridge, J 1998, 'On the contested nature of the public good', in WW Powell & ES Clemens (eds.), *Private action and the public good,* Yale University Press, New Haven, CT, pp. 3–19.

Messina, A 2007, 'Public relations, the public interest and persuasion: an ethical approach', *Journal of Communication Management,* vol. 11, no. 1, pp. 29–52.

Mitnick, B 1980, *The political economy of regulation: creating, designing, and removing regulatory forms,* Columbia University Press, New York.

Mitnick, B & Getz, KA 2008, 'Regulation and regulatory practices', in RW Kolb (ed.), *Encyclopedia of Business Ethics and Society Vol 5,* Sage, Thousand Oaks CA, pp. 1787–1802.

Sanday PR, & Jannowitz C 2004, 'Public interest anthropology: a Boasian service-learning initiative', *Michigan Journal of Community Service Learning,* Summer, pp. 64–75.

Sallot, LM, Cameron, GT &Lariscy, RAW, 1997, Professional standards in public relations, *Public Relations Review,* vol. 23, no. 3, pp. 197–216.

Sorauf, FJ 1957, 'The public interest reconsidered', *The Journal of Politics,* vol. 19 no. 4, pp. 616–39.

Seib, P & Fitzpatrick, K 1995, *Public relations ethics,* Harcourt Brace, Orlando, FL.

Wheeler, C 2006, 'The public interest: we know it's important, but do we know what it means', in R Creyke & A Mantel (eds.), *AIAL Forum no. 48,* Australian Institute of Administrative Law, pp. 12–26, viewed 1 September 2013, http://150.203.86.5/aial/Publications/webdocuments/Forums/forum48.pdf.

Index

For Product Safety Concerns and Information please contact our EU
representative GPSR@taylorandfrancis.com
Taylor & Francis Verlag GmbH, Kaufingerstraße 24, 80331 München, Germany